Neighborhood Policy and Planning

Politics of Planning Series

Barry Checkoway, Editor

Neighborhood Policy and Planning

Edited by
Phillip L. Clay
Massachusetts Institute of
Technology
Robert M. Hollister
Tufts University

LexingtonBooks
D.C. Heath and Company
Lexington, Massachusetts
Toronto

Library of Congress Cataloging in Publication Data
Main entry under title:

Neighborhood policy and planning.

Includes index.
1. Neighborhood—United States—Addresses, essays,
lectures.   2. City planning—United States—Addresses,
essays, lectures.   3. Urban renewal—United States—Ad-
dresses, essays, lectures.   4. Quality of life—United
States—Addresses, essays, lectures.   5. United States—
Social policy—Addresses, essays, lectures.   I. Clay,
Phillip L.   II. Hollister, Robert M.
HT167.N39 1983   307′.3362   82–48559
ISBN 0–669–06302–9 casebound
ISBN 0–669–06936–1 paperback

Copyright © 1983 by D.C. Heath and Company

Published simultaneously in Canada

Printed in the United States of America

Casebound International Standard Book Number: 0–669–06302–9

Paperback International Standard Book Number: 0–669–06936–1

Library of Congress Catalog Card Number: 82–48559

*To our students and colleagues
and to citizens everywhere who are
working to improve the quality of
life in America's neighborhoods.*

Contents

Preface

This book grows out of several years of research and professional involvement on the part of the editors and the contributors. The work emerged from our observation—and that of our colleagues—that planning at the neighborhood level was going on without a real framework for action. Similarly, research proceeded without clear linkages to the practical concerns that fuel neighborhood action. Independently, researchers were coming up with useful insights that needed testing and translation, and practitioners were making gains in promoting neighborhood redevelopment that seemed impossible only a few, short years ago—gains that needed to be put in context, evaluated, and documented for replication.

To bring together the worlds of practice and research, we organized colloquia, workshops, and seminars at the Massachusetts Institute of Technology (MIT) and at the Boston Neighborhood Network. Much that was presented at these sessions is included in this book. Other chapters come from colleagues who were undertaking similar efforts in other cities.

We are very grateful to the contributors and to the dozens of colleagues who over the years made immeasurable contributions to the efforts that are captured in this book. We are particularly grateful to our colleagues at MIT and Tufts University who have been most supportive of these efforts.

We began the process of editing this reader in 1978, during a period of rapidly escalating interest in U.S. neighborhoods and in the public and private sector policies that influence them. While there have been significant political and economic shifts at both national and local levels since the neighborhood movement peaked in the late 1970s, the issues addressed here are enduring. Our hope is that this book will help to refocus academic, professional, and community attention on these continuing challenges—how to improve the quality of neighborhood life, how to strengthen the public and private choices that determine the future of neighborhoods, and how to better understand the internal and external forces that shape neighborhood dynamics. We are hopeful that this book will spark a second generation of research and give encouragement to practitioners to extend the frontier of neighborhood planning.

Part I
The Emergence of Urban Neighborhoods

The current renewal of public interest in neighborhoods and in public policies toward neighborhoods has produced a great deal of research prose, political rhetoric, and media comment. The policy debates about neighborhood development focus on present-day choices and controversies, but it is essential to address these issues as contemporary instances of what are more enduring dilemmas with respect to neighborhood and community development.

The new attention to neighborhood issues reflects, in part, greater public support for neglected neighborhoods as well as new interest in private reinvestment. Analysis of these developments promises to advance our knowledge of how neighborhoods emerge and change—questions that are still a matter of some mystery and intellectual curiosity.

There is some confusion about what neighborhood-focused analysis means. Confusion results, in part, from the disparate reasons for the reemergence of urban neighborhoods on the public-policy agenda. The factors that have generated heightened activity with respect to neighborhoods have converged, but they are hardly a consistent set of themes. They mask divergent meanings of the term *neighborhood,* and they blur conflicting goals for neighborhoods, for the people who inhabit them, and for planners who seek to intervene in them.

Historically planners have had shifting allegiance to, and uses of, neighborhood goals and concepts. During the twentieth century, urban professionals have moved cyclically toward and away from neighborhood concepts—tending toward affirmation of neighborhoods as desirable and real at one point in time then shifting toward a more critical posture. Nothing in our recent experience, or in our repeated pattern of embracing then rejecting the U.S. neighborhood, suggests that the cycle is likely to be broken. We can, however, improve the utility, efficiency, and equity of action as well as the rigor of analysis at the neighborhood scale. A major purpose of this book is to record the lessons and insights that emerge from the recent period of neighborhood policy initiatives.

The introductory chapter by Albert Hunter summarizes three analytical approaches to the study of the neighborhood context—typologies, stages of change, and functions (including economic, administrative, political, and social). Hunter explores the conflict between the neighborhood as an informal and sentimental entity versus the neighborhood as an organization of interests. The discussion is especially significant for its distinction between the sentimental and the instrumental aspects of the neighborhood and for its identification of interrelationships among them.

However, a major aspect of recent concern about neighborhoods is the dynamics of revitalization and reinvestment. The chapter by Phillip Clay sets up some key distinctions—between revitalizing neighborhoods *(gentrification)* and incumbent upgrading (reinvestment by long-term residents). He suggests that neighborhood planning requires that we know the difference and act accordingly.

Dennis Gale's chapter goes into much more detail on gentrification and explores some of the dynamics imbedded in it, including displacement and the implications of demographic shifts. Part I sets the stage for the more detailed discussion that follows in later sections.

What should be clear is that this book is not about neighborhoods in general; it is about intervening in neighborhoods—to promote revitalization and strengthen the capacity for residents to improve the quality of their environment and residential life.

1

The Urban Neighborhood: Its Analytical and Social Contexts

Albert Hunter

Why the Neighborhood? Why Now?

As interest in the neighborhoods of U.S. cities once again emerges, it is appropriate that we pause to consider the nature of this unit—not simply as an academic exercise but also in order that policy and planning recommendations may take advantage of recent developments, the state of the art, in thinking about urban neighborhoods. This chapter at times advances specific policy recommendations within given problem areas; but more importantly, it poses a more general set of persistent and emergent issues that will confront most, if not all, specific policy and planning considerations. Therefore, the reader should not approach this chapter with the hope of finding specific recommendations that will be implemented within six months—leading to the saving of the nation's neighborhoods, its cities, and ultimately itself. Rather, the general problems posed in this chapter are more apt to be irresolvable dilemmas than quick solutions, but it is hoped their serious consideration will lead to more informed and judicious policy choices.

The generality of the issues addressed is indicated by the recurrent themes that run throughout—power, sustenance in housing and work, inequality, community, and sociability. Though the neighborhood may be small as a social/spatial unit, it looms large as a locus for many of the issues confronting contemporary urban society.

The neighborhood is nothing new, but the issues that center on the neighborhood are both new and old. After a long period of research and a policy of benign neglect, the urban neighborhood is seen to be the locus of many social problems and the appropriate unit of intervention for their solution. Therefore, it is fitting to ask our opening questions—Why the neighborhood? Why now?

The transformation of contemporary society beginning with the in-

Reprinted from Albert Hunter, "The Urban Neighborhood: Its Analytical and Social Contexts," *Urban Affairs Quarterly* 14, 3 (March 1979):267–288, © 1979 Sage Publications, Inc., with permission.

3

dustrial revolution and its allied global processes of urbanization, bureau-
cratization, immigration, and the rise of the modern nation-state have all
had impact upon local urban neighborhoods—their creation, variation,
demise, and rebirth. These are the processes that shape and change urban
neighborhoods and, as these processes have altered, the nature of urban
neighborhoods has altered in turn. The links between urban neighborhood life and these general processes are highly variable, some impacting
more directly, some more torturously, through the maze of social organization these processes have produced.

Emile Durkheim, Adam Smith, Ferdinand Tonnies, Marx, and En-
gels, among others, theoretically addressed the issues relating the nature
of urban neighborhoods and their fate to the forces operating within the
emerging modern system. Empirical concern with urban neighborhoods
was also early evidenced by Charles Booth's detailed research on the
neighborhoods of London; and the need for altering the impact of these
forces was seen in the early concerns of Clarence Perry and his use of
the neighborhood as the basic unit of urban planning. It is at times
difficult and of questionable utility to trace neighborhood phenomena
always to their links with the modern world system (Wallerstein 1974).
However, it is important to see that they may be so linked, and especially
for policy and planning considerations. When neighborhood programs
are repeatedly judged as failures (for example, when federal housing
programs do not appear to thwart the decline of urban neighborhoods),
then it becomes imperative to assess the reasons for these failures. Such
evaluations require broader considerations than the specific organizational characteristics of the programs; more than a judgment of the intentions, motives, or performance of individuals involved; and even more
than an assessment of the neighborhood's internal characteristics. Rather,
it becomes clear that we must study the larger structural constraints that
set the parameters within which the problems are being generated and
the solutions sought.

The central thesis of this chapter is that the neighborhood is a uniquely
linked unit of social/spatial organization between the forces and institutions of the larger society and the localized routines of individuals in
their everyday lives. To try to understand the neighborhood solely by
focusing on its internal structure and dynamics is to end up with carefully
documented descriptions but a persistent failure to grasp the causal explanations of the processes that create the variety of neighborhood forms
and constrain the conduct of neighborhood life. If one does not view the
neighborhood within its context, in short, one ends up with description
not explanation. The focus of this chapter, therefore, is upon the position
of the urban neighborhood within the larger society and the nature of its
linkages to this context. The focus is upward, not downward. It does at

times and to varying degrees touch upon the neighborhood's microsocial relationships and the social-psychological sentiments and attitudes of neighborhood residents. However, for the most part and more centrally, it focuses upon this vertical link (Warren 1972), and the way in which this sets the parameters within which neighborhood life takes place. This is not an entirely new perspective, for it may be viewed as a further extension of Ernest Burgess's early advice (1973:42):

> In the study of the growth of the city it is found that the life of any neighborhood is determined, in the long run, not altogether by the forces within itself, but even more by the total course of city life. To think of the neighborhood or the community in isolation from the rest of the city is to disregard the biggest fact about the neighborhood.

What is a Neighborhood?

As to a definition of the urban neighborhood there is relatively little consensus that one can find within the scholarly literature (Keller 1968). We can state that uniformly it is considered a social/spatial unit of social organization and that it is larger than a household and smaller than a city. The problem with presenting a further list of definitive characteristics is that they often become normative rather than descriptive (in Weber's terms, "ideal types"), which when held up to reality leave one still looking in vain for a neighborhood. Academicians may easily bypass this definitional problem by invoking a consensual faith in common language and shared experience—which is to say, we cannot define neighborhoods precisely, but we all know what they are and what they mean when we talk about them. However, for those concerned with policy and planning the definitional problem is more central because the very nature of a program may depend upon what working definition of a neighborhood is established. A neighborhood often becomes operationally defined in terms of a specific program and its explicit policy objectives—some emphasizing physical or housing characteristics, some social relationships of residents, and some retreating to some administratively defined districts. As social scientists we cannot at this time offer a single, credible alternative to these a priori, operationally defined neighborhoods. We can, however, as several social scientists have demonstrated, treat the very definition of neighborhood itself as a problem for empirical investigation (Firey 1945; Lynch 1960; Hunter 1974a). We can, in turn, caution planners and policymakers to be aware of the diversity of alternative definitions that may be invoked and of the implications of choosing one over others.

Neighborhood Analysis: Typologies,
Stages, and Functions

The study of neighborhoods by social scientists often still draws upon the structural-functional perspective of morphologically identifying different types of neighborhoods, specifying the processes of morphological change by a set of sequential stages, and listing functions that neighborhoods perform as units of social organization both for their residents and as units within the larger society. Precursors of these three approaches are found in the early writings of Park and Burgess (1921) and the old Chicago School, which defined different types of "natural areas," described their sequential changes through the expansion of Burgess's classical concentric-ring model of cities, and traced the interdependencies between these "functional niches." Contemporary human ecologists, sociologists, geographers, planners, and neighborhood analysts still operate, by and large, within some variant of these three approaches.

Neighborhood Typologies

The more simple neighborhood typologies are usually defined by some relative distribution of demographic and compositional characteristics of neighborhood residents and their housing. Relative rankings based upon social class, race and ethnicity, family composition, and housing stock, or any of a number of such variables taken singly or in combination, often are considered relevant and sufficient for analytical purposes. For example, there are numerous studies that explain variation in individual characteristics, behaviors, or attitudes by relating them to these contextual variables of neighborhood composition (Greer 1962b; Bell and Boat 1957). Similarly, other structural or institutional characteristics of neighborhoods may be related to neighborhood composition, such as the number and intensity of local organizations (Warren 1975) or the characteristics of schools, churches, and other local institutions (Zald 1970). For all of the above typologies, the neighborhood is often little more than a spatial, statistical aggregation of individual characteristics.

A more sophisticated derivative of these descriptive typologies is the recent work in *social-area analysis* and *factorial ecology*. Stemming from the early work by Eshrev Shevky (1955) and its further elaboration by Brian J.L. Berry (1967), this approach attempts to identify major dimensions or factors that summarize the relative and varying spatial distributions of a wide number of variables. The three most commonly found factors in U.S. metropolitan areas have been socioeconomic status, race and ethnicity, and some combination of life-style and life-cycle characteristics of residents. The post hoc theorizing aside, this research has produced a widely generalized and replicated set of dimensions by which local neighborhoods may be typed. Such analytical typologies have also been related to residents' own *social typologies* used in characterizing the image of their local neighborhood (Hunter 1974a).

There are, of course, other dimensions by which neighborhood typologies may be developed than those relying upon compositional characteristics leading to descriptive typologies. For example, there are typologies based upon residents' perceptions of their local neighborhoods (Lynch 1960) and typologies based upon functional characteristics of neighborhoods, which will be addressed shortly. There are, in short, different types of typologies for analyzing local neighborhoods. Given the large number of variables and dimensions that might be used in developing typologies, it becomes futile to list them all or to attempt to define the best typology. Debates between this or that typology must ultimately rest upon utilitarian questions—is it useful and does it work? These questions may be raised analytically in terms of whether or not a typology is useful in organizing a diversity of research findings and conceptual elements; and they may be raised operationally in terms of whether or not they are useful in differentiating among neighborhoods for specific policies and programs. And although typologies are useful and often necessary, for neither analysis nor policy should they be considered an outcome, but rather, the first step.

Neighborhood Stages

The dynamic aspect of cities—their growth, expansion, decline, or rebirth—is often translated at the neighborhood level into sequential stages of neighborhood change. Again, the early Burgess concentric-zone model of cities with its outward expansion from a central core produced a series of neighborhood transitions captured in the famous *invasion-succession sequence*. Populations, institutions, and functional shifts in land use resulted from outward expansion of inner zones (invasion), followed by competition manifest either in economic land markets or in social conflict between diverse social groups. The outcome of the competition according to these early ecologists was not the maintenance of a self-sustaining competitive market envisioned by economists but rather dominance (succession) by a particular function or group. For the city as a whole the process was like the ripple effect produced by a stone dropped into the middle of a pond. For a given neighborhood, spatially fixed, the ripples were successive waves that over time resulted in the neighborhood going through a sequence of states—from new to old, from birth to death, from development to decline.

As with the descriptive typologies, attempts at defining stages of neighborhood changes are often posited as universal, generalized patterns (Hoover and Vernon 1962; Downs 1970; Hunter 1974b). One of the ironies that Calvin Bradford points out (1979) is that the widespread acceptance of these stages of change by decision makers resulted in a self-fulfilling prophecy that abetted the stages of neighborhood transition and decline. Also, similar to the descriptive typologies, the focus in these stages of change is mostly upon population and housing characteristics of the neighborhood. For example, the *trickle-down theory* of housing is a direct descendent of these earlier theories of neighborhood change.

The policy implications of such sequential stages of neighborhood change center upon identification of targeted neighborhoods and designing programs that will strategically intervene to abate the process. Intervention may occur at the tail end in attempts at redevelopment or massive urban (neighborhood) renewal or at some midpoint in the process in an attempt to keep it from going full cycle and arresting or reversing the sequence. It has been observed that the widespread acceptance of these general sequential models—even by those attempting to abate them— does not deal fully with the social and political factors that may have to be considered; and more importantly, an entirely different sequence may have to be developed to deal with revitalization than the sequence that initially led to decline.

The positing of a universal, generalized sequence of neighborhood change is a logical outcome of both the macrotheories of the early human ecologists and the more contemporary political-economy perspective. Both perspectives, in effect, present the somewhat somber view that to the degree that these macroforces of change operate, the microforces of neighborhood intervention, organization, and control are quixotic. The mills of the modern city, driven either by the "natural" winds of the ecologists or by the engines and machinery of industrial capitalism will continue to grind to dust the whims and wishes of local neighborhood residents. A more complete dialectic, however, would entertain the possibility that these forces would produce a dust out of which would rise new neighborhood forms and countervailing local forces.

A focus upon stages of neighborhood change emphasizes a dynamic, treats time as a variable, and points to the need for historical analysis as well as holding out the opportunity for prediction. However, to be more than description, the stages, like the typologies, must be linked to the forces of the larger society. This is not to suggest that empirically grounded sequences are not without utility, for their aggregation and replication point to the nature of the forces that must be considered in developing a more linked and integrated picture—a picture not only of what is happening and why but of what must be changed to alter the sequence to maximize alternative values, and how to do it.

The conclusion often drawn from an analysis of stages of neighborhood change is that there are inexorable macroforces that act upon neighborhoods, leaving the view that urban neighborhoods are dependent units lacking initiatory powers and unable to impact upon these larger forces. They are residues and repositories, and their relative significance and importance in modern urban life are questioned. One way to address this issue is by posing it in a somewhat older form by asking what functions do or can neighborhoods play within the modern urban system?

Neighborhood Functions

The potential number of functions that may be attributed to neighborhoods, as to any social unit, is limited only by one's imagination. I have chosen, therefore, to focus upon a limited set of functions that are germane to the issue of the vertical linkage of neighborhoods to their larger context—and also functions that are related to current public issues and policy concerns. These functions are ones that neighborhoods might potentially perform, but it remains an empirical question to what degree they actually do perform them or to what degree programs might be developed to increase a neighborhood's ability to perform them. The four functions considered are: (1) the economic function, both production and consumption, (2) the administrative and control function, (3) the political function, and (4) the socialization and sociability function.

A recurrent theme running throughout this functional analysis is the differentiation among neighborhoods and its linkage to systems of inequality and stratification. A second theme is the historical question of whether or not neighborhoods are *losing* functions to other institutions and to other levels of social organization. This second theme relates directly to the issue of the *increasing scale* of the metropolis and the public and private institutions of society as a whole. The increase-in-scale argument has been posited as one of the major dynamics leading to the local neighborhood's functional demise (Greer 1962a).

The Neighborhood's Economic Function. Economically, the local neighborhood has been viewed primarily as a unit of consumption not of production. Home and work in the modern U.S. metropolis have become separated, though within highly variable limits. Home is the house and the local neighborhood, the locus of consumption; work is the office and the factory, the locus of production.

Housing is the major element in the view of the neighborhood as an economic consumption unit, and the fate of a neighborhood often is tied directly to the dynamics of the housing market. The traditional economic theories focus upon the demand side of this market, analyzing the rise and fall of housing/land values as a function of changes in aggregate demand for housing/land. However, both Harvey Molotch (1979), and Bradford (1979) highlight the impact that major institutional actors, both public and private, have upon this market. The parameters within which individual housing decisions are made are set by the decisions of these larger-scale institutions, whether they are major developers, banks and mortgage institutions, or agencies of local and federal government. It is the increasing awareness of these larger-scale decisional impacts that has catapulted housing and neighborhood interests into the political spotlight. The role of the Federal Housing Administration (FHA) in the housing market, the so-called redlining of older urban neighborhoods by banks and insurance companies, and the impact of real-estate speculators and developers in bringing about neighborhood change have led to increasing political demands from the neighborhoods for controlling legislation at local, state, and federal levels. The dynamics of urban growth or decline and, at the local level, of neighborhood change are now being questioned. The impetus for change, the circulation of capital and of people through urban neighborhoods, the creation of new suburban housing, and the abandonment of older central-city housing have been increasingly defined as costs no longer to be borne by local urban neighborhoods and their residents. With increasing inflation, high interest rates on mortgages, and the general deterioration of the economic climate, the traditional demand for new housing has turned inward toward maintenance of existing urban neighborhoods and revitalization of older ones. The reemergence of so-called fashionable neighborhoods in city after city is still operating within these broader parameters, but it does imply an altering of residential values more beneficial to central cities.

A second nexus of the neighborhood as a consumption unit focuses upon commercial and retail sales. Here, the pattern is very clear. The increase in scale of marketing, related to the increasing reliance upon automobiles, has led to the proliferation of large-scale regional shopping centers, within both central cities and suburbs. For the local neighborhood, the result has been the abandonment of many local retail outlets and the boarding-up of whole commercial strips. To be sure, certain local retail functions still remain, drug and hardware stores, barbershops and beauticians; but these and others are continuing to feel the competitive threat from large-scale regional and national chains located in central shopping centers (Hunter 1975; Berry 1967).

Although I referred to the neighborhood primarily as a consumption unit, there are two aspects of the neighborhood as a production unit that have been somewhat neglected by social scientists. The first focuses again upon housing, but on the production side. Housing as a product is one of the last in terms of work and product to fall within the mass centralized-production sphere of bureaucratic industry. The building industry has been slow to move from craft to industrial labor, to shift from small-scale, on-site production to centralized factory production. The building of denser, larger, multiple units and the prefabrication of parts and pieces in factories to be assembled on site have been dominant trends within this industry in recent years. The "rationalization" of the housing industry, like that of agriculture, has been increasing, as Molotch (1979) notes, since large corporations and national banking and insurance interests have entered the development market. However, the contempory focus upon housing as a policy issue appears to link it almost wholly to the intermediate consumption role of capital circulation at the local level in the issues of redlining, so-called residential steering by realtors, and other issues related to local capital flows.

A second element of viewing the neighborhood as a production unit focuses upon the variable of home/work separation mentioned earlier. The interdependencies of these two spheres of activity have been neglected since their separation was often taken as one of the defining characteristics of the modern metropolis. However, the recent work by Kornblum (1974) points to a persistent linkage between primary social ties, such as neighborhood and ethnicity, and the activities of work in local neighborhood industries. A second indicator of this important linkage is the increasing suburbanization of industry, which is bringing about a reduced home/work separation, especially since corporate headquarters have joined this movement. The disarticulation between home and the neighborhood and work may have costs whose limits have been reached and whose benefits are being reevaluated.

The Neighborhood's Administrative Function. Viewing the neighborhood as an administered unit focuses attention upon the provision and distribution of public services. All bureaucracies, as Scott Greer (1962a) has observed, must at some point literally come down to earth, operate on the ground, and when they do, they find that they must deal with local neighborhoods. This is especially true of governmental agencies, which within the so-called contemporary welfare state are increasingly concerned about the efficient and equitable distribution and provision of public services. The surrounding issues of efficiency, equality, and control are much too complex to address fully here (see Lineberry 1977); but we can explore briefly the implications for the neighborhood of viewing it as a bureaucratically defined, administered social unit.

One of the consequences of viewing the neighborhood as an administered unit is the increasing number of service districts that are being delimited throughout urban areas. These districts are often overlapping and noncoterminous and range in scale for specific functions and agencies from small police and school districts to mental-health catchment areas to large, regional water and sewage districts. One of the forces behind the creation of these districts is the desire for efficiency and equitability in matching an agency's service districts to the particular population that is the beneficiary of the services and to the tax-funding base. This desire is also a dilemma, especially when coupled with the second major force behind the proliferation of these districts—the push for local community input and influence over the provision of these services. The pushes and pulls of centralization versus decentralization often pit agency against neighborhood, bureaucratic interests against neighborhood needs.

A second consequence of the proliferation of administered neighborhood districts is the specialization, the compartmentalization of services. One of the unique features of the neighborhood is that it is a small-scale social unit where diverse problems and issues often coalesce, where the intercorrelationships between issues of housing, schools, police, crime, and so on are directly experienced and more readily understood. Therefore, agency specialization and proliferation of districts tend to crosscut the neighborhood as a single collective unit capable of dealing with a diverse set of interrelated issues. Given the somewhat ambiguous lay definition of neighborhoods (Hunter 1974a), neighborhoods are very readily defined authoritatively—they are what the agencies say they are. The diverse interests of residents are more likely to become equally specialized and delimited, both functionally and spatially. Agencies, for the most part, do not deal with *the* neighborhood; rather, they create and maintain specialized neighborhood interest groups. This creation of a neighborhood clientele provides agencies with local support and legitimacy, at the same time providing potential cooptation of local neighborhood leaders.

A third consequence of the increasing administration of neighborhoods by governmental agencies relates directly to the issue of social control (Janowitz 1976). The *deinstitutionalization* movement, for example, implies movement away from professionals and institutions (anything resembling asylums); but, more ambiguously, it also implies a movement toward the local community and the neighborhood as the appropriate unit for the provision of services. One implication of this may be a variant of blaming the victim, wherein the source of the problem and the inability to alleviate it is deflected from the professionals and the agencies and placed upon the neighborhood itself. Relatedly, defining the neighborhood as the unit of intervention allows agencies to reach out more aggressively in broadening and expanding their serviceable clientele. Rather than identifying an appropriate clientele through costly individual-search procedures or waiting for self-selection by those who walk through the door, by defining the neighborhood as the unit, they encompass all who may reside within the spatially defined district. Furthermore, the neighborhood definition of a clientele allows agencies to link up with other institutions, such as schools, churches, employers, and such, thereby extending their network of service and control.

In summary, the neighborhood as an administered unit highlights the increasingly important link that it forms between individuals and the provision of services by the state and the recurring tensions and dilemmas surrounding equality and control that will continue to be played out within local neighborhoods.

The Neighborhood's Political Function. The function of the neighborhood as a political unit is closely related to the above considerations of the neighborhood as an administered unit. Where the latter focuses upon the *delivery* side of the 3–D model of the political process (demand, decision, delivery), the former focuses upon the process of definition, aggregation, and organization of demand. The neighborhood has historically had an essential function to play in this regard; and, more importantly, it continues to do so, though in new organizational forms.

The political machines of U.S. cities were built upon the primary ties and loyalties of ethnic ghettos that became established near the turn of the century. The general demise of such machines has been traced to the social and spatial mobility of various ethnic groups that respectively reduced their dependency upon the spoils of the machine and dispersed the voting blocks upon which it was built. Significantly, a major tenet of the reform movement was a shift from small districts to at-large electoral districts, a shift that has tended to deny neighborhoods a formal position within the polictical process. However, the relative vacuum that this shift created was filled—sometimes explosively, as in the riots of the sixties, but more often by local community organizations whose tactics ranged from conflict, to compromise, to cooperation. The political function of the neighborhood is to be found, primarily, within such local groups.

One of the significant qualities of these groups is that they tend to be reactive; that is, rather than initiating activities, they tend to respond (often negatively as veto groups) to policies and programs being initiated by governmental structures. As Robert Dahl (1961) has noted, echoing the increase-in-scale thesis, there has been a shift in government from providing *individual benefits* to providing *collective benefits*. Fluoridation, school busing, expressway construction, and urban renewal have been among the issues in recent decades that have seen the mobilization of local neighborhood interests rising up in opposition to these so-called collective goods.

More recently, this aggregation of reaction has taken a new form—the rise of federations of local neighborhood groups. Beginning as metropolitan federations, they have in the last decade emerged as national federations and have become powerful lobbying groups for local neighborhood interests at the federal level. National People's Action, the National Association of Neighborhoods, and National Neighbors are three exemplary groups that have been pressuring legislative assemblies at local, state, and federal levels to act upon a variety of issues that are seen to be directly impacting the quality of life in urban neighborhoods. The targets are not only governments but also include banks, insurance companies, and other private corporations. The types of institutional targets and exemplary issues were spelled out in a recent issue of *Disclosure,* the newsletter of National People's Action: "neighborhood people, through their determination, won major commitments from LEAA (Law Enforcement Assistance Administration), HUD (Housing and Urban Development) and some of the biggest insurance companies to sit down and resolve the issues of crime, HUD abuses and insurance redlining" (1978).

As Cohen (1979) points out, the process of neighborhood politicization often begins with concerns relating to economic and housing decline. He suggests that these should be transformed into a positive spiral of political mobilization and organization. This appears to be increasingly the case, for the politics of community is no longer local politics. As the chains of decision making that impact local areas are traced up the vertical hierarchy, neighborhood politics becomes national politics.

The Neighborhood's Socialization and Sociability Function. The sociability function has received much attention from neighborhood analysts and is often seen as a necessary definitional characteristic of a neighborhood. However, as Suzanne Keller (1968) suggests, in today's cities *neighbor* is an extremely limited and narrowly circumscribed role. Wellman (1979) also points out that the metropolitan area, not the local neighborhood, is the domain of most of today's friendship networks. We should be cautious, however, not to romanticize the past by seeing today's urban life as less neighborly than that of a previous period (Hunter 1975).

Important though the historical question may be, most analysis has focused upon variations in sociability, which Janowitz (1967) refers to as the community of "limited liability." From this perspective local neighborhood interaction, identification, and commitment are seen as highly variable and increasingly voluntaristic; that is, people may choose to become involved in the local neighborhood to varying degrees. There are, however, systematic variations in the degree and nature of this local involvement.

Sociability within local neighborhoods has been found to vary directly with social-class composition, or resource distribution, of local areas. As Wellman (1979) concludes, the "saved" community, with its dense local networks, is perhaps an anachronisitic residual neighborliness carried on by those with limited resources and few linkages to the larger society. This is exemplified by the poorer, working-class neighborhoods studied by Suttles (1968) in Chicago, and Gans (1962) in Boston. In these cases local linkages and sociability appear to be the result not of choice but of constraint. Those with more resources and broader opportunities for interaction characterize the "liberated" community. The choice of friends becomes separated from neighbors resulting in more limited local commitments.

A second variable that appears to impact strongly upon local neighborhood sociability is the family and life-style character of a neighborhood. Repeatedly, findings have shown that those with children residing in areas with many families are more likely to engage in informal and formal participation in local groups. By contrast, the single person or childless couple in less familistic neighborhoods is less likely to engage in such locally circumscribed interactions. Instead, these individuals are more likely to have interests and engage in activities that transcend the local neighborhood, or they are less likely to be drawn out of the home into the local neighborhood through the concerns and interests of children. In short, this population is either more cosmopolitan or more isolated than those leading a more familistic life-style.

The role of children as the essential denizens of neighborhoods has been linked directly to the importance of the neighborhood in the socialization and social control of children. Beshers (1962), for example, linked the class segregation of urban neighborhoods to the desire of parents to indirectly constrain the social-interaction patterns of children, thereby preserving or increasing intergenerational status attainment. Forbidding a child to cross a street may be as much a result of a concern for preserving one's social position as for protecting the child's physical safety. Though economic interests loom large in many neighborhood issues, the degree to which the primary relationships within the family may be mobilized at the neighborhood level into passionate political protest is nowhere more clearly demonstrated than in the issue of school busing and school integration.

In summary, it appears that the socialization and sociability functions of urban neighborhoods are still important, though variable from neighborhood to neighborhood. This variation appears to be related to the life-style or family composition of the neighborhood, and also to the degree of vertical linkage to the centers of power, privilege, and wealth. It is this link that allows some populations to opt in or out of the neighborhood by choice, while constraining others to the more limited interactional domain of the local neighborhood.

Toward the Future: New Structures and Persistent Dilemmas

Having reviewed some of the more central contemporary issues relating to urban neighborhoods, I will turn briefly now to a discussion of two general points that may be of assistance in thinking about the future of urban neighborhoods. The first focuses upon the newly emerging organization of neighborhoods into a *hierarchy of community;* and the second deals with the persistent dilemma Durkheim and Weber defined as the conflict between sentiments of place and the organization of interest.

The Emerging Hierarchy of Neighborhoods

The historical reality of the embeddedness of local neighborhoods in larger vertical structures is beginning to generate new and visible forms of organization that suggest the neighborhood will be a persistent and viable unit within modern urban life. I have suggested elsewhere (Hunter 1974a) that the proper way to view local urban areas is as a hierarchy of community. *My* neighborhood and *your* neighborhood may be differentiated and distinct; but on a larger scale, a higher level, they become fused into *our* area. These communal hierarchies may range from small social blocks surrounding the home, to local neighborhoods, to larger communities, and even whole regions. The fusion of identification, interest, and sentiment is a process that may be progressive, with larger units building upon, rather than detracting from, the smaller units.

How much lower units persist as basic building blocks in this process of hierarchical fusion is nowhere better evidenced than in the degree of vertical federation of urban neighborhoods that is now emerging. This organization of neighborhoods is experiential, and the result is a heightened consciousness about the chains of power and decision making that are critical in the vertical linkage of local neighborhoods. In the early days of community organizing, the local neighborhood was most often seen to be battling local city halls (Alinsky 1946), and it remains an important arena for political action. However, several structural changes, such as the increasing scale of bureaucratic organization both by governments and corporations, the increasing growth of metropolitan areas, and the split between city and suburb have reoriented the political battles, redefined the arenas, and changed the organization and dynamics of local community politics.

The local neighborhood's federated reorganization has resulted from a historical process of learning through previous political battles that power and decision making at lower levels are constrained. Agreements reached, concessions gained, and victories won at local levels were ultimately seen to be limited, if not worthless, as the seemingly powerful proved powerless to alter the forces that were impinging upon the local neighborhood. As inexorably as moths are drawn to light, local neighborhoods are coalescing around the centers of power and decision making, growing more numerous, agitated, and louder as they press their demands for state and federal politics that will improve the quality of neighborhood life. The organization of this demand has taken the form of federated national associations built up from neighborhoods throughout the nation's cities. This is a parallel increase in scale to that of the bureaucracies themselves, a structure that has given local neighborhoods a power that, if not equal, is at least comparable in form and that the centers of power cannot ignore. It is ironic, perhaps dialectical, that the argument of many mass-society theorists about the increase in scale that was supposedly leading to the demise of local neighborhoods may in fact be used to explain the rise of this hierarchical organization of neighborhood interests. The increased mobility of the population on a national scale, the increased facilities of mass communication and transportation, have made people in the neighborhoods increasingly aware of their shared fate and have provided them with the instruments for coalescing their interests into this federated organization. With its social base in the urban working-class and lower-middle-class neighborhoods, and with its emerging ideology of redirection and restriction of large-scale centers of wealth and power, both public and private, the emerging hierarchy of neighborhoods is a new urban populism.

Sentiments of Place and the Organization of Interests

In whatever form and over whatever issue, the local neighborhood will remain a persistent and central locus of the clash between local sentiments and large-scale interests. The diffuse attachments and collective bonds of the neighborhood will continue to interact dialectically with the rational, goal-directed pursuit of organized interests. There is a parallel that may be drawn, both metaphorical and real, between the fate of the neighborhood and the fate of the family in modern urban life. What were previously multifunctional primary units are seen to be losing functions to professionals, to other institutions, and to organized interests. Not only do these activities draw people out of the home and the neighborhood, but they functionally compartmentalize the life space of individual family members and neighbors. Men (and increasingly women) are at work, children are at school, and the elderly are in secluded retirement. What role is left for these primary units to perform? Why do they persist?

Most family researchers now agree that the family's persisting central function is the provision of socioemotional support out of the sentiments that inhere within long-term, intimate, personal relationships. So too with the neighborhood. Though more limited and circumscribed than within the family, it is the sentiment that inheres in personal relationships of proximity, the common fate of shared space, that defines the neighborhood's essential social bond. For both the family and the neighborhood, without such sentiments, they would cease to exist. They would become physically coexisting individuals—the home would become merely a house, the neighborhood, merely space—the social unit would be gone. In an urban society increasingly organized bureaucratically around the rational pursuit of narrowly defined goals, the diffuse and limited sentiments of locale are often considered troublesome anachronisms, irreducible to a rational calculus.

The rational pursuit of interest requires adjustment, mobility, and change; it is unrooted at its base. The personal, social, and physical distances that are often created by this pursuit of interest will continue to clash with the grounded, conservative, nonrational sentiments of place. When workers refuse to move from their local community to their relocated jobs in a new factory hundreds or thousands of miles away, then corporate interests may be acting rationally, the workers are not. When local residents organize to protest an expressway through their neighborhood that will speed them more readily between home and work, but uproot neighbors, then governmental planners may be acting rationally, but local residents are not. When oil leaks from a well drilled for corporate profits and national energy needs, and local residents protest the smudging of the community's beach and image, bureaucracies are acting rationally, local residents are not. This is not to deny that local residents are in fact pursuing their self-interest, but it is often a self-interest that is not translated into the metrics of cost/benefit analyses.

The unique features of the local neighborhood, its locus as the grounded point of intersection of diverse interests from the larger society, coupled with the sentiments of place that inhere within it, will keep the neighborhood alive as an important social unit. It is up to social scientists to continue to explore the intersection of these sentiments and interests, and it is up to social planners to design programs that will be sensitive to the needs of both. It is hoped the chapters in this book will contribute to this task.

References

Alinsky, S. 1946. *Reveille for radicals*. Chicago: University of Chicago Press.

Bell, W., and M. Boat. 1957. "Urban neighborhoods and informal social relations." *American Journal of Sociology* 62 (January):391–398.

Berry, B.J.L. 1967. *Geography of market centers and retail distribution*. Englewood Cliffs, N.J.: Prentice-Hall.

Berry, B.J.L.; and P. Rees 1969. "The factorial ecology of Calcutta." *American Journal of Sociology* 74 (March):445–491.

Beshers, J. 1962. *Urban social structure*. New York: Free Press.

Bradford, C. 1979. "Financing homeownership: the federal role in neighborhood decline." *Urban Affairs Quarterly* 14 (March):313–335.

Burgess, E.W. 1973. *On community, family, and delinquency*. L. Cottrell, A. Hunter, and J. Short, eds., Chicago: University of Chicago Press.

Dahl, R. 1961. *Who governs?* New Haven: Yale University Press.

Downs, A. 1970. *Urban problems and prospects*. Chicago: Markham.

Firey, W. 1945. "Sentiment and symbolism as ecological variables." *American Sociological Review* 10 (April):140–148.

Gans, H. 1962. *The urban villagers*. New York: Free Press.

Greer, S. 1962a. *The emerging city*. New York: Free Press.

———. 1962b. "The mass society and the parapolitical structure." *American Sociological Review* 27 (October):634–646.

Hoover, E.; and R. Vernon 1962. *Anatomy of a metropolis*. Garden City, N.Y.: Doubleday.

Hunter, A. 1975. "The loss of community." *American Sociological Review* 40 (October):537–552.

———. 1974a. *Symbolic communities*. Chicago: University of Chicago Press.

———. 1974b. "Community change." *American Journal of Sociology* 79 (January):923–947.

Janowitz, M. 1976. *Social control of the welfare state*. New York: Elsevier.

———. 1967. *The community press in an urban setting*. Chicago: University of Chicago Press.

Keller, S. 1968. *The urban neighborhood*, New York: Random House.

Kornblum, W. 1974. *Blue collar community*. Chicago: University of Chicago Press.

Lineberry, R., ed., 1977. "The politics and economics of urban services." *Urban Affairs Quarterly* 12: entire issue.

Lynch, K. 1960. *The image of the city*. Cambridge, Mass.: MIT Press.

Molotch, H. 1979. "Capital and neighborhood in U.S.: some conceptual links." *Urban Affairs Quarterly* 14 (March):289–312.

National People's Action. 1978. *Disclosure* 39 (July):1.

Park, R.; and E.W. Burgess 1921. *Introduction to the science of sociology*. Chicago: University of Chicago Press.

Shevky, E.; and W. Bell 1955. *Social area analysis*. Stanford: Stanford University Press.

Suttles, G. 1968. *The social order of the slum*. Chicago: University of Chicago Press.

Wallerstein, I. 1974. *The modern world system*. New York: Academic Press.

Warren, D.I. 1975. *Black neighborhoods*. Ann Arbor: University of Michigan Press.

Warren, R.L. 1972. *The community in America*. Chicago: Rand McNally.

Wellman, B.; and Barry Leighton. 1979. "Network, neighborhoods and communities: approaches to the study of the community question." *Urban Affairs Quarterly* 14 (March):363–390.

Zald, M.N. 1970. *Organizational change: the political economy of the YMCA*. Chicago: University of Chicago Press.

2

Urban Reinvestment: Process and Trends

Phillip L. Clay

The emergence of neighborhood revitalization in recent years has attracted the gaze of the public and practitioners alike. Observers view the rehabilitation phenomenon as significant for its immediate neighborhood improvements and for its catalytic potential for the quality of life in central cities.

In 1977 the U.S. Congress created a National Commission on Neighborhoods to identify trends and to explore possibilities for more public- and private-sector initiatives to help older urban areas.[1] In 1978 President Carter climaxed his administration's focus on neighborhood revitalization with the announcement of a new urban policy plus a series of legislative and administrative initiatives designed to accelerate neighborhood improvements, to secure neighborhood stability, and to establish the neighborhood as one cornerstone of an overall national city policy.[2] While the Reagan administration has not offered new programs and has even reduced federal activities in cities, the effect has been, in part, to stimulate local groups and local government to look for more creative and small-scale interventions to reverse decline in urban communities.[3]

What is less well known, however, is that neighborhood-based change (especially revitalization) is rooted in local interests activated by individuals and groups long before the government's recent and much publicized attention. Years prior to the government's recognition of the importance of urban neighborhoods as a locus for change, public discussion of neighborhood revitalization was limited to analyses based on local observations and to anecdotes. We have no empirically based hypotheses for the original spark of the developmental processes attending neighborhood revitalization. The government introduced policy proposals and program initiatives without the concrete data to understand the dynamics of current neighborhood changes. Individual actors and organizations likewise took initiatives without grounding in a theory of process. Only recently have systematic observations of the process and the extent of neighborhood revitalization taken place.

This chapter seeks to fill a conceptual void by examining the nature and extent of neighborhood revitalization in the major central cities in the United States. In particular, the aim is to complement other studies that focus on gentrification with a comparative analysis of the reinvestment process as carried out by long-term residents (incumbents) in an urban neighborhood as compared to the experience of middle-class resettlers, as documented in this book by Gale and others.

The issue of revitalization is more than an issue of private housing rehabilitation; housing is more than shelter. Neighborhood revitalization is a complex mixture of housing-market dynamics, neighborhood image-changing and promotion, demographic trends, conflicting life styles, and a significant element of expectation based on faith.

The neighborhood revitalization process requires private investment (including bank lending) in areas where it has not been attractive before. It also requires a willingness by outside investors to take what they have in the past viewed as risks. Where the investment does not involve immigration, the process has to generate some greater confidence on the part of incumbents that improving their housing is justified both as an economic investment and as a personal commitment. In other words, there must be an improvement in what Rolf Goetze calls "neighborhood confidence." Such confidence could emerge from successful neighborhood-development activities, from increased neighborhood consciousness, and from increased strength in the market, (resulting from either reduced supply in given price ranges or an increase in the size of demanding cohort.)

The maturation of the postwar baby boom will, over the next decade increase the young-adult population, though not as dramatically as in the 1970s. The extremely rapid growth in the price of new housing and existing suburban housing yields price differences between city and suburban housing that make some city housing a relative bargain.

The current paradigm for neighborhood change is one in which the important features are private, locally generated, residential development activity in small areas. This paradigm contrasts sharply with earlier experiences in urban-development programs with their public financing, federal initiation and design, city-wide or district-wide scope, and artificial boundaries drawn to meet guidelines established in Washington and gerrymandered by the pressures of local politics.

The points made in the preceeding paragraphs might be viewed as a set of informal hypotheses or a contextual backdrop for the examination of the revitalization process. To test these hypotheses and to provide a context for the recent experiences, we examined 105 revitalizing neighborhoods in the thirty largest central cities. These neighborhoods included areas with some evidence of private-market rehabilitation undertaken either by long-term residents or by mainly middle-class investors. The analysis of that data and information from field visits and secondary sources comprise the basis for the discussion in this chapter.[4]

Analysis of Data

The data indicate that there are two types of revitalized neighborhoods. The first type we might refer to as *incumbent upgrading*. This type occurs in a moderate-income neighborhood where the revitalization has been accomplished primarily by long-term residents. Additionally some new residents, usually of the same socioeconomic class, join them as part of a natural turnover. These neighborhoods generally have strong organizations and a strong sense of neighborhood identification. Often the revitalization is done in conjunction with organizations such as Neighborhood Housing Services (NHS), which is a partnership of local residents, lenders, and city officials. These organizations provide technical assistance, access to financing, and public services that when applied to a blighted but reasonably sound neighborhood dominated by owner-occupants can lead to significant, if not dramatic, increases in reinvestment by long-term residents. By June 1982, for example, NHS programs were formed in 170 neighborhoods in more than 120 cities. While the neighborhoods tend not be large, the scale is sufficient to demonstrate the viability of reinvestment by moderate-income families when the appropriate range of resources is available. The number of NHS and non-NHS reinvestment efforts is substantial enough to suggest that the idea is catching on.[5]

The second type revitalization is *gentrification* and describes neighborhoods where the private rehabilitation comes substantially from middle-class new residents to the neighborhood. The newcomers are primarily young households with professional occupations. This type of neighborhood change is more often the result of individual effort than organizational initiative. Older residents or incumbent residents are often displaced from such neighborhoods.[6] Gentrification often results in substantially higher prices and rents. The following sections outline our findings with respect to important aspects of the revitalization process for each of these two types of revitalization.

Extent of Revitalization

Revitalization in U.S. cities is extensive. The survey reveals some revitalization in all of the major U.S. cities, including some that are not large, such as Savannah and Charleston.

Nearly half of the neighborhoods in both categories of revitalization began their improvement process after 1975. Upgrading neighborhoods are nearly twice as likely to have begun since 1975—24 percent to 13 percent of the cases. The two types of neighborhoods vary significantly in their first reported signs of revitalization. For the majority of gentrification neighborhoods, improvements in the housing stock, new residents, speculator activity, or some combination of these were the first signs. Public action was significant in less than 10 percent of the cases and neighborhood initiative hardly mattered (4 percent). For upgrading neighborhoods, organized neighborhood or public initiatives were first signs for 47 percent of these neighborhoods. This finding highlights the success of such neighborhood initiatives as Neighborhood Housing Services when individual investor/buyer interest may be weak.

While the revitalization phenomenon is widespread, the percentage of central-city neighborhoods or structures involved in revitalization efforts is still rather small when compared to all city neighborhoods. Decline and blight are still significant realities—in some cities, the dominant reality.[7] For every neighborhood that has been revitalized in recent years, several have slipped into a more intractable state of disinvestment and decay.

It is significant that the size of the neighborhoods included in this survey ranges from the equivalent of a few square blocks to areas that are a square mile or more. Upgrading neighborhoods tend to be larger (4,000 to 10,000 households) than gentrification neighborhoods, (typically less than 4,000 households) and in the upgrading neighborhoods the improvements seem to be more modest and more generalized than in gentrification neighborhoods, where substantial improvements are concentrated in a smaller area.

Characteristics of the Neighborhoods
prior to Revitalization

The neighborhoods that are revitalized are in most cases older neighborhoods with most of their houses constructed before 1900. Gentrified neighborhoods are more likely to be older, turn-of-the-century areas than are the upgrading neighborhoods. Forty-six percent of gentrification neighborhoods in our sample are one hundred years or older, compared to only 11 percent of upgraded areas, which tend to reflect the more recent vintages. Turn-of-the-century neighborhoods are more often settled in the latter quarter of the nineteenth century, with distinctive Victorian architecture and carefully planned construction to provide features and amenities preferred by the middle class for whom they often were constructed originally.

The neighborhoods that underwent upgrading have fewer professional or white-collar workers and are slightly more likely to include substantial populations of households with older heads. The populations of neighborhoods that have become gentrified are different. They more often have populations that are particularly susceptible to displacement. As table 2–1 shows they include more households whose heads are black, poor, elderly, or transient. These are households least able to protect their turf or to organize or articulate their own interests in the neighborhood. They are also the households who were more often renters than owners.

Housing Condition and Locational Features of Neighborhoods Experiencing Revitalization

Table 2–2 illustrates some of the major housing characteristics of neighborhoods that underwent revitalization. The major finding is that gentrification neighborhoods are more often neighborhoods that have more dilapidated housing or some evidence of abandonment. The value of the housing was not significantly different in the two types prior to revitalization although our data suggests that the gentrification neighborhoods more often contained housing with serious structural problems.

The price of housing in the two types of neighborhoods diverges significantly as revitalization proceeds. Few, if any, units are available for sale in a range affordable by modest-income people in gentrification

Table 2–1
Selected Social Characteristics of Neighborhoods prior to Upgrading
(in percentage)

Characteristics	Upgraded Neighborhoods N = 48	Gentrified Neighborhoods N = 57
Neighborhoods seventy-five years or older	46	57
Neighborhoods where the predominant population was white	44	53
Neighborhoods considered so-called ethnic communities	35	40
Neighborhoods that mainly had settled families or elderly households	29	20
Neighborhoods that mainly had transient or single-person households	4	18
Neighborhoods where predominant occupations had been professional or other white collar	10	6

Source: National Endowment for the Arts data.

Note: N = 105, however, because of missing data, calculations for all variables are not always based on 105 cases.

Table 2–2
Structural Features of Housing in Revitalized Neighborhoods
(in percentage)

Characteristics	Upgraded Neighborhoods N = 48	Gentrified Neighborhoods N = 57
Neighborhoods where housing was mainly one- and two-unit structures	64	54
Neighborhoods with significant abandonment	2	6
Neighborhoods where most housing was considered structurally sound	87	71
Revitalized neighborhoods where less than 10 percent of units were improved	33	15
Revitalized neighborhoods where more than 40 percent of units were improved	27	33
Neighborhoods with public-housing development	4	none
Neighborhoods with typical sales prices equal to or greater than $40,000[a]	22	92
Neighborhoods with typical sales prices less than $25,000[a]	55	none

Source: National Endowment for the Arts data.

Note: N = 105, however, because of missing data, calculations for all variables are not always based on 105 cases.

[a]Sales information available on only twenty-one neighborhoods.

areas. Values of $40,000 (1977 values) are common. Values in the $20,000 and $30,000 range are more common in upgrading areas. The rents in both categories reflect values of owner-occupied housing.

The type of work actually completed on the structures includes a mixture of modernization, restoration, and gut rehabilitation. This pattern of improvement exists whether revitalization is upgrading or gentrification. The actual features of the rehabilitation work (as opposed to type) are substantially different, reflecting the level of investment the respective households are able to afford. Incumbents make more modest improvements; NHS data show this figure to be typically less than $6,000.[8] The gentry, on average, spend considerably more and do more structural upgrading.

The major features that differentiate upgrading from gentrification areas emerge more clearly in locational features than in housing features.

Table 2–3 presents important locational features of the two types of areas. Gentrification neighborhoods, but not upgrading neighborhoods, are either within the central business district (CBD) or within one-half mile of the district. Few gentrified neighborhoods, but no upgrading

Table 2–3
Selected Locational Features of Neighborhoods
by Revitalization Types
(in percentage)

Characteristics	Upgraded Neighborhoods N = 48	Gentrified Neighborhoods N = 57
Neighborhoods within central business district or within one mile of central business district	34	49
Neighborhoods more than two miles from central business district	47	30
Neighborhoods with positive topographic or locational features[a]	46	78
Neighborhoods with distinctive eighteenth- or nineteenth-century architecture	39	44
Neighborhoods with recent nonresidential upgrading or construction	68	81
Neighborhoods where land use is entirely residential	22	6
Neighborhoods where other land use includes institutional, commercial, or combinations of these	51	82

Source: National Endowment for the Arts data.

Note: N = 105, however, because of missing data, calculations for all variables are not always based on 105 cases.

[a]Includes location in connection with seashore, high elevation, public open space, river. There is no implied judgment about quality of these features.

neighborhoods, are more than two miles from the central city, and hardly any are as many as five from the CBD. The gentrification neighborhoods are also much more likely to have attractive topographic locations such as high elevations, proximity to open space, or location on the shore of a river or lake or near an important public landmark. Gentrification neighborhoods are more likely to have some distinctive historical significance, such as an area of former middle-class settlement or an area of distinctive architectural or historic interest.

Gentrification neighborhoods are also much more likely to be located near substantial, recent nonresidential upgrading (including new construction.) This construction varies from one city to another and includes expansion of medical or other institutional facilities, construction of office space, and the construction of in-town areas with new hotels or exhibition complexes. Gentrification and nonresidential upgrading in such cases complement each other by bringing life to an activity center. In short the gentrification process has taken advantage of the amenities of city living and has sought to locate itself near other kinds of investments and ongoing reinvestment in the city.

These findings about locational features have implications both for predicting where future revitalization might occur and for identifying the revitalization potential in areas located at some distance from the CBD. These findings also suggest that at least in the first round of gentrification, there has been a so-called creaming of the best neighborhoods (defined here as closest to the center of action and most stylish) and a simultaneous attempt to reclaim neighborhoods originally constructed for the middle and upper class. There are still unimproved areas that may be attractive for the gentry. It remains to be seen whether these areas, and only these areas, undergo gentrification, or whether the middle class will seek to establish beachheads in less attractive areas. This future trend may be particularly interesting as we enter a period in which the middle class attracted to living in the city faces affordability problems, are less risk-accepting, or are even less handy than the first round of modern-day pioneers whose experience we are documenting presently. In addition much of the speculative fever of the 1970s is past, since in the last two years housing appears less attractive as an investment medium.

It also remains to be seen where incumbent upgrading goes. While the maturation of the postwar baby boom will assure some growth in the number of new households in the low and moderate-income range to support the revitalization of more modest neighborhoods, there are many uncertainties that still remain—these range from the quality of local public services, especially schools, on which they (unlike the gentry) have to depend, to trends in racial attitudes and management of racial change, to interest and affordability of homeownership and the capacity of neighborhood organizations such as NHS to be effective in ways that organizations such as NHS to be effective in ways that organizations have been effective in the past. It need not be belabored here that there is plenty of housing stock in neighborhoods all over our large cities where such incumbent upgrading can emerge. Other issues about the future in this regard are explored later.

Neighborhood organizations such as NHS (and unlike the more individualistic gentrification) seem to be critical to revitalization in non-middle-class neighborhoods. Their roles (see table 2–4) include technical assistance, promotion, advocacy, and in some cases, direct development. The initiative on the part of neighborhood organizations in upgrading areas also seems to rally support and interest and to provide assistance to break the so-called prisoner's dilemma, (that is, convincing significant numbers of people to invest in their property and in soliciting the local government and institutions for assistance so that each actor is assured that their investment will be reinforced by the actions of others.)

Table 2–4

Selected Roles of Key Actors in Neighborhood by Revitalization Type
(in percentage)

Characteristics	Upgraded Neighborhoods N = 48	Gentrified Neighborhoods N = 57
Neighborhoods where activity was generated mainly by new residents	21	70
Neighborhoods where developers played some role from the start of the process	25	43
Neighborhoods where realtors never played a key role in the process	48	19
Neighborhoods where local government role included allocation of local funds or use of federal funds at an early stage in the process	29	24
Neighborhoods where local government played no role in revitalization	16	9
Neighborhoods where Community Development Block Grants funds were used	28	20
Neighborhoods where conflict was reported among neighborhood residents, city, or local institutions	33	60

Source: National Endowment for the Arts data.

Note: N = 105, however, because of missing data, calculations for all variables are not always based on 105 cases.

Local governments play a major role in the revitalization process, although usually their role emerges only after the process has begun. There does not appear to be a significant variation in the types of roles government plays; but of neighborhoods receiving several types of government attention—regulation, planning, allocation of federal funds, preservation, historic designation, and other activities—gentrification neighborhoods are much more likely to have received this multiple assistance than upgrading neighborhoods, while in upgrading areas it is regulation and allocation of resources such as Community Development Block Grant funds (CDBG) that are most common.

It is also significant to find that gentrification areas are almost as likely to have benefited from block-grant funds as are upgrading areas, since 28 percent of upgrading neighborhoods and 20 percent of gentrification neighborhoods have received (by 1979) some assistance under the CDBG program. This figure is particularly signficant since many of the variables analyzed distinguish so well the characteristics of the two types of areas and the beneficiaries of the investment in each. These findings lend support to the argument that block-grant funds have been dispersed, rather than targeted to the most needy areas, and that, whether intentionally or not, it is sometimes gentrification, not low- and moderate-income benefit, that is provided.

The Postreinvestment Character of Neighborhoods

Chapter 3 in this book, by Gale, documents and highlights the character of the population of gentrified neighborhoods. Gale notes that dramatic changes occur with gentrification such that the nature of everything from home prices to types of public services in demand changes. Dealing with the change in the neighborhood and dealing with those who are displaced are major issues for local urban planning.

For the neighborhood where long-term residents reinvest, the changes are less dramatic but nevertheless important. Property maintenance is improved. Values and rents rise modestly by comparision with gentrified neighborhoods. The changes are consistent with the kind of perceptual and behavioral change that Goetze and Colton describe in chapter 4. Replicating this process is the major goal of the neighborhood-planning thrust examined in part IV of this book.

Some Notes on Neighborhoods Not Revitalized

While survey and field data we have presented to this point focus on neighborhoods that underwent revitalization, we have also been able to make some observations about neighborhoods that did not undergo revitalization during the late 1970s and seem to have been consistently if not systematically passed over by private-investment initiatives. There are several general conclusions about the features of such neighborhoods:

1. *Neighborhoods that have a substantial number of large multifamily housing structures or developments, especially those that are publically assisted.* (The exception is those areas that attracted condominum conversion.) This is perhaps expected, given the important role played by small owner-investors and the importance of private money in the initial stages of the process. It requires some capital on the part of the individual or small speculator to do the substantial rehabilitation and to expose himself to the substantial financial risk involved in rehabilitating large structures—especially when such structures would not be marketable without a subsidy, and then only as rental units. (Condominiums, while noted widely in the popular literature, account for less than 2 percent of the 1970 housing stock.) Areas dominated by public housing or assisted housing also have difficulty attracting private investment.

2. *Housing condition is less important than housing location, so neighborhoods with less attractive locational and physical features (as opposed to poor condition) are overlooked.* Often the gentry pay more for housing that is in poor condition to get attractive locational or physical features. The gentry are interested in locating near the central business district. Distant areas are more inaccessible or isolated and are therefore relatively less attractive to the gentry who desire city life not the serenity of distant more suburbanlike residential areas. These more distant areas are more likely candidates for upgrading, since residents have firmer ties to their neighborhoods. But even for this group, isolation is a negative feature.

For upgrading neighborhoods, however, condition is important. These neighborhoods tend to be areas where the housing, while showing some signs of blight, are nevertheless quite sound. A fundamental commitment by owners seems to be a prerequisite for success of such efforts.

3. *Areas with very mixed and incompatible land use discourage revitalization.* Our findings indicate that the gentry do not mind locating in areas of mixed land use, as long as the land uses are attractive and consistent with their life style and tastes. Gentry do not mind for example, a bakery or a delicatessen or even a college or office building. What they do mind are so-called nuisance uses—gas stations, bars, garages, liquor stores, fast-food places, drug clinics, and the like. The nuisances often exist on main thoroughfares between downtown and the outlying communities. Areas where these uses have concentrated are feared as sources of traffic, crime, blight, and congestion. Where these uses or their impact cannot be controlled, and especially where the neighborhood is some distance from the core, the chances of private reinvestment by anyone, including incumbents, are more limited.

This chapter summarizes the experience of large cities undergoing neighborhood revitalization. Our findings do not suggest that cities have turned the corner in meeting the tremendous problems they face in providing decent housing and neighborhood environments for their citizens or in reversing the decline that is so widespread. All of the problems remain.[9] Yet we have found: (1) a more positive attitude about the possibility of improvement; (2) the rediscovery of a few areas by the middle class; (3) new confidence by long-term residents in selected areas; and (4) new nonresidential investment in many downtowns that attracts and complements residential investment.

While impressive, these new developments reflect relatively little change in overall conditions of urban distress. During the five-to-seven-year period of revitalization reported in this survey there was much more decline than revitalization in traditional inner-city neighborhoods. The experience documented in this study merely documents possibilities for city neighborhoods and explains aspects of the process by which change occurs.

While we do not want to encourage undue optimism, neither do we wish to encourage naïveté or paralyzing pessimism. Devising public and private interventions to replicate the revitalization that the experience we have documented suggests is possible is likely to be more difficult in the future than any projects cities will attempt.

Policy Implications

The reader might now ask what is the outlook for reinvestment as we move through the 1980s. What is reported on here are mostly developments that began in the mid-1970s and reached their high point in the late 1970s. The recession and high interest rates have slowed activity since 1981.

Assuming the economic recovery takes place, we can expect reinvestment to pick up. There are some neighborhoods ripe for gentrification. There are some modest apartment buildings in good locations that will be converted to condominiums. Our view is that the pace of the late 1970s will not be equaled in the 1980s in most cities. The investment outlook for gentrification is less favorable with variable interest rates, alternative urban housing options, and so on. Values are flat and whole new areas (older suburbs nears cities, recycled nonresidential structures, and such) offer alternative frontiers for the urban pioneers. Local groups and local government are more sensitive to the displacement issue so that some initiatives that would have occurred in the 1970s—preconscious of displacement—will not be allowed in the 1980s.

For neighborhoods of long-term residents, we think there will be an increase in the pace of reinvestment if economic conditions improve. The possibility that these households could improve their housing by moving is now largely limited by higher home prices and the tendency of older people to be more stable in their location. The potential for significant expansion in this area is directly related to the ability of local-government and community-based organizations to orchestrate the process for incumbent upgrading. Many of the chapters that follow address the specifics of what these efforts might include.

While there is a federal role—housing assistance, block grants, credit, tax and regulatory policy, and so on—most of the programs to revitalize neighborhoods in the United States will have to originate locally (and with states.) Here lies both the challenge and opportunity of neighborhood planning.

Notes

1. See generally, The National Commission on Neighborhood, *People, Building Neighborhood: Final Report to the President and the Congress of the United States* (Washington: U.S. Government Printing Office, 1979).

2. See generally U.S. White House Interagency Coordinating Council, *Urban Action: A New Partnership to Conserve America's Communities* (Washington: U.S. Government Printing Office, 1979).

3. See Department of Housing and Urban Development, *The President's National Urban Policy Report—1982* (Washington: Department of Housing and Urban Development, 1982), pp. 1–24.

4. For a description of sample and methodology as well as a fuller discussion of findings, see Phillip L. Clay, *Neighborhood Renewal* (Lexington, Mass.: D.C. Heath and Co., Lexington Books, 1979), ch. 1, appendix B.

5. For a detailed description and evaluation of the NHS program, see Phillip L. Clay, *Neighborhood Partnerships in Action* (Washington: Neighborhood Reinvestment Corporation, 1981).

6. For a discussion of the displacement see Gale (chapter 3, this book) and Chester Hartman et al., *Displacement: How to Fight It* (Berkeley: National Housing Law Project, 1981), chs. 2–4.

7. For a recent assessment of urban decline, see generally Katherine Bradbury and Anthony Downs, *Urban Decline and the Future of American Cities* (Washington, D.C.: Brookings Institution, 1982).

8. For a detailed analysis of the financial aspects of incumbent reinvestment in NHS neighborhoods, see Maynard Robison and Gary Ferguson, *Evaluation of the Urban Reinvestment Task Force* (Cambridge, Mass.: Urban Systems Research and Engineering, Inc., 1981), parts 1, 3.

9. Katherine Bradbury and Anthony Downs, *Urban Decline and the Future of American Cities* (Washington, D.C.: Brookings Institution, 1982).

3

Middle-Class Resettlement in Older Urban Neighborhoods: The Evidence and Implications

Dennis E. Gale

In recent years, a small but growing number of middle-class households have moved into declining, older central-city neighborhoods in the United States. Though a few of these areas were the sites of urban-renewal programs, most have undergone renovation and restoration through private-investment activity. The significance of this movement, termed *neighborhood resettlement* here, lies in its stark contrast to the urban-to-suburban migration patterns that have predominated in metropolitan areas at least since the 1950s. Indeed, an elaborate body of residential-location theory has developed since the 1920s, much of which assumes that households filter up through the housing supply as their family size and economic status grow. Housing and neighborhoods, on the other hand, filter downward as increasing age renders both architectural styles and technological features obsolete (Lowry 1960) and these areas became economic for progressively lower-income groups (Grigsby 1963). One common result in older urban residential areas is invasion and succession, whereby households of lower socioeconomic status displace those of higher status (Duncan and Duncan 1957). Conversely, there is evidence that in the 1970s significant numbers of young households have filtered downward to an older housing stock and, consequently, their neighborhoods have filtered upward through a myriad of individual rehabilitations. In effect, a reverse invasion-and-succession process is replacing households of lower socioeconomic circumstances with those of higher circumstances.

In a survey of public officials and real-estate officials in 143 cities, J. Thomas Black found that 48 percent of communities over 50,000 population had some degree of private-market, nonsubsidized housing renovation underway in older deteriorated neighborhoods (1975). Another survey, of public officials and local citizen organizations in the thirty largest U.S. cities, discovered that resettlement was occurring in

Reprinted by permission of the *Journal of the American Planning Association* 45 (July 1979).

almost all of them. Fifty-three such neighborhoods were found (Clay 1978). In a study of forty-four cities, substantial private-market rehabilitation was identified in almost 75 percent (National Urban Coalition 1978). Sixty-five resettlement neighborhoods were located.

One important key to understanding the reasons for this apparent departure from classical precepts of residential-location theory is the development of broad-based data from opinion surveys of resettlement households. Unfortunately, such comprehensive statistics do not yet exist. Nevertheless, a number of individual, separately conducted surveys have been performed recently in U.S. resettlement neighborhoods and together their results provide some important indications as to the identity of the resettlers, their geographic origins, and the reasons for their residential-location choice. These studies were conducted in Atlanta (McWilliams 1975), Boston and Cambridge (Pattison 1977), New Orleans (Ragas and Miestchovich 1977), New York (New York Landmarks Conservancy 1977), St. Paul (Urban Land Institute 1976), and Washington, D.C. (Gale 1977a, 1976).

Other evidence indicates that negative externalities occur in the form of the displacement of many low- and moderate-income households by the renovation process. Together these data form a preliminary composite description of the extent and character of neighborhood resettlement. Though the condition of this evidence does not permit more sophisticated analyses, the sheer paucity of published quantitative studies and the critical nature of the subject itself warrant the present preliminary investigation.

Demographic Characteristics of Resettlers

Data sources are sufficient to permit observations on six demographic characteristics of resettler households: household size, racial composition, annual income, and the age, education, and occupation of the household head. (See table 3–1.)

Household Size

With comparatively few exceptions, resettler households tend to be small. At least one-half (48 percent) in one Boston neighborhood and as many as 97 percent in an Atlanta area are composed of one or two persons. Nationwide, about one-half of all households are composed of one or two persons (U.S. Bureau of the Census 1977, I). At least 60 percent in each neighborhood have no children present. Household size in the New

York neighborhood tended to be larger, though this may be attributable to the fact that it underwent resettlement several years ago.

Racial Composition

With pitifully few exceptions, the resettler households were composed of whites. In a few cases, mixed households (one black and one white) appeared. In three cities white households composed between 94 and 97 percent of all resettler households. One Washington neighborhood showed a black resettler proportion of 14 percent, though blacks make up 75 percent of the city's population. By contrast, the mean proportions of whites and blacks in metropolitan central cities in the United States in 1970 were 75 and 23 percent, respectively (Advisory Commission on Intergovernment Relations 1977).

Annual Income

Neighborhoods in only four cities provided data on household income and it is not apparent whether gross or net income figures were presented. Nonetheless, the evidence confirms suspicions that resettler households generally are comfortably middle income. More than one-half (56 percent) in the Atlanta neighborhood and 88 percent in the New York area had incomes of $15,000 or more. Almost one-half (46 percent) in New Orleans reported incomes of $20,000 or more while 73 percent and 90 percent in two Washington neighborhoods had such incomes. These figures compare closely to the 49.4 percent of families nationally earning $15,000 or more in 1975, when the median family income was almost $14,900 (U.S. Bureau of the Census 1977, I).

Age

Clearly, the largest group of household heads in resettlement families tends to range in age from the mid-twenties to the mid-thirties. No city reported less than 40 percent in this age group. Nationally, only 20 percent of household heads fell in this range in 1976 (U.S. Bureau of the Census 1977, I). Those resettlers in the age thirty-five to forty-four interval represent the next largest group; at least 20 percent fell in this range while nationally 16 percent did so.

Table 3–1
Demographic Characteristics of Recent In-Migrants in Individual Resettlement Neighborhoods in Selected Cities
(in percentage)

City in Which Resettlement Neighborhood Is Located	Household Size[b]				Age of Household Head[b]				Racial Makeup of Household			Household Annual Income[b]				Highest Education of Household Head			Occupation of Household Head		
	One-Person	Two-Person	Two or Fewer	No Children Present	20–29	25–34	30–39	35–44	White	Black	Mixed	Under $15,000	$15,000 or More	Under $20,000	$20,000 or More	Less than Four-Year College Degree	Four-Year College Degree	Graduate Degree or Graduate Work	Professional and Technical	Managerial	Other
Atlanta (1975)	27	70		66	41		39		99			39	56			38	38	24	57	12	31
New Orleans (1977)	45	27	72	75+		43		24	97						46						
New York (1977)	8		42	64		74[d]										20	18	61	57	10	33
St. Paul (1975)							46[f]					4	88[g]				80[e]		55	27	8
Washington, D.C.[a] (1977/1976)	29/23	55/60		74/61		59/63		21/23	94/77	0/14	0/7			7/22	90/73	3/13	10/21	87/65			
Boston (1972–1975)		48[c]				63		21											60	5	35
Cambridge (1972–1975)		80[c]				50		39											82	–	18

Sources: Sybil W. McWilliams, *Recycling a Declining Community: Middle Class Migration to Virginia-Highlands*, School of Urban Life, Georgia State University, December 1975; Wade R. Ragas and Ivan J. Miestchovich, *Summary Analysis of Households in the Lower Garden District*, Urban Studies Institute, University of New Orleans, New Orleans, 1977; *The Impacts of Historic District Designation*, New York

Landmarks Conservancy, New York, 1977; *Private Market Housing Renovation: A Case Study of the Hill District of St. Paul*, Urban Land Institute, Washington, D.C., 1976; Dennis E. Gale, *The Back-to-the-City Movement . . . or Is It?*, occasional paper, Department of Urban and Regional Planning, George Washington University, Washington, D.C., 1976; Gale, *The Back-to-the-City Movement Revisited*, occasional paper, Department of Urban and Regional Planning, George Washington University, Washington, D.C., 1977; Timothy Pattison, *The Process of Neighborhood Upgrading and Gentrification*, Unpublished thesis, Massachusetts Institute of Technology, Cambridge, Mass., 1977.

[a]Two neighborhoods reported.

[b]Categories are not mutually exclusive because each study was conducted independently of the others.

[c]Data for the period 1957–1975.

[d]Data for ages twenty-one through thirty-nine.

[e]Eight percent have at least four years of college.

[f]Forty-six percent were between ages twenty-five and forty-four. Fifty-four percent were over age forty-four. None were under age twenty-five.

[g]Twelve percent earned $15,000 to $24,999. Forty-two percent earned $25,000 to $49,999. Thirty-five percent earned $50,000 or more.

Education

No other indicators are as impressive as those on the level of education achieved by resettler household heads. Most had completed at least a four-year college-degree program in Atlanta (62 percent), New York (79 percent), St. Paul (80 percent), and Washington (97/86 percent). By comparison, only 14.7 percent of the U.S. population age twenty-five and older held a four-year college degree in 1976 (U.S. Bureau of the Census 1977, II). In highly competitive employment markets such as New York and Washington, where specialized graduate education is often required, 61 percent and 87 percent had achieved graduate degrees. But, even in Atlanta, a rapidly growing regional center, fully one-fourth (24 percent) of resettlers hold graduate degrees.

Occupation

Closely correlated to education is the head-of-household's occupation. More than one-half of household heads in resettlement neighborhoods in Atlanta, New York, St. Paul, Boston, and Cambridge, Massachusetts, were classified as professionals. Managerial and administrative occupations were much less in evidence in most neighborhoods, though in St. Paul 27 percent were found to fall in this category. Clerical, sales, and blue-collar employees constituted as much as 35 percent of the remaining portion. As a rough basis of comparison, 15.2 percent of U.S. employed persons were classified as professional or technical workers in 1976 and 10.6 percent were in managerial and administrative positions (U.S. Bureau of the Census 1977, II).

Collectively, these data lend considerable weight to popular characterizations of resettlers. The most typical such household is childless and composed of one or two white adults in their late twenties or thirties. College educated, often possessing graduate education, the household head is most likely a professional or (less commonly) a manager. The annual household income varies among metropolitan areas but is likely to range between $15,000 and $30,000, with several resettlers earning more than $40,000. Doubtless, many of those earning higher incomes are composed of two workers. For the most part, the above evidence seems to be supported by more descriptive accounts of resettlement in several U.S. cities.

Geographic Origins of Resettlers

One of the most misunderstood notions about the inner-city neighborhood-resettlement phenomenon is the origin of its participants. Where are the resettlers moving from? The answer is important for obvious reasons. To the extent that the reinvestment process continues and grows, it could have a substantial effect on the future viability of central cities. The list of benefits municipal governments derive from this process— improved housing stock, lower demands for social services, higher real-estate taxes and other revenues, more affluent consumer participation in the central-city economy—are considerable.

If the resettlers were migrating in from the surrounding suburbs in sufficient numbers, they would help to offset the well-documented suburban movement of city dwellers, the bane of large-city governments for many years. For public officials to stimulate private-market investment in older urban neighborhoods, it is important for them to understand from where the current resettlers—and therefore, potential future resettlers—are coming.

Unfortunately, a popular wisdom has developed that refers to resettlement as the *back-to-the-city movement*. Thus many observers have assumed, with little or no evidence, that most resettlers are dissatisfied former suburbanites:

> What is beginning to happen now in America is a flowback of people from suburbs. . . . They rehabilitate old housing because it is cheaper than building new homes. Older people flow back because their children . . . are now grown and departed. Young couples do it because they can't afford the suburbs and because they prefer the life style of the cities. (Eric Sevareid, CBS Evening News, 8 July 1977)

To the contrary, evidence indicates that a relatively small minority of households moved into resettlement neighborhoods from the city's encircling suburbs (see table 3–2). Less than 20 percent of resettlers surveyed in Atlanta, Boston, Cambridge, and Washington said that they had done so. In fact, more appear to have located in some cities from outside the metropolitan area altogether (that is, from communities in other parts of the United States). The data indicate that more than one-half (and in some cases as many as 90 percent) already were seasoned urbanites, having moved to the renovating area from somewhere within the city's municipal boundaries.

Not only do few resettlers appear to be exsuburbanites, there is evidence that most consciously embraced inner-city living and/or rejected a suburban location when looking for a house to purchase. In other words, few appear to have "settled" for an inner-city dwelling as a second-best alternative to a suburban home. On the contrary, other observers suggest that the life style associated with suburban residence and/or the presumed ideology of its inhabitants is at odds with those of most resettlers.

> There is a very conscious rejection of suburbia, or rather a conscious

Table 3–2

Previous Location of Recent In-Migrants to Resettlement Neighborhoods

(in percentage)

City in Which Resettlement Neighborhood Is Located	Lived in the Central City	Lived in the Suburbs	Lived Outside the Metropolitan Area
Atlanta (1975)	57	8	35
Boston (1972–1975)	72	15[b]	–
Cambridge (1972–1975)	90	15[b]	–
New Orleans (1977)	–	–	26
Washington (1977/1976)[a]	71/67	15/18	14/16

Sources: Sybil W. McWilliams, *Recycling a Declining Community: Middle Class Migration to Virginia-Highlands,* School of Urban Life, Georgia State University, December 1975; Timothy Pattison, *The Process of Neighborhood Upgrading and Gentrification,* Unpublished thesis, Massachusetts Institute of Technology, Cambridge, Mass., 1977; Wade R. Ragas and Ivan J. Miestchovich, *Summary Analysis of Housholds in the Lower Garden District,* Urban Studies Institute, University of New Orleans, New Orleans, 1977; Dennis E. Gale, *The Back-to-the-City Movement . . . or Is It?,* occasional paper, Department of Urban and Regional Planning, George Washington University, Washington, D.C., 1976; Gale, *The Back-to-the-City Movement Revisited,* occasional paper, Department of Urban and Regional Planning, George Washington University, Washington, D.C., 1977.

[a]Two neighborhoods reported.

[b]The maximum proportion of housholds from the suburbs or elsewhere in Massachusetts was 15 percent.

> rejection of the somewhat stereotyped "image" of suburbia . . . by residents in the area, and a correspondingly positive assertion of the values of "urban living". . . . From this perspective suburbia is seen as a retreat from the reality of major social problems facing American society; and residents who . . . move from the area are defined by others and to a degree, themselves as "selling out"—not simply a house—but an ideology and a movement (Hunter 1975).

Statistics from a survey of resettlers in an Atlanta neighborhood indicate that over two-thirds (69 percent) preferred a central-city, rather than a suburban, residential setting. More than one-third looked only in the study neighborhood for a home. More than one-half of the remainder (51 percent) looked only in city neighborhoods, mostly renovation areas (McWilliams 1975).

The strongly urban-oriented predilections of resettlers, at least in transitional neighborhoods, contrast sharply with their earlier experiences, if the results of the Washington surveys are representative of most resettlers nationwide (Gale 1977a, 1976). Slightly less than two-thirds

(64 percent and 61 percent) in two such neighborhoods reported that they had spent all or most of their childhood years in a suburban, small town, or rural setting. In addition, at least three-fourths (77 percent and 88 percent) spent those years living in a single-family detached house, the style most associated with suburban and suburbanlike living. This latter finding is significant because most Washington resettlers (indeed, it appears, most resettlers nationwide) live in row houses located in higher density areas, a dwelling type more commonly linked to inner-city living. Hence, their current locational choice, although a continuation of their adult urban locational preference, represents a decided departure from their childhood experiences.

Why Did They Move to the Neighborhood?

No factor related to the resettlement phenomenon so intrigues some researchers and public officials as the explanation of why it is happening at all. Though the varied sources of the data discussed here permit only loose comparisons, it is clear that four conditions most appealed to the respondents: an acceptable housing price, the investment potential of the property, accessibility to place of employment, and the architectural/historical character of the house and/or neighborhood (see table 3–3). Of these four, the last showed the most consistently high ratings. From 72 to 85 percent of the respondents in Atlanta, New Orleans, and New York rated architectural/historical character highly, and those in Washington valued it only slightly less so than their property's investment potential.

Generally, economic variables related to the price and the investment potential of the house and to the employment accessibility variable appear to be of approximately equal importance overall. Though individual resettlers vary in the relative weight they ascribe to each characteristic, there are few who are likely not to cite one or more as critical in their locational choice. From 42 to 70 percent of resettlers in three cities rated an acceptable housing price as among their highest concerns in locational choice; in Washington, it was comparably rated. Though data is sparse, table 3–3 hints that the resettler's concern over the investment potential of his property was an even more compelling consideration than its price. Because most resettlers are purchasing their first home, it is likely that they do so with an especially critical eye to the promise of a substantial, relatively rapid, capital gain in the future.

Easy access to place of employment was a salient matter also, ranging from 39 to 70 percent in the proportion of resettlers who rated it

Table 3–3
Reasons Given by Resettlers for Their Residential Location Choice
(in percentage)

Cities in Which Resettlement Neighborhood is Located	Acceptable Housing Price	Investment Potential of the Property	Accessibility to Place of Employment	Architectural-Historical Character of House and/or Neighborhood	Cultural, Social, and/or Shopping Opportunities Available in the City	Desire to Live in a Racially Integrated, Diverse Neighborhood	Desire to Live near Friends Who Reside In or near the Neighborhood	Proximity to a University
Atlanta (1975)[a]	70	–	66	72	73	–	27	29
New Orleans (1977)[a]	60	75	70	83	–	–	–	–
New York (1977)[a,b]	42	–	39	85	23	4	19	–
Washington (1977/1976)[c]	17/19	22/24	16/13	18/14	14/10	6/14	7/7	–

Sources: Sybil W. McWilliams, *Recycling a Declining Community: Middle Class Migration to Virginia-Highlands*, School of Urban Life, Georgia State University, December 1975; Ralph Thayer and Paul Waidhas, "What Do In-Town Investors Want?" *Urban Land*, June 1977, p. 77; *The Impacts of Historic District Designation*, New York Landmarks Conservancy, New York, 1977; Dennis E. Gale, *The Back-to-the-City Movement . . . or Is It?*, occasional paper, Department of Urban and Regional Planning, George Washington University, Washington, D.C., 1976; Gale, *The Back-to-the-City Movement Revisited*, occasional paper, Department of Urban and Regional Planning, George Washington University, Washington, D.C., 1977.

[a]Respondents could choose more than one highly favorable characteristic. Thus, percentages do not equal 100.

[b]Some figures represent responses from residents who moved into the neighborhood before historic designation and others from those who moved in afterward.

[c]Two neighborhoods reported. Figures represent the proportion of respondents identifying each factor as among the three most important in influencing their locational choice.

highly in three renovation neighborhoods. Again, in Washington, results were comparable.

Implications for Theory

These data, though limited geographically, are important for the light they shed on the complex of factors that enter into the resettler's locational decision. Unfortunately, the few published attempts at this subject have been confined to arguments based largely on economic assumptions. For example, one observer claims that rapidly rising suburban prices for new homes, due to inflation in labor, materials, and financing costs and to restrictive growth controls, have "forced many homebuyers with limited economic means to stay in cities" (James 1978). As the evidence previously cited indicates though, most resettlers eschew suburban living not for economic reasons but due to matters of taste related to their lifestyles. And, because few have children, most such households are not compelled to leave the cities to seek better public education. The absence of children and the high incidence of two-worker households increase family per-capita income and, if anything, render many suburban housing opportunities quite affordable. Clearly, most resettlers' urban locational choices are their first preferences and not a second-best alternative to suburban living.

Another researcher presents an interesting theoretical model to explain resettler behavior and concludes that two variables predominate: the number of household workers and household size (Yezer 1977). He argues that in many resettler households both husband and wife are employed. Hence, commuting costs are considerably higher. Therefore, it becomes economically rational to minimize commuting costs by living close to the central-business-district employment center. This argument, though plausible, ignores the fact that with two breadwinners household income also rises. It is likely that this condition will overcome most increases in commuting costs and, hence, two-worker resettler households will have great flexibility of locational choice within the metropolitan area.

The second variable, household size, is somewhat more helpful in contributing to an explanation of the resettler's locational choice. It is claimed that because most such households are childless and, therefore, need less dwelling and yard space, they act rationally in choosing the generally smaller properties available in older urban neighborhoods. Of course, it could be argued that many inner-city homes in fact, are quite spacious when compared to new suburban dwellings. Built in the nineteenth century when larger numbers of children and extended families were de rigueur, many of these properties compete quite well with all but the most affluent suburban subdivision homes. It is true however, that inner-city yard space is not likely to be as large. This argument aside, it is apparent that young singles and couples without children do have the option of reducing housing costs by purchasing less space. Therefore, the resettler's locational preference is economically rational (Gale 1977a).

Residential-location models based on economic rationale provide a critically important theoretical framework for understanding metropolitan development patterns. However, most such constructs have assumed that it is economically rational behavior for younger middle-income households to move outward from the central business district to progressively more affluent neighborhoods as they pass through a conventional life cycle (Hoover and Vernon 1959). In doing so, they make a choice to trade off greater commuting distance (that is, time and expense) for more living space, as well as a better package of public services. Generally, the models presuppose that these households will aspire to new housing and neighborhoods, leaving behind older areas as soon as economic circumstances permit (Birch 1971). Yet, as Firey demonstrated in the 1940s, many locational choices ignore these attractions (1947). Instead, they place an economic value on the cultural, historical, or architectural character of an area, as well as accessibility to the central business district. Consequently, small, centralized enclaves of older, well-maintained housing such as Boston's Beacon Hill or New York City's Grammercy Park have survived the normal deterioration process that accompanies architectural and technological obsolescence. The neighborhood-resettlement phenomenon of the 1970s demonstrates a significant growth in this ethic. It is expressed in rising sales prices in neighborhoods where property values previously remained stagnant or declined. To the extent that this reinvestment process continues to burgeon, it will require planners and model builders to reinterpret the filtering-up process, so as to include alternative economic choices based on architectural, historical, cultural, and accessibility values. The use of opinion-survey data in conjunction with studies of economic indicators such as property-value trends (Meadows and Call 1978) should help to explain the resettlement phenomenon and give insights as to its future.

The Displacement Dilemma

Neighborhood resettlement gives prima facie evidence of providing myriad benefits to local governments at very little cost. Improvement of the housing stock, increased real-estate taxes and other revenues, reduced demand for social-welfare services, lower serious crime rates, diminished neighborhood population densities, higher home-ownership rates, and reduced enrollment pressures on neighborhood schools are all probable outcomes of middle-class reinvestment in many older urban neighborhoods. Yet, it is apparent from mass-media accounts and protests by neighborhood organizations that the rate at which disadvantaged households are being involuntarily displaced has increased significantly in recent years.

Typically, dislocation results when rapid reinvestment in formerly declining neighborhoods stimulates inflation in property values, causing rents and property taxes to rise and evictions for renovation to increase. Because most neighborhood resettlement is the result of private-market investment activities and not a publicly controlled program such as urban renewal, the displacement impact is considerably more difficult to evaluate than it was when relocation programs were available to monitor and subsidize the process. The Uniform Relocation Assistance Act of 1970 does not provide for those uprooted by private rehabilitation efforts. Hence, the few dislocation relief programs that exist have been developed by local governments (Gale 1978a and b).

Evidence on the magnitude and dimensions of displacement, especially by private-market forces, is not yet in very precise form. One survey of realtors, public officials, and civic leaders in the thirty largest cities has concluded that significant dislocation was occurring in 82 percent of the neighborhoods undergoing middle-class renovation (Clay 1978). An analysis of R.L. Polk Company data and other sources estimated that in no community were more than 100 to 200 households being displaced annually by private-market forces except for a few cities such as Washington, D.C., and San Francisco (Grier and Grier 1978). The U.S. Department of Housing and Urban Development studied unpublished tabulations of the 1974–1976 Annual Housing Surveys and estimated that the annual number of metropolitan households displaced by public and private actions ranged from 364,000 to 373,000. These households constituted slightly less than 4 percent of the total population of movers in each year. The highest proportion of those displaced among all movers occurred in the northeast region of the United States (4.3 percent) and the lowest, in the West (3.8 percent). Unfortunately, these data do not include moves due to rental increases, a major impetus in many household displacements (Cousar 1978).

The racial implications of resettlement were examined in a survey of local observers in forty-four cities by the National Urban Coalition (1978). About one-half of neighborhoods undergoing renovation were thought to have lost minority-group members since resettlement began and about one-third experienced no change. Thirteen percent were thought to have had an increase. An analysis of a resettlement area in Alexandria, Virginia, projected an average decline in black housing occupancy of 85 households per year between 1975 and 1980. Many of these would be at or near retirement age (Hammer, Siler, George Associates 1976).

Other neighborhood surveys have touched upon the social effects of displacement but have been inconclusive about the costs of replacement housing for rental dislocatees. Estimates in a renovation neighborhood in St. Louis (Hu 1978) and in New Orleans (Ragas and Miestchovich 1977) concluded that about one-half of renovated homes in each had been vacant prior to renovation. Both implied that evictions for reinvestment purposes in these units do not appear to have occurred. Hu found that nearly all owner-households leaving the renovation area did so because of life-cycle factors related to "old age, illness, and family problems." However, his study could not determine the reasons for which renters left the area. Ragas and Miestchovich discovered that most outmigrating households had little difficulty locating another nearby rental unit of comparable quality and size but may have had to pay a higher rent. They concluded that about fifty to sixty persons were displaced in the neighborhoods each year.

Collectively, these studies suggest that the involuntary movement of households, usually low- or moderate-income ones, in response to private-market rehabilitation of neighborhoods has grown significantly in the 1970s. Blacks and other minorities, as well as the elderly, appear to be disproportionately affected. Yet, there is little evidence that, except for a few cities, dislocation directly affects a very large number of households per year. Where middle-class rehabilitation proceeds at a moderate pace and where the vacancy rate in the existing housing stock approximates national averages, the impact of resettlement is likely to be modest. Nonetheless, it will be important, on both political and humanitarian grounds, for local governments to carefully monitor the reinvestment process. Where the social costs become excessive, planners and public officials should be prepared to respond with effective measures to mitigate the rate and intensity of displacement.

Implications for Policy

The primary significance of the present review is in its implications for urban planners and policy professionals concerned with central-city revitalization. First, it is clear that there has been a small but growing market among middle-class households in many urban areas for housing in older neighborhoods. However, it probably does not compose more than 25 percent of potential first-home buyers in the twenties and thirties age groups currently living in central cities. Secondly, there is proportionately, a much smaller market among suburbanites for such housing. In part, this may be due to poor information about inner-city housing opportunities and liabilities.

Thirdly, those factors that most attract resettlers to buy an older dwelling—sales price and investment *potential*—obviously, are least susceptible to manipulation by planners and public officials. Only the architectural and historical character of housing and neighborhoods and employment accessibility offer possibilities for policy intervention. Thus, preservation of such neighborhoods, adaptive reuse of older structures, careful blending of new and existing architecture, and improved public services and facilities may be the most promising programmatic activities for central-city planners. Just as important, although somewhat more difficult, is the attraction of new employment opportunities to the city and, especially, to the central business district. Unfortunately, neighborhood revitalization and economic development activities have sometimes been in conflict. This occurs when attractive older buildings in the CBD or in adjacent neighborhoods are demolished for higher-density uses such as office, commercial, or industrial activities. Attracting both neighborhood revitalization and new employment generation, while achieving a proper balance between the two, continues to be one of the most compelling, yet difficult, challenges facing planners in the future.

A fourth implication of the present research is in the notion of a stage theory of resettlement. Certainly, the observations herein are tentative at present; yet, the logic of such a theory seems highly plausible. It suggests that neighborhood resettlement takes place in increments and that overlapping but relatively distinct demographic subgroups may enter such neighborhoods at different phases during the reinvestment process. Planners and policymakers therefore, may want to view this as a kind of reverse filtering process. Hence, any strategy to attract middle-income households to older neighborhoods would concentrate first on younger singles and childless couples. Efforts to improve property values, such as historic districts and zoning, code enforcement, and public improvements, seem most appropriate at Stage One.

However, efforts to attract families with children and those with long-term commitment to the neighborhood will encompass not only these, but other activities, as well. Active and well-supported neighborhood advisory organizations are needed to encourage advocacy and political impact. The quality of public services—but especially education and crime control—will have to be raised. It seems apparent that any local government with a serious commitment to attracting and holding Stage Two households will have to be able to compete with the quality of these services in at least some of the surrounding municipalities.

Nonetheless, the disruptive effects of resettlement on some low- and moderate-income households cannot be ignored, either. Two roles for planners are suggested. First, efforts should be made to monitor the extent and severity of displacement of low- and moderate-income households, especially renters, due to private-reinvestment activity (Houstoun 1976). Secondly, where dislocation rates become excessive, displacement relief programs should be implemented (Gale 1978a and b, Weiler 1978). Certainly, some displaced households should be assigned a high priority for existing and future publicly subsidized units in programs such as Community Development Block Grants, Section 8, and Section 312.

Finally, thus far the present analysis has failed to ask, What happens to those central-city neighborhoods from which households migrate in order to settle in reinvestment areas? Will they decline? No evidence has been found by the author to suggest that the resettlement phenomenon is robbing Peter to pay Paul. Most resettlers appear to have been renters prior to buying a home in an older neighborhood. They appear to be exercising normal life-cycle options in acquiring a first dwelling in their late twenties and thirties. In previous decades most would have purchased in the suburbs or in a more affluent neighborhood in the city. Meanwhile, new renters, it would seem, move into the resettler's previous neighborhoods, replacing them. In other words, the resettlement phenomenon would seem not to affect these rental areas either positively or negatively. Admittedly however, the position is only conjecture and more substantive comment will have to await further empirical research.

The Future of Neighborhood Resettlement

Thus far this discussion has been limited to the current extent and character of neighborhood resettlement in the United States. What is the likelihood that this phenomenon will continue at the same rate or perhaps increase in the future? As the previous data indicate, most resettler households are composed of one or two members. Very few have children present and recent national statistics indicate that the number and proportion of these types of households have increased and are likely to continue doing so. The number of one-person households grew 29 percent between 1970 and 1975 while two-person households rose 19 percent. These two groups now comprise almost one-half of all U.S. households (U.S. Bureau of the Census 1977, I). The incidences of other demographic conditions such as the postponement of marriage and of childbearing, divorce rates, and cohabitation of unmarried couples have increased significantly in the 1970s (Population Reference Bureau 1977).

Many observers foresee a general continuation of these trends into the 1980s (Alonso 1977, Goetze 1976).

National demographic trends however, present only one dimension of the possible future of neighborhood resettlement. Decline or growth in white-collar employment in central cities, the impact of urban real-estate taxes and other exactions, and the extent and character of criminal activity also will influence this recently emergent phenomenon. The extent to which it can reach beyond young singles and couples and attract families with children is related primarily to the future quality of inner-city public education. At the present time though, it is clear that resettlement is limited largely to childless households whose life-styles embrace careerism and consumerism rather than "familism" (Johnston 1972). Because increasing numbers of these persons are postponing childbearing or are having smaller families, they have more income and time to devote to other pursuits. It is not apparent from the present analysis that neighborhood resettlement, *in vacuo*, can reverse the tide of net out-migration from central cities to suburbs that has continued since the postwar era. But, it is reasonable to suspect that this movement, an anomaly in metropolitan residential mobility patterns, will continue to grow in most central cities in the ensuing decade. To that extent, then, it could help to mitigate some of the debilitating effects of suburban magnetism.

References

Advisory Commission on Intergovernmental Relations. 1977. *Trends in metropolitan America*. Washington, D.C.

Alonso, William. 1977. *The population factor and urban structure*. Working paper no. 102. Cambridge, Mass.: Center for Population Studies, Harvard University.

Birch, David L. 1971. Toward a stage theory of urban growth. *Journal of the American Institute of Planners* 37 (March):78–87.

Black, J. Thomas. 1975. Private-market housing renovation in central cities: a ULI survey. *Urban Land* 34 (November):3–9.

Clay, Phillip L. 1978. *Neighborhood revitalization: issues, trends and strategies*. Cambridge, Mass.: Massachusetts Institute of Technology, Department of Urban Studies and Planning.

Cousar, Gloria. 1978. *Bulletin on HUD estimates of national displacement and pertinent program information*. Mimeographed. Washington, D.C.: U.S. Department of Housing and Urban Development.

Duncan, Otis D.; and Duncan, Beverly. 1957. *The Negro population of Chicago*. Chicago: The University of Chicago Press.

Firey, Walter. 1947. *Land use in central Boston.* Cambridge, Mass.: Harvard University Press.

Gale, Dennis E. 1978a. Dislocation of residents, *Journal of Housing* 35 (May):232–235.

————. 1978b. *Neighborhood resettlement and displacement: people and policies.* Occasional Paper. Washington, D.C.: George Washington University, Department of Urban and Regional Planning.

————. 1976. *The back-to-the-city movement . . . or is it?* Occasional paper. Washington, D.C.: George Washington University, Department of Urban and Regional Planning.

————. 1977a. *The back-to-the-city movement revisited.* Occasional paper. Washington, D.C.: George Washington University, Department of Urban and Regional Planning.

————. 1977b. The unpredictable reasons for inner-city living, *The Washington Post.* August 6, 1977: A 17.

Goetze, Rolf. 1976. *Building neighborhood confidence.* Cambridge, Mass.: Ballinger Publishing Company.

Grier, George; and Grier, Eunice. 1978. *Urban displacement: a reconnaissance.* Washington, D.C.: U.S. Department of Housing and Urban Development.

Grigsby, William G. 1963. *Housing markets and public policy.* Philadelphia: University of Pennsylvania Press.

Hammer, Siler, George Associates. 1976. *Final N.E.A. study report to the City of Alexandria, Virginia.* Mimeographed. Alexandria, Virginia: City of Alexandria.

Hoover, E.M.; and Vernon, R. 1959. *Anatomy of a metropolis.* Cambridge, Mass.: Harvard University Press.

Houstoun, Lawrence O., Jr. 1976. Neighborhood change and city policy. *Urban Land* 35 (July–August):3–9.

Hu, Joseph. 1978. Who's moving in and who's moving out—and why. *Seller/Servicer* 5 (May–June):19–29.

Hunter, Albert. 1975. The loss of community: an empirical test through replication. *American Sociological Review* 40 (October):537–558.

James, Franklin. 1978. *The revitalization of older urban neighborhoods: trends, forces and the future of cities.* Washington, D.C.: The Urban Institute.

Johnston, Ronald J. 1972. *Urban residential patterns.* New York: Praeger Publishers.

Lipton, S. Gregory. 1977. Evidence of central city revival. *Journal of the American Institute of Planners* 43 (April):136–147.

Lowry, Ira. 1960. Filtering and housing standards: a conceptual analysis. *Land Economics* 36 (November):362–370.

McWilliams, Sybil W. 1975. *Recycling a declining community: middle* class *migration to Virginia-Highlands*. Unpublished thesis. Georgia State University.

Meadows, George R.; and Call, Steven T. 1978. Combining housing market trends and resident attitudes in planning urban revitalization. *Journal of the American Institute of Planners* 44 (July):297–305.

National Urban Coalition. 1978. *City neighborhoods in transition*. Washington, D.C.

New York Landmarks Conservancy. 1977. *Impacts of historic district designation*. New York.

Parkman Center for Urban Affairs. 1977. *Young professionals and city neighborhoods*. Boston: City of Boston.

Pattison, Timothy. 1977. *The process of neighborhood upgrading and gentrification*. Unpublished thesis. Massachusetts Institute of Technology.

Population Reference Bureau. 1977. *Marrying, divorcing and living together*. Population Bulletin 32 (October):1–41.

Ragas, Wade R.; and Miestchovich, Ivan. 1977. *Summary analysis of households in the Lower Garden District*. New Orleans: University of New Orleans, Urban Studies Institute.

Urban Land Institute. 1976. *Private market housing renovation: a case study of the Hill District of St. Paul*. Washington, D.C.

U.S. Bureau of the Census. 1977. I. *Household and family characteristics, March 1976*. Series P–20, no. 311. Washington, D.C.

———. 1977. II. *Population characteristics, 1976*. Series P–20, no. 307. Washington, D.C.

Weiler, Conrad. 1978. *Handbook on reinvestment displacement*. Washington, D.C.: National Association of Neighborhoods.

Yezer, Anthony. 1977. Living patterns: why people move into the inner city. *Washington Post*, June 25: A 17.

Part II
The Dynamics of
Neighborhood Change

The present era of preoccupation with neighborhoods holds great promise for refining and strengthening theories of neighborhood change. In the recent past there have been several major theoretical contributions, each based upon many years of research and, in some cases, community action. The merits and demerits of the major theories—including those of David Birch, Rolf Goetze, Roger Ahlbrandt, Anthony Downs, Art Naparstek, and Gail Cincotta—have been debated vigorously by academics and also by practicing planners and community activists. An important feature of the present period is the high level of articulate criticism of all available theory by practicing professionals and activists. The strength of this criticism poses a major challenge to researchers to develop theory that more accurately describes neighborhood realities and provides a better basis for predicting the future and for assessing the consequences of alternative public and private policies.

Part II presents and compares major theoretical perspectives. The chapters discuss the relative significance of factors of population composition, rates of population change, physical condition, and perceptual factors. They contrast stage and homeostatic theories and examine the influences of variables external to individual neighborhoods. Part II includes a stages-of-demographic-change framework for viewing neighborhood change, an analysis of the attitudinal dimensions of change, and a discussion of the policy implications of alternative theoretical perspectives.

Chapter 4 by Rolf Goetze and Kent Colton moves beyond conventional stage theories by offering a model of steps in the processes of neighborhood development that is not unidirectional. The Goetze and Colton scheme for classifying neighborhoods focuses on the two key variables of housing condition and market perception. Their approach departs from that of Birch and Downs by placing greater emphasis on perceptual factors—the attitudes of present and prospective home buyers, realtors, bankers, and public officials.

Chapter 5, by Timothy Pattison, is a theoretically instructive case account of changes in the population and physical characteristics of a Boston neighborhood. While Pattison's account basically confirms the theoretical notions advanced by Goetze and Colton, he adds to the available theory about neighborhood change by refining our understanding of the stages of change. His particular contribution lies in documenting the characteristics of the different types of residents who move in and out during each period and analyzing the factors that influence their attitudes and their behavior.

In Chapter 6 Robert Kolodny reviews alternative theories—*Life-cycle* and *push-pull* perspectives, neighborhood change as an evolutionary process, and equilibrium theory. In tracing the consequences of competing theories, Kolodny examines the major policy options of accepting, slowing, or attempting to stop change. He argues that the policy dilemmas ultimately reduce to the question, For whom should neighborhoods be preserved? Kolodny advocates an approach of *managing* change on behalf of the *stayers* and the *in-movers*. He concludes with a critique of the behavioral theories espoused by Birch and Downs and with a discussion of the limits of local strategies for dealing with neighborhood change.

4

The Dynamics of Neighborhoods: A Fresh Approach to Understanding Housing and Neighborhood Change

Rolf Goetze and
Kent W. Colton

There is widespread confusion concerning the causes of neighborhood decline. In this confusion various interests argue from differing premises for conflicting solutions. It's an income problem. No, it's a race problem. No, the problem is lack of financial support from the banks; city complacency; corruption; and on and on.

This chapter will show that, rather than relying on any one causal force, the dynamics of cities evolve around a combination of influences.[1] The future of our cities in this country is not impossible. In fact, the demographic trends over the next decade provide a unique opportunity for city revitalization—although they also bring new challenges (Alonso 1977). However, the emphasis in formulating policy must be on understanding the dynamics of the urban marketplace and neighborhood change, and strategies must be tailored according to these neighborhood dynamics.

To highlight possible opportunities for the future, the next section of this chapter will review some of the influences that may contribute to a new life for the city, with a special emphasis on the underlying demographic trends. Following that, two sections will discuss the importance of understanding neighborhood market dynamics. Using Boston as an illustration, a classification scheme will be developed to explain the patterns of change that exist and to show how housing strategies must be tailored according to these dynamics. The concluding section will offer a recommended approach to achieve the so-called golden mean of neighborhood stability.

A New Life for the City?

Until quite recently it was fashionable to debate whether cities were worth saving. Housing experts seemed to be on an endless quest to cure blight,

Reprinted by permission of the *Journal of the American Planning Association* 46 (April 1980).

and the focus was on efforts to arrest decline and to restore the tax base for struggling urban areas. Although problems of blight still persist in many neighborhoods, a countermovement is also building. Suddenly urban neighborhoods are being rediscovered, urban chic is becoming in, and the cultural excitement and vitality of cities is receiving increasing attention (Allman 1978; Peirce 1977; Black 1975; Lipton 1977). Experts now seek a cure for *displacement,* a new term describing existing residents being priced out of their own neighborhoods. Magazine articles feature the "Middle Class Poor," and declare "Housing Outasight," while Sunday magazine supplements dwell on *brownstoning,* the restoration of nineteenth-century city residences that fell into neglect (Anderson 1977; Peirce 1977; Reinhold 1977).

A growing variety of influences have contributed to this renewed attention to urban neighborhoods. First, the 1973 oil shortages and embargo challenged people's beliefs that energy would always remain cheap and that commuting times would always improve. And shortages in 1979 have confirmed these concerns. Suddenly urban density, public transit, and even the availability of buses and taxicabs demonstrated their advantages. Not only is living in the city fun and culturally exciting for some, it may also have economic advantages.

Second, the bicentennial fostered a reappraisal of our American heritage. Many now place a greater value on older things. And experience has taught us that newness sometimes means shoddiness, advertisers' claims notwithstanding (Fichter 1977).

Third, and unobserved by many, an unprecedented flood of new households is forming from the babies born after World War II. These individuals crowded the suburban classrooms in the Kennedy years and then clamored to get into (and change) the universities in the Johnson years. Large numbers of these young now seek to own houses of their own. Some of these households, with a penchant or life style that thrives on urbanizing, are returning to the city. What percent will actually choose to buy in the city as compared to the suburbs is still undetermined, but undoubtedly demand for the existing stock will sharply increase.

Finally, housing is no longer viewed solely as shelter; rather it is a form of investment, a way to keep pace or ahead of inflation. With more women working—either to keep up with inflation or to seek a new life style—young, childless couples are less concerned with the quality of inner-city schools and two-wage households can afford to spend more on housing (Alonso 1977). By outbidding the single-earner family, though, they may also add to the growing inflation in property values.

It will not be known for a number of years whether these forces actually portend a permanent and significant return to city living or whether it is a transitory phenomenon hyped by the media.[2] However, some type of change is occurring and we can no longer look back. We must focus at least part of our attention on housing and urban neighborhoods and the interaction that is underway. One of the biggest determinants of this interaction is the post–World War II baby boom.

The Challenges and Opportunities of the Baby Boom

Most know of the baby bulge—the large number of children born between 1940 and 1965. While we have heard of overcrowded classrooms (now empty), the crush on colleges (with overbuilt dormitories), and the current intractable unemployment problems, we seldom connect these events. At each turn, accommodating this bulge has strained the system, and housing is no exception.

Figure 4–1 shows this national bulge of people turning thirty, the time of settling down. Until 1955 there was a steady progression as the system accommodated a regularly increasing number of people. Then, between 1955 and 1975, there was a relative shortfall. In this period, the nation was short an average 14 percent of the normal number of people turning thirty. But even more drama is in store for the period from 1975 to the year 2000, because during this period 16 percent more than normal will seek to settle. The stresses this will cause are hard to visualize in advance. Those who have spent the last twenty years fighting blight will be unprepared.

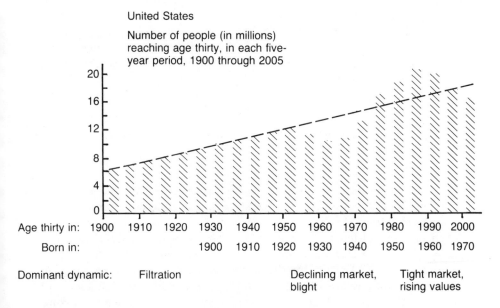

Figure 4–1. Number of People Reaching Age Thirty, 1900–2005

Decline is difficult to adjust to in our growth-oriented society, but between 1950 and 1965, the system was forced to adjust to a reduced rate in the number of people entering the housing market. Just about the time the system became reconciled with this slack period as a normal state, the baby bulge intruded, with staggering numbers trying to form independent households and become wage earners. From the late 1960s on through the mid-1990s, increases will be stunning.

Tidal-wave accounts describe how the wave first pulls the waters back, exposing the hidden ocean floor, before rushing in swamping everything in sight. In the decade of the sixties and the early seventies, we puzzled, exploring the mysterious ocean floor and arguing about questions of neighborhood blight, lack of mortgage credit, and dwindling city revenues. When the tidal wave of new households engulfs urban areas in the late seventies and eighties, most of the existing housing supply will be brought into play because the nation simply cannot produce enough new housing in the next fifteen or twenty years to meet the new demand.

For policymakers, the implications should be clear. The last twenty years can be characterized as the period when problems of urban blight caused special stress; and the coming twenty years may become the period of reinvestment, displacement, and speculation.[3] Lest we confuse this shift with the biblical image of the lean years followed by years of plenty, we must realize that increased demand brings benefits but also a measure of trauma, particularly for existing residents. Since all neighborhoods in urban areas are not influenced concurrently, policymakers will have to learn to separate healthy from pathological neighborhood evolution. Blight and deterioration will continue to be a problem, only less frequently. The new challenge will be to promote neighborhood stability and revitalization without displacement.

Neighborhood Market Dynamics: Boston as an Illustration

Housing condition alone is not a sufficient criterion for understanding neighborhood dynamics or for allocating housing and community-development resources. In the analysis described here, it is assumed that, left to themselves, different neighborhoods naturally evolve in different ways. A neighborhood-classification scheme will be introduced—using data from the city of Boston for illustrative purposes—that corresponds to these different patterns of change. In turn this classification scheme will be used in recommending policy choices. Only when the natural evolution of neighborhood housing markets is understood can the impact of various public-sector housing-program interventions be projected reliably.[4]

The key dimensions for the classification scheme are housing condition and market perception. Housing-condition data are essential for the analysis of various public interventions in different neighborhoods, serving both to indicate the need for such programs and to set limits on the potential cost of a given program. However, although necessary, housing-condition data are not sufficient for the purpose of determining housing policies appropriate to different neighborhoods. A host of other factors come into play in determining the future of a neighborhood, and in this chapter we have characterized this interaction of factors as *market perception*. (For an interesting discussion of citizen perception of their neighborhoods, see Ahlbrandt 1977.) These two dimensions—housing condition and market perception—provide the basis for the neighborhood-classification framework described below.

Based on an analysis of the city's housing condition, housing units in the neighborhoods in Boston were somewhat loosely classed into three categories: *good* condition requiring at most minor repairs such as exterior painting (no more than $1,000 per unit); *fair* condition requiring moderate repairs to deal with deferred maintenance ($1,000 to $3,000 per unit); and *poor* condition requiring major rehabilitation ($3,000 to $10,000) or demolition.[5]

Regarding market perception, the strength of the housing market in a neighborhood can be defined in terms of the relative number of households desiring to move into, stay in, or leave that neighborhood.[6] Three types of markets were identified. In the first—a strong, *rising* market— there are more applicants than vacancies, or more households who wish to live in the neighborhood than there are available dwelling units. In the second, a *stable* neighborhood, supply and demand balance out. And in the third, a *weak* market area, there are fewer households seeking to remain than available dwellings.

It is important to realize that variations in housing-market strength do not necessarily parallel housing condition. For example, comparison of housing condition and market strength in Boston revealed that areas in similar condition were subject to different market influences. There were neighborhoods—for example, the South End of Boston—that were in poor condition but where the market was strong. And in turn, some neighborhoods were in fair to good condition but the markets were weak and owners of sound houses were disinvesting because of fear that a lack of qualified buyers might result in possible neighborhood change.

A matrix results from combining the housing-condition dimension with the market-perception dimension, as shown in table 4–1. Some of the characteristics associated with different types of neighborhoods are

Table 4-1
Neighborhood Characteristics Associated with Housing Market Condition Classifications

Housing Condition	Market Perception				
	Rising (R)	Stable (S)	Declining (D)	Rapidly Declining (RD)	Total
Good (G) minor repairs required	G/R Rising values Rising rents 15 percent 33,400 dwelling units	G/S Ideal neighborhood 17 percent 39,700 dwelling units			32 percent 73,100 dwelling units
Fair (F) moderate repairs required	F/R Reverse filtration Absentees taking over Existing tenants being displaced Speculation 21 percent 48,300 dwelling units	F/S Greying Low turnover 23 percent 56,400 dwelling units	F/D Blockbusting Unrealistic expectations Arterial or industrial blight Racial fears 6 percent 12,800 dwelling units		50 percent 117,500 dwelling units
Poor (P) major repairs required		P/S Market bottomed out Some abandonment Realistic expectations 9 percent 22,000 dwelling units	P/D Abandonment Foreclosures Multi-problems 8 percent 17,300 dwelling units	P/RD Firebombing Disaster wholesale 1 percent 1,600 dwelling units	18 percent 40,900 dwelling units
Total	36 percent 81,700 dwelling units	49 percent 118,100 dwelling units	14 percent 30,100 dwelling units	1 percent 1,600 dwelling units	

Source: Rolf Goetze, *Building Neighborhood Confidence*, Ballinger, Cambridge, Mass., 1976, p. 35.

also identified. The *cost* of maintaining and upgrading is a function of condition; but the *incentive* to do so depends in many cases on the strength of housing demand and the change in market value resulting from upgrading. Markets perceived by key actors as rising or declining differ sharply in their behavior, and the futures, even of superficially similar neighborhoods with essentially the same housing condition, will differ widely.[7]

As an illustration, table 4–1 also shows the estimated percentage of Boston units that fell into each of the various neighborhood types. Only about half of Boston's stock was located in neighborhoods where housing supply and demand were in a state of balance, whereas one-third of the stock was affected by strong demand; that is, by forces where the number of prospective buyers and tenants exceed the opportunities coming on the market. On the other hand, one-sixth of the housing stock was estimated to be in areas experiencing disinvestment, reflecting a weak and ineffective housing demand.

The significance of the classification scheme outlined above lies primarily in the fact that neighborhoods belonging to various cells in the matrix framework tend to be quite different and will accordingly respond in a different manner to the same housing-policy intervention. That it is essential to be sensitive to these differences in market forces and neighborhood dynamics in designing housing strategies will be discussed next.

Policy Recommendations: Housing Strategies Tailored to Neighborhood Dynamics

As yet there has been little research on how neighborhood well-being can be monitored and confidence built.[8] Without this sensitivity, policymakers who seek to revitalize neighborhoods are confused by conflicting objectives, and as a consequence it is difficult for clear policy recommendations to emerge. The national housing policy debate revolves around which is more important: maximizing housing choice, fixing up houses, restoring the tax base, promoting integration, housing the disadvantaged, or bringing the middle class back to urban living. Failure to rank these objectives in some order or priority as well as to identify explicitly the optimal strategies for each objective, underlies the continuing housing-policy debate. Explicit discussion of these objectives and their inherent conflicts is vital before the national policy dilemma can be resolved.

To help such issues fall into place this chapter asserts that the primary role of public policy is to build neighborhood stability (or, if one prefers, to bring neighborhoods to the stable column of the conceptual framework presented in table 4–1.) Further, strategies must be tailored to neighborhood housing-market dynamics.

Based on an understanding of neighborhood dynamics it is possible to outline a series of strategies tailored to neighborhood dynamics depending on whether the market reflects stable, rising, or declining dynamics. Table 4–2 summarizes these revitalization strategies in general terms.[9]

Strategies for Stable Markets

Markets where housing is in good condition (G/S) do not require special neighborhood housing actions by the city beyond appropriate routine public improvements, city services, and equitable shares of general city-wide housing credit and services. Where areas are stable but require moderate fix up (F/S), technical assistance, housing-code enforcement, and possible property-tax incentives linked to repairs will usually maintain stability and improve conditions. Stable areas needing major repairs (P/S) often require additional government or private-sector support such as special bank-loan funds, federally assisted rehabilitation loans, or a homesteading program, if they are to be restored to good repair. As long as the market is stable such programs have a fairly good chance of success, but an entirely different approach is required if the market is declining.

Strategies for Declining Markets

The strategies for assisting areas that are declining must differ radically from those appropriate for sound and rising market areas because the challenge is to increase housing demand appreciably. Home owners, if they are concerned about the condition of their property, feel that decline is caused by forces they cannot fight: curtailed availability of lending and insurance; fear of lower rental incomes from new residents; racial change; and, as the self-fulfilling trend continues, visible deterioration, accumulating debris, and trash. Those who see housing primarily as an investment—both absentee property owners and banks—are inclined to overreact at the early stages of decline. Fearing deteriorating property values, they begin to disinvest, curtail maintenance, and extract what they still can out of their properties.

Under these circumstances, a very unstable situation results, changing long-term resident owners into sellers. Statistics in Boston, for example, indicate that annual owner turnover is normally between 4 and 8

Table 4–2
Strategies for Neighborhood Housing Revitalization

Housing Condition	Market Perception			
	Rising (R)	Stable (S)	Declining (D)	Rapidly Declining (RD)
Good (G) minor repairs required	G/R Dampen outside demand Assist residents to remain Construct additional housing	G/S No special neighborhood actions		
Fair (F) moderate repairs required	F/R Code enforcement Prevent illegal conversions Increase resident ownership liNew elderly and mixed income housing	F/S Code enforcement Technical assistance Tax incentives for repairs	F/D Demolish excess housing Value insurance Neighborhood Housing Services, if requested Direct household assistance Quotas on occupancy	
Poor (P) major repairs required		P/S Code enforcement Technical assistance Special loan fund Homesteading Demolition New elderly and mixed income housing	P/D Direct household assistance Demolition	P/RD Direct household assistance Relocation Demolition

Source: Rolf Goetze, *Building Neighborhood Confidence*, Ballinger, Cambridge, Mass., 1976, p. 45.

percent, meaning that among a thousand structures perhaps fifty seek a buyer annually (see Goetze; Colton; and O'Donnell 1977). As long as there are over fifty willing and qualified buyers, the neighborhood remains stable, but if only forty buyers show up, the remaining owners become inclined to disinvest unless active neighborhood promotion begins. Suddenly, there are many more sellers than buyers. Some owners may panic, willing to sell now rather than face the uncertainty of obtaining less later on. Others, hearing of price declines, may become frightened and also start dumping their property for whatever price, however low, it can bring. As people overreact, the bottom falls out of the market.

Many people are forced to remain because they cannot sell, but they begin to undermaintain. Others sell to buyers like absentee owners, communes, or minorities that price and social norms previously excluded. As appraisers, real-estate brokers, and lenders become aware of the changing situation, the stage becomes set for disinvestment and abandonment that is hard to turn around. Media sensationalizing about the neighborhood only discourages its residents all the more.

Any effective fight against decline in neighborhoods such as F/D or P/D in table 4–2 must first change the market perception of the area and this often depends on initiative and promotion from within the neighborhoods. Attempts to save a declining neighborhood solely from the outside through government action generally fail. The attitudes of residents are key variables. Will the most capable local leaders stay and promote the neighborhood, or will they flee? City services and the strategies previously discussed for stable neighborhoods can prevent decay only in neighborhoods that have confidence in their own future. Code enforcement, technical assistance, and even special-loan funds are useful only when they complement neighborhood self-initiatives. Imposed from the outside, or brought in by an insignificant minority of residents, they will be unable to effect housing upgrading (see U.S. Department of Housing and Urban Development 1975c; Turner 1977; Urban Homesteading Assistance Board 1977; and Rogg 1977).

To make public improvements visible and to promise an improvement in city services are not enough. Rebuilding or replacing existing housing under the programs similar to the federal subsidy programs of the 1960s is not only too cumbersome but tends to undermine neighborhood confidence and to reduce market demand when the subsidized beneficiaries are not seen as meritorious by the existing residents. The housing and urban-renewal programs of the 1960s were largely oriented toward increasing the supply of housing and often provided few benefits for the existing neighborhood residents. They did not reckon with the need of low-income households for jobs and more income resources. Too often they rehoused a few while scattering the majority and provoking resident owners to depart.

If programs in declining neighborhoods are to be successful, direct household assistance to all eligible residents of declining areas may be necessary as an alternative to housing-production assistance. Direct financial assistance in the form of either housing allowances or income supports coupled with job training and counseling gives priority to helping households, rather than saving or replacing specific residential structures in declining areas. Although there is no guarantee that an income approach would result in better *housing* (by objective standards) this approach could open up a wider range of housing choices for such households. The focus in declining areas, then, must be on the household instead of the housing—and upon changing market perceptions and demand as opposed simply to providing greater government assistance focused on physical improvements.

Strategies for Rising Markets

The posture in rising markets must obviously be different than in stable or declining market areas. The likelihood of housing revitalization is high due to private-market forces and the emphasis is on assisting the current residents—particularly renters—and on preventing or easing the problems of dislocation. Speculative rent increases should not be necessary since the housing stock in these areas is basically in good repair and outlays are needed only rarely to correct deficiencies or to modernize. However, in such areas speculatively inclined owners are tempted to reap the gains of rising market values without any improvements in services (see Whiteside 1977; Embry 1977; Kotler 1977; The National Urban Coalition 1978; Weiler 1977; and Naparstek and Cincotta 1976). Proper code enforcement on those who sharply inflate rents can help encourage responsible ownership.

When speculation does get out of hand, tenant-landlord polarization increases, and formerly sound housing can erode at an alarming rate. When such collapse of the housing market occurs the shrewdest owners usually have already taken their windfall gains elsewhere and sold their properties to less experienced amateurs or newcomers.

Appropriate neighborhood strategies for F/R areas include special emphasis on code enforcement, monitoring illegal conversions, and widening ownership options. Wherever repairs are required amidst a strong market demand, the dilemma is to clarify the rights of tenants with limited incomes who remain. Should they be allowed to live in substandard dwellings? If not, how much of the improvement costs should be passed on in increased low-interest loans or direct rental assistance to tenants (for example, through Section 8 leased housing)? Such subsidies could be granted to owners upon the condition that they make the improvements and continue to serve the existing tenants. But at present, neither subsidy nor direct assistance is available generally, and conditions involving income limitations tend to develop into an administrative nightmare even when such assistance programs are operative. Creating condominium options for present tenants may therefore offer promise. This would enable tenants to become owners and thus share in the rising market instead of being displaced by it.

General Strategies

Besides the specific program recommendations noted in table 4–2 and discussed above, several general points should be stressed. First, public policy must be designed to increase the confidence in the future, not simply to underwrite fix-up costs. Boosting the image of urban living is appropriate wherever central-city housing demand is slack in the face of a tight regional housing market. Without replacement residents to fill the vacancies of those who move away through natural turnover, any neighborhood quickly becomes blighted. In some no-growth cities there may not be enough housing demand to go around even as the baby-boom generation settles down. The market is the best agent to identify the least desirable areas, but public priority should be given to aiding residents of these areas with special housing assistance like Section 8 certificates and relocation assistance.

Second, a housing-restoration program must distinguish between strategies that are designed to upgrade the housing in a neighborhood and those that are designed to help the people. For example, in a rising market, private forces may assure the upgrading of the physical attributes of the neighborhood, and it is the needs of the residents being forced to relocate that must be dealt with.

Third, neighborhood strategies must be formulated within a citywide, statewide, and nationwide housing-policy context. Certain elements are essential in almost all programs; it is their application that must vary. These elements include adequate credit; equity in and reduction of the burden of property taxation; reorientation of city agencies (such as code-enforcement agencies) toward serving the housing consumer; availability of public-sector funds to inject at the margin so as to stimulate confidence; reorganization of city agencies to improve the delivery of housing services; and development of better partnerships between public and private efforts.

Finally, a housing-restoration program must distinguish between problems that can be solved by a single injection of public resources as opposed to problems that will require more sustained public support like income maintenance, employment opportunities, or transfer payments. In areas where household income is adequate to guarantee routine up-keep, one-shot fix-up funds through government subsidized loans and grants coupled with areawide code enforcement may be effective in re-turning areas to good condition. But in some lower-income areas, such tactics will only improve housing temporarily because inadequate cash flow will soon again lead to deferred maintenance.

The emerging policy recommendations set forth in this chapter, then, add the dimension of neighborhood dynamics to housing condition in an effort to arrive at a newly orchestrated set of housing tools. Many of these tools have been available for a number of years, and there is nothing magic or absolute about them. Based on individual needs, preferences, and experience, particular cities may want to alter or shift the emphasis of the program outlines. The most important point is that strategies must be tailored to neighborhood dynamics—what may prove effective in one neighborhood facing one set of market and housing dimensions may be counterproductive in another.

Conclusions and Recommendations: the Golden Mean of Neighborhood Stability

Maintaining the health of existing urban neighborhoods requires an ap-proach radically different from the special interventions devised during the 1960s, such as urban renewal, FHA mortgage insurance, programs to build subsidized housing, and the like. Not only is it becoming clear that resources are inadequate to serve all of the potentially eligible house-holds equitably, but the programs themselves often appear to be coun-tereffective. We currently have in our arsenal of public policy a wide range of housing programs and tools. However, before remedies can be applied a diagnosis is required.

A medical analogy furnishes some insights. The human body has a complex system for maintaining health that we only partially understand. When the system experiences infection, combat mechanisms are brought into play. A doctor assists these coping mechanisms in administering treatment, but he looks for contraindications that signal when the assis-tance is doing more harm than good. This same bodily system may also react allergically to something in its environment and that is a quite different matter. An allergy is not an infection, but an overresponse of the coping mechanisms to some outside agent, such as a pollen. Here the doctor attempts to suppress the coping mechanisms just enough to restore homeostasis, but not so much as to impair the normal defenses against infection. If we can associate disinvestment with infection, and speculation with allergies, then the public-policy course is defined as aiding the neighborhood forces to combat the extremes of disinvestment on one hand and speculation on the other.

Once we differentiate the pathologies it is relatively simple. Just as a patient may develop an allergy to penicillin administered to combat an infection, so a neighborhood can develop a serious reaction in response to well-intended policy interventions. Iatrogenic, or doctor-induced, illness is an important concept in medicine. It seems likely many of our neighborhoods can suffer similarly from misguided interventions into the neighborhoods' housing dynamics.

Much of our housing-policy system in the past has been formulated on the idea of filtering or trickling down, which accepts deterioration as inevitable. An examination of the curve of household settlement noted earlier in figure 4–1, suggests that filtration theory was most appropriate to the steady growth period ending around 1955. While we may consider the last twenty years normal, the curve shows they were not. Blight may be sharply exacerbated by an overall slackening in settlement, the rate of new households forming and settling down. The nation is now entering a new period of settlement rapidly accelerating beyond the response capacity of the home-building system. This threatens to sharply inflate the value of the existing stock, and indeed, this process of inflation has already begun in many areas throughout the country.

Since the filtration theory only accounts for one form of neighborhood deterioration, the analysis in this chapter demonstrates that filtration fails to fit the current situation. Instead, a stabilization approach to cover the period of 1970 to 2000, based on the concepts of supply and demand, is proposed. The stabilization approach identifies a *golden mean* between market extremes as shown in table 4–3. As market demand surges, areas considered declining will be rediscovered and will rise. Unless policymakers are aware of the shift, special public assistance like subsidized loans or special revitalization programs will simply aid the so-called gentry in taking over the neighborhood from absentee owners and lower-income tenants, displacing the latter.

In conclusion, a number of observations can be drawn for managers in both the public and private sector based on the dynamics described above:

1.   Revitalization strategies must be tailored to stabilize neighborhood dynamics.

Table 4–3
Stabilizing Neighborhoods

Neighborhood Market Types	Declining (disinvesting)	Stable or Ideal	Rising (gentrifying)
	– –		+ +
Symptoms: indicators (or causes?)	Excess supply Uncertainty in property values Redlining Negative press image Departure of the able Discretionary sales Increase in low down payment and/or government-insured lending Increase in absentee ownership Rising tax delinquency Property abandonment	G O L D E N	Excess demand Price inflation (real or anticipated) Speculation Strong press image Immigration of higher class Investment purchases Conversion of marginal space into more dwellings
Corrective Remedies	Boost neighborhood image Value insurance for resident owners Improve jobs/income without stigma Support neighborhood housing services if requested Demolish excess housing (or mothballs) Land-bank vacant lots until stable	M E A N	Dampen outside demand Assist disadvantaged to remain Enforce codes Prevent illegal conversions Reassess only upon sale Construct additional housing

2. To design sensitive revitalization strategies, further indicators must be developed to monitor neighborhood status and change.

3. Public and private resources should be used in cooperation so as to stimulate private investment.

4. Federal, state, and local government programs should be inventoried and reviewed in light of the realities of neighborhood market dynamics.

As we monitor neighborhood dynamics and change, perhaps a relevant illustration lies in driving down the road into the future. All neighborhoods can be seen as traveling into the future. The demographic trends noted in figure 4–1 provide an influx of demand that may help to support revitalization within our cities over the next decade. This new demand may provide an opportunity to overcome disinvestment, but it is also accompanied by a new set of problems—speculation and displacement. What we need is a feedback system to track our progress into the future to help identify when we are moving toward the edge. As long as we move on course, there is no need for intervention. However, if the course begins to veer, if the neighborhood path moves erratically into speculation and displacement on the one side or disinvestment on the other (or if a neighborhood is caught oscillating between speculation and disinvestment), then certain actions such as those discussed previously might be triggered by both the private and the public sector so as to help redirect neighborhood dynamics towards stability and the golden mean.

In a few years it will be apparent how extraordinary the chances are at this time. The time of opportunity is now and ripe, but fleeting.

Notes

1. In preparing this chapter the authors drew heavily from a research project and report funded by the U.S. Department of Housing and Urban Development, Office of Policy Development and Research. The origins of the research trace back to June 1972, when Rolf Goetze and Kent Colton began examining housing dynamics and census and market trends at the Boston Redevelopment Authority (BRA) Research Department. A purchase order from the Department of Housing and Urban Development in the summer of 1977 to Public Systems Evaluation enabled the synthesis of this initial research with the subsequent research efforts at the BRA continued under the direction of Rolf Goetze. For further description of the research see Goetze (1979).

2. For further discussion of the dialogue concerning the back-to-the-city movement, see James (1977); Gale (1977); Clay (1978a); Fichter (1977); and Grier and Grier (1978).

3. Although not the subject of this chapter, it is important to note that the trend will shift back around the turn of the century. As the number of households seeking housing drops around the year 2000, demand will fall, and a new set of problems will develop. Also see Alonso (1977).

4. The belief that neighborhoods can be placed on a single linear continuum has long been in currency. The best-known work of this belief, *Dynamics of Neighborhood Change* (U.S. Department of Housing and Urban Development 1975a) ranked neighborhoods from Stage 1, stable and viable, to Stage 5, unhealthy and nonviable. This was on the right track because it put a national focus on neighborhood context, but it was too simple to be useful directly. Neighborhood rediscovery was asserted to be simply reverse filtration in this model, but closer inspection has revealed that various types of revitalization have entirely different dynamics as will be shown throughout this chapter.

5. There are a wide range of definitions related to housing quality ranging from census definitions (tied to such features as lack of plumbing and overcrowding) to actual inspections of houses to see if they are above or below housing-code standards. To develop data in Boston on housing condition, trained housing inspectors conducted a so-called windshield

survey, driving by each of the houses in the city and making estimates as to condition. For a further discussion of the methodology, see Goetze; Colton; and O'Donnell (1977).

6. This chapter maintains that marked perception is often the critical factor in neighborhood dynamics, although it is sometimes difficult to measure. This seems more intuitive when one remembers that perceptions are also important in a number of other areas of human behavior, for example, stock-market interactions, decisions to buy or sell a liquid investment, and overall consumer purchasing.

7. Some of the dynamics of neighborhoods were first noted by the authors in research conducted at the Boston Redevelopment Authority on triple-decker housing in Boston. For a discussion of the factors, see Boston Redevelopment Authority and Boston Urban Observatory (1975).

8. Some of the most interesting data and research relative to tracking neighborhood change has been done by R.L. Polk and Company. For a discussion of some of these ideas, see R.L. Polk and Company (undated).

9. If the readers are interested in a more detailed discussion of these strategies they should see Goetze; Colton; and O'Donnell (1977), or Goetze (1976). The reader may also find it interesting to relate the programs described here to those discussed in Kollias (1977).

References

Ahlbrandt, R.; Charny, M.; and Cunningham, J. 1977. Citizen perceptions of their neighborhoods. *Journal of Housing* 34, 7:338–41.

Allman, T. 1978. The urban crisis leaves town. *Harpers* (December):41–56.

Alonso, W. 1977. *The population factor and urban structure.* Working Paper Number 102. Cambridge, Mass.: Harvard University, Center for Population Studies. August.

Anderson, J. 1977. Reporter at large: the making of Boerum Hill. *New Yorker,* November 14.

Black, J.T. 1975. Private market housing renovation in central cities: a U.L.I. survey. *Urban Land* (November):3–9.

Boston Redevelopment Authority and Boston Urban Observatory. 1975. *Working class housing: a study of triple deckers in Boston.* Boston: Boston Redevelopment Authority.

————. 1973. *Subsidized multifamily rental housing in the Boston metropolitan area: analysis and prognosis.* Boston: Boston Redevelopment Authority.

Clay, P. 1978a. *Neighborhood revitalization: issues, trends, and strat-*

egies. National Endowment for the Arts. Cambridge, Mass.: Massachusetts Institute of Technology, Urban Studies Department.

————. 1978b. Neighborhood revitalization and community development: the experience and the promise. *Center for Community Economic Development Newsletter* (August–October):1–9.

Colton, K. 1978. The future of the nation's housing finance system: reform or paralysis. *Journal of the American Institute of Planners* 44 (July):306–316.

Colton, K.; Lessard, D.; Modest, D.; and Solomon, A. 1977. National survey of borrower's housing characteristics, attitudes and preferences. *Alternative Mortgage Instruments Research Study,* vol. I. Washington D.C.: Federal Home Loan Bank Board.

Downs, A.; and Lachman, J.L. The role of neighborhoods in the mature metropolis. Paper prepared for Symposium on Challenges and Opportunities in the Mature Metropolis, St. Louis Exhibition and Convention Center, Missouri, June 6–8.

Embry, R. 1977. Urban reinvestment and the effects of displacement of low and moderate income persons. Testimony before the Senate Committee on Banking, Housing and Urban Affairs. July 7.

Fichter, R. 1977. *Young professionals and city neighborhoods*. Boston: Parkman Center for Urban Affairs.

Gale, D. 1977. The back-to-the-city movement . . . or is it?: A survey of recent homeowners in the Mount Pleasant neighborhood of Washington, D.C. Washington, D.C.: George Washington University, Department of Urban and Regional Planning.

Goetze, R. 1979. *Understanding neighborhood change, the role of confidence in urban revitalization*. Cambridge, Mass.: Ballinger Publishing Company.

————. Avoiding both disinvestment and speculation in private multifamily housing. *Journal of the American Real Estate and Urban Economics Association* 6, 2:175–185.

————. *Building neighborhood confidence: a humanistic strategy for urban housing*. Cambridge, Mass.: Ballinger Publishing Company.

Goetze, R.; Colton, K.; and O'Donnell, V. 1977. *Stabilizing neighborhoods: a fresh approach to housing dynamics and perceptions*. Prepared for HUD, Office of Policy Development and Research, Cambridge, Mass.: Public Systems Evaluation, Inc. and Boston Redevelopment Authority. November.

Grier, G.; and Grier, E. 1978. Urban displacement: a reconnaissance. Memo report prepared for the U.S. Department of Housing and Urban Development. March.

————. 1977. *Movers to the city: new data on the housing market for Washington, D.C.* Washington, D.C.: Washington Center for Metropolitan Studies. May.

Holman, C. 1977. Neighborhood revitalization and dislocation. Testimony before the Senate Committee on Banking, Housing and Urban Affairs. July 8.

James, F. 1977. *Back to the city: an appraisal of housing reinvestment and population change in urban America.* Washington, D.C.: The Urban Institute.

Kollias, K.; with Naparstek, A.; and Haskell, C. 1977. *Neighborhood reinvestment: a citizen's compendium for programs and strategies.* Washington, D.C.: National Center for Urban Ethnic Affairs.

Kotler, M. 1977. Dislocation of long time residents caused by the growing pace of neighborhood revitalization in many of our older cities. Testimony before the Senate Committee on Banking, Housing and Urban Affairs. July 8.

Leven, C.; Little, J.; Nourse, M.; and Read, R. 1976. *Neighborhood change, lessons in the dynamics of urban decay.* New York: Praeger Publishers.

Lipton, G. 1977. Evidence of central city revival. *Journal of the American Institute of Planners* 43 (April):136–147.

Myers, P.; and Binder, G. 1977. *Neighborhood conservation: lessons from three cities, an issue report.* Washington, D.C.: The Conservation Foundation.

Naparstek, A.; and Cincotta, G. 1976. *Urban disinvestment: new implications for community organization, research and public policy.* Washington, D.C.: National Center for Urban Ethnic Affairs and Chicago: National Training and Information Center.

The National Urban Coalition. 1978. *Displacement: city neighborhoods in transition.* Washington, D.C.

Peirce, N. 1977. Nation's cities poised for a stunning comeback. *Washington Post* July 3.

President's Urban and Regional Policy Group. 1978. *A new partnership to conserve America's communities.* Washington, D.C.

R.L. Polk and Company. Undated. The T.E.A.M. approach. *Update: Profiles of Change* 8.

Reinhold, R. 1977. Middle-class return displaces some urban poor. *New York Times* June 5:1.

Rogg, N. 1977. *Urban housing rehabilitation in the United States.* Washington, D.C.: United States League of Savings Associations.

Schur, R.; and Sherry, V. 1977. *The neighborhood housing movement.* New York: Association of Neighborhood Housing Developers.

SRI International. 1979. *Using new governance tools to solve local government problems.* Menlo Park, Calif.: Center for Urban and Regional Planning.

Stanfield, R. 1976. Cities being rehabilitated, though housing ills remain. *National Journal* 17(July):1004–1009.

Sumka, H. 1978. Displacement in revitalizing neighborhoods: a review and research strategy. *Occasional Papers in Housing and Urban*

Affairs 2. Washington, D.C.: U.S. Department of Housing and Urban Development, Office of Policy Development and Research. Pp. 134–167.

Turner, J. 1977. *Housing by people: towards autonomy in building environments*. New York: Pantheon Books.

Urban Consortium. 1977. *The displacement problem in revitalized urban neighborhoods*. Washington, D.C.: Report of the Community and Economic Development Task Force.

Urban Homesteading Assistance Board (UHAB). 1977. The urban homesteading assistance board: third annual progress report. New York: Cathedral House.

U.S. Department of Housing and Urban Development. Office of Policy Development and Research. 1975a. *The dynamics of neighborhood change*. San Francisco: Public Affairs Counseling.

————. 1975b. *The neighborhood succession process* (edited by Nourse, H.). Washington, D.C.

————. 1975c. The neighborhood housing services model (by ACTION-Housing, Inc.). Washington, D.C.

U.S. House of Representatives, Committee on Banking, Currency and Housing. 1976. Hearings on the rebirth of the American city. September 20–October 1.

U.S. Senate, Committee on Banking, Housing and Urban Affairs. 1977. Hearings on neighborhood diversity, problems of dislocation and diversity in communities undergoing neighborhood revitalization activity. 95th Congress, first session, July 7, 8.

Warren, R.; and Warren, D. 1977. *The neighborhood organizer's handbook*. South Bend: University of Notre Dame Press.

Weiler, C. 1978. *Reinvestment displacement: HUD's role in a new housing issue*. Paper prepared for the Office of Community Planning and Development, U.S. Department of Housing and Urban Development.

————. 1977. Urban reinvestment and its effects on displacement of low- and moderate-income residents. Testimony before Senate Committee on Banking, Housing and Urban Affairs. July 8.

Whiteside, W. 1977. Dislocation of poor and minorities caused by neighborhood revitalization in older cities. Testimony before Senate Committee on Banking, Housing and Urban Affairs. July 8.

5

The Stages of Gentrification: The Case of Bay Village

Timothy Pattison

Middle-class reinvestment in selected urban neighborhoods gathered considerable momentum in the 1970s. Popularly labeled *gentrification* or the back-to-the-city movement, this trend has been documented by various surveys and countless newspaper and magazine features. It has been viewed alternately as a blessing and a problem. Local governments, faced with diminishing federal funds and sagging tax rolls, have considered private reinvestment as one of the more positive trends to occur in cities in years and there are many who would happily see it continue unabated. Others have not shared this viewpoint, seeing reinvestment as just another way of dislodging low-income residents from neighborhoods they have long considered their own. Judging the pros and cons of the process is a debate that will doubtless continue for a while among academics, concerned citizen activists, planners, and elected officials. In an academic sense, however, reinvestment has served a major purpose by throwing into question the hitherto largely unchallenged housing-market theory that neighborhoods only trickle down. There is ample literature on downward filtration, the process of neighborhood decline and a related stage theory. There has been little consideration, however, of these dynamics in reverse, namely disaggregating the gentrification process in older urban neighborhoods into a similar stage sequence.

Studies conducted on neighborhood reinvestment have been generally for the purpose of either ascertaining the extent of the phenomemon throughout the United States (Black 1975, Clay 1978) or examining a gentrifying neighborhood at a given point in time (Gale 1976). Contrastingly, this chapter traces the process of gentrification over a twenty-year period in one of its earlier instances in the United States, in Boston's Bay Village.[1]

Bay Village Prior to Gentrification (Pre-1957)

Bay Village is a small neighborhood of approximately one-hundred-and-fifteen street addresses and three-hundred-fifty housing units sitting on the edge of Boston's central business district. It did not get its name until

77

1959, but the area first developed as a residential community in the 1820s, its construction coinciding with that of Boston's prestigious Beacon Hill. In fact, many of the artisans responsible for Beacon Hill built houses, albeit in a less grand manner, in Bay Village for themselves. A deed accompanying the sale of original lots prescribed height and construction materials. As a result, two- to three-story red-brick, federal-style rowhouses predominate. The scale and visual harmony in Bay Village, combined with its proximity to the central business district, make it somewhat typical of other urban neighborhoods across the United States that recently have attracted middle-class interest (Clay 1978).

The popular image of Bay Village in the late 1940s and early 1950s, immediately prior to upgrading, is one of blight, with lodging houses catering to a predominantly low-income population. One resident complained that these establishments fostered "a sense of anonymity about the neighborhood . . . with a lot of transients who just didn't care." The area's proximity to both the central business and theater districts meant that vacancies were few and landlords consequently felt little pressure to improve their properties to attract tenants. Moreover, there were "some very sloppy rooming houses . . . there were those who had houses who didn't care who they rented to," recalled one resident in a discreet reference to the prostitutes and alcoholics that many harbored. A strip of bars along the area's perimeter also contributed to the area's poor public image. To cast the Bay Village of the early 1950s in an entirely negative light, however, would be to distort the picture. While a considerable number of rooming houses were sanctuaries for prostitution and alcoholism, there were indeed more respectable establishments housing a largely retired population. Moreover, as one long-term resident recalled, "there was always a hard core of middle-class business and professional people . . . people here from time immemorial . . . with waspish names." Lawyers, architects, and schoolteachers were mentioned among these home owners.

Gentrification: Stage One (1957–1959)

Key Actors

In the fieldwork associated with this study, artists and gays were mentioned most frequently as being responsible for the initial renovation activity. One banker remembered that "there were a lot of homosexuals who had been pushed out of Beacon Hill and went into the Bay Village area . . . they were very intelligent and very innovative . . . it was amazing the various restoration jobs they'd done.'' Indeed the drive, initiative, and artistic talent of members of the gay community were frequently lauded by those interviewed. One realtor-resident felt that upgrading began when two gays bought a building on Melrose Street, "fixed it up, and added window boxes and shutters . . . window boxes and shutters were the start.'' Another admitted to having had a genuine commitment to the neighborhood, wanting more than simply a place to live, and accordingly set out to renovate property for his own use and to assist and encourage others. His motto was "Let's buy all the bad properties . . . to hell with the good ones, they stand on their own merit.'' In other words, these so-called pioneers were not only rehabilitating properties that would demonstrate the area's residential potential, but they were simultaneously *eliminating* from the area's housing stock the particularly deteriorated structures that might otherwise deter prospective residents.

One realtor noted that among the first round of renovators were many gay tenants who made internal and external improvements—with the permission of landlords yet at their own expense. He felt that, even as renters, their life styles contributed to and sometimes precipitated broader physical-improvement efforts: "Gay kids were very clean, very artistic, very determined to have a home . . . not a warehouse. Married couples don't put up curtains and they live with boxes around them for months. I rented . . . and would rent to the gays far sooner than the straights.''

One of the people responsible for some of the initial major renovation work suggested that the first people to move in had very little money and simply wanted a place to live. They would take a house wherever one came up for sale. In fixing their homes, with their limited incomes, these people "didn't believe financial benefits would come of their efforts, but when they did, they sold their houses and got out.''

While interviews reveal, therefore, that gays were the primary moving force behind early restoration activity, public records add yet another perspective. They indicate that for the first three years buyers were drawn primarily from the professional job categories, that they were of all ages, and that almost all moved from within the city itself. Only two artists were listed as buyers, which suggests that their supposed influence on early renovation efforts was either as renters or that a limited few undertook rehabilitation work on behalf of others.

Financing

Four people interviewed bought or attempted to buy Bay Village properties in the latter half of the 1950s. All met considerable intransigence on the part of lending institutions, one recalling having gone to twenty banks to get a mortgage. One respondent attributed the banks' reluctance to their having suffered losses in the area during the Depression and to the area's infamous speak-easy reputation from previous decades.

One person sought to purchase a house in 1955 but was refused by one bank who "thought they were in the neighborhood deep enough . . . that it was a poor fire risk area . . . and that it might be taken by the BRA." He finally solved his problem by taking advantage of his GI rights. Nevertheless, insured mortgages appear to have played very little role in the resurgence of Bay Village. Instead, persistence, ingenuity, or the reliance on personal resources appear to account for the initial upgrading effort. One ex-resident, for example, was told by a bank in 1957 that they had to lend in the area of their depositors; they were interested in Bay Village and would grant a mortgage once the proposed property was 80-percent renovated. Financially strapped, however, the buyer recalled that with "a stroke of genius . . . I painted the basement . . . the bank thought that anyone who would finish the basement would finish the rest of the house . . . they gave me the mortgage forty-eight hours later, the time it took to process the forms." For the remaining transactions recorded during the first few years of Bay Village's resurgence, seller mortgages and second mortgages emerge as important factors.

One bank made significantly more loans to Bay Village during the entire upgrading process. The loan officer at that bank recalled how some of Bay Village's gay community approached the bank in 1958. Noting that Bay Village "was not an area conducive to lending," he was nevertheless convinced by several factors that the area had potential. He acknowledged being struck by the salesmanship and zeal of one particular individual who had contacted him and was impressed by the work already completed, recalling that "when you saw that someone cared enough to remove all the lead paint to reveal the natural wood, you believed (in them)." He also credited the board of his bank with the initiative to want to "create business in an innovative way."

Gentrification: Stage Two (1960–1965)

Key Actors

The efforts of the gay community—both the cosmetic touches and the practice of rehabilitating the most deteriorated structures—set the stage for the entrance of one particular realtor. As one long-term incumbent noted, "the real breakthrough came when (the realtor) made a determined drive to make the place a desirable neighborhood.'' The realtor was already a resident in the neighborhood and had been involved in the renovation of several properties for personal use. While the importance of the commission accompanying each sale cannot be discounted, it was clear from interviews that this particular realtor was convinced deeply of the area's potential appeal to people seeking a house in the downtown area—a conviction grounded in the experience of also being a resident there. The realtor began a promotional campaign for the area, building upon the foundation laid largely by the gays. Using personal property and the buildings renovated by the pioneering gays to demonstrate the area's potential, the realtor began to attract a clientele different from those who had been gutting properties themselves. As one of the original renovators noted, these people were more ''the carriage trade, told (by the realtor) that if you go in and dust (an older property) you're a pioneer . . . but they were not the gutsy pioneers . . . there weren't too many do-it-yourselfers in that group.''

The realtor recalled the early resistance encountered when trying to appeal to a clientele more inclined to look at Beacon Hill, stating that ''good old Yankees think address first . . . cash value, rather than a spiritual value.'' Indeed, Bay Village was perceived initially by many potential buyers as a ''poor man's Beacon Hill'' because of its location, its housing stock—and most importantly—what one resident described its ''easy-to-take price tag.'' Besides the prospect of a bargain, many reportedly saw in Bay Village another distinct advantage over Beacon Hill. The size and scale of the neighborhood imparted a sense of intimacy and neighborliness that appealed to many newcomers and also lent high visibility to initial private improvement efforts.

The area's reputation doubtless deterred many from buying in the early years. During the prohibition era the bars on the edge of the neighborhood had created a speak-easy image for the area. One ex-resident, who was not a realtor but who played an almost evangelistic role in attracting potential residents in the late 1950s, discovered that he could not appeal readily to people who were aware of this aspect of Bay Village's history. Instead, he sought out a younger group who had not been around for the bad press the neighborhood had received in the past and were thus not bothered by any lingering reputation.

As in the first stage, those drawn to Bay Village during this period were employed primarily in the professional job category. Indeed, the professional and managerial ranks accounted for 58 percent of all buyers in the years 1960 to 1965; or, including sales and clerical workers, white-collar workers constituted 94 percent of all buyers during this period. Fifty-nine percent of all buyers were under forty-five, leaving a surprisingly high proportion of buyers forty-five and over. Sixty-eight percent of the home buyers were from within the city itself and, of these, almost three-quarters moved from either elsewhere in the neighborhood or the downtown area. Most of the remainder moved in from out of state, not the suburbs.

Many bought having been shown renovated properties in the neighborhood, a strategy designed by the realtor and the pioneer to demonstrate renovation potential. Yet having bought, some were still uncertain about the neighborhood as a place to live. Some did nothing, waited for the neighborhood to improve, and then sold—reaping the financial gains accompanying increased demand. There were others who wanted to renovate but were wary about the investment without additional signs that the neighborhood would improve. There were, of course, people less risk averse, who were prepared to gamble on the neighborhood's future in renovating their buildings. They were attaching considerable importance to the scattered-site private renovations in an area that was still surrounded by extensive physical deterioration. The formation of a neighborhood association perhaps also encouraged some prospective buyers. A small group of predominantly long-term residents felt that it was important to give the neighborhood an identity. One of them explained that not long after they had coined the name Bay Village and formed the Bay Village Neighborhood Association, their poster campaign to demand improved services from city hall, their window-box contests, and the Bay Village renovations featured in magazine design sections soon served to raise public awareness of the neighborhood's existence.

Displacement

One of the people involved in the earliest renovation work remembered that many existing home owners reacted favorably to his and other people's efforts, noticing that "everyone likes the interest . . . whenever you see improvements that's a sign that people care." Several long-term residents interviewed certainly corroborated this view, noting that some of their work was replicated by existing residents. Indeed, it should be stated at the outset that in Bay Village displacement of *home owners* does not appear to have been a major characteristic of the gentrification process. There was no mention of rising property taxes or sense of alienation by newcomers forcing out long-term residents. Rather, properties became available through death or because, as one ex-resident recalled, there were those "who really wanted out . . . (they) had lived in the neighborhood through the bad times and decided that it couldn't get better . . . and they stuck with their attitudes," the visible signs of upgrading notwithstanding. Instead, upgrading and the accompanying increased demand provided some incumbents with the financial opportunity to fulfill a long-term goal—to leave the neighborhood and move to the suburbs.

Most incumbent home owners appear to have reacted favorably to the influx of newcomers and to their renovation activity—whether simply enjoying the neighborhood's improving physical appearance, welcoming the incentive to make similar modifications to their own structures, or appreciating the newfound means by which to escape to a more "desirable" suburban location. But owner-occupied properties did not constitute a large proportion of all structures in the Bay Village area in the late-1950s-to-early-1960s period. Many structures had, a decade or so earlier, been converted into rooming houses. Discussions with both realtors and older residents indicated that the lodging house appears to have been relatively easy prey for the person seeking a property to renovate or have renovated. For an absentee owner, the prospect of considerable financial gain on an investment made only several years earlier was almost irresistible. One ex-resident noted that, in particular, "those who were running cheap flophouses . . . bought for $3–6,000 (in the early 1950s) and when the revival came a few years later they sold for $8–12,000." The final disappearance of the less reputable establishments came with urban renewal, which involved a conscious decision to eliminate those remaining. Yet not all rooming houses in Bay Village had been disreputable. Indeed, lodging houses were the backbone of low-income housing at this time, frequently providing residents with a family situation, albeit in many cases temporary. That there was a reduction in the supply of rooming houses meant that displacement of a lower-income rental population was a characteristic of the Bay Village upgrading process. An examination of resident lists reveals that renters from the service and other blue-collar occupational categories peaked in 1963–1965 and thereafter declined as a proportion of incoming renters. The nonworking population declined consistently from the earliest period. These groups were doubtless forced out as the supply of rooming houses that probably housed a large proportion of them were converted into more expensive apartments. That the service and "other" occupations survived longer than the nonworking population doubtless reflects their ability to outbid the latter in an ever-diminishing market of rooming houses.

Financing

In this stage, financing was still not easy. Nevertheless, the bank described in Stage One acceded to what one ex-resident described as a "people-rather-than-building policy" and began to make 50-percent loans. The bank officer claimed that his approach had been to consider the neighborhood's strengths and potential on a block-by-block basis, encouraged by ''nucleii of stability''—where rehabilitation work was already completed and where there was a solid core of long-term middleclass professional residents. He claimed that the risk factor was small, weighed against the neighborhood's potential. Acquisition costs in the early years were very low, and the bank protected itself by lending only on buildings with strong, sound shells, by insisting on owner occupancy (''since the absentee landlords were responsible for much of the degradation''), and by ''looking at the signature''—that is, the earning capacity of the mortgagor. This willingness to factor the person into the loan decision contrasted sharply with the attitude of officers of other banks interviewed. While real-estate data indicates that banks during this period were approving mortgages for an average of 65 to 70 percent, this data does not reflect the entire financing picture. Indeed, assumed mortgages, seller mortgages, second mortgages, and straight cash transactions (that is, no mortgage) all played a signficant role in this stage.

Gentrification: Stage Three (1965–1971)

Key Actors

Public-sector improvements in Bay Village under the urban-renewal program were extensive. Materializing from a series of BRA-community meetings held in the mid-1960s, the improvements were designed to complement growing private investment.

The BRA's earliest overtures were met with hostility from Bay Village residents. When it was discovered that several Bay Village rowhouses were scheduled for demolition as part of the South Cove Urban Renewal District, some were fearful that this action would be the wedge in the door leading to a total razing of the Bay Village Neighborhood such as happened in the West End. The city's code-enforcements' inspections in the early 1960s were interpreted by some as simply a precondemnation inspection. Whatever the initial intentions of the BRA, it found in 1962 a neighborhood of considerable strength and cohesion, anxious that renovation efforts thus far undertaken be reinforced by public-infrastructure investment. The neighborhood association was quick to see the advantages of a good working relationship with the BRA. The BRA, recoiling from a black eye acquired in the West End and considerable bruising from its forays into Charlestown, saw the opportunity to rebuild its tarnished urban-renewal image by accommodating the needs and requests of the Bay Village residents.

Extensive BRA-Bay Village negotiations between 1964 and 1966 resulted in a series of public investments that reinforced the residential character of the neighborhood. Disreputable bars and lodging houses on the periphery were eliminated. Boundary streets were realigned and widened, which reduced vehicular traffic within Bay Village. The area was rezoned to halt further nonresidential use and an entirely new, below-street infrastructure was installed. Finally, the public sector played a key role in developing Bay Village's present intimate character—its brick sidewalks, narrower streets, its trees, a small park, and gas lamps simulated to look antique—all designed "to restore the context within which the neighborhood was built," asserted one BRA official.

There were few significant changes in the type of newcomer in this stage. Sixty-eight percent of all buyers were in the professional and managerial job categories and 96 percent were in white-collar occupations. The buyers were becoming younger—46 percent between the ages twenty-five and thirty-four, and 81 percent less than forty-five. Moreover, the pattern of the seasoned urban dweller continued with 82 percent of all buyers moving from within the city, 75 percent of these having previously lived in the neighborhood itself or the adjoining downtown/core area. Indeed, of those interviewed, three people began by renting in Bay Village and then, having tested the neighborhood, opted to purchase a property during this stage. It was clear that they, along with others during this period, attached considerable importance to the aesthetic qualities of a neighborhood. Knowing that the city intended to commit public funds to strengthen these qualities in Bay Village undoubtedly helped dispel any fears they might have had regarding the neighborhood's direction. The Beacon Hill model also appears to have continued to direct the residential decision of a number of Bay Village home buyers in the late 1960s. However, the price differential that originally made Bay Village much more feasible financially eroded as prices inevitably rose with increased demand.

Displacement

Displacement at this stage was restricted to occupants of a few remaining lodging houses that, because of their reputation, were designated for demolition under urban renewal. The advent of renewal was seen by some long-term home owners as a blessing. Many had opted not to move along with their peers in the early years of upgrading. Instead, they held onto their properties until public-sector improvements were underway, in the hope of realizing significant profits on sale. This strategy particularly applied to Fayette Street residents who, some observers noted, waited not just for street improvements within Bay Village but, more importantly, for the demolition of an adjoining street on the edge of the neighborhood, complete with its honky-tonk bars and so-called flea hotels. Indeed, real-estate-transaction data indicate that Fayette Street sales did not match those on Melrose Street (the other major residential street with approximately the same number of properties) until the late 1960s.

Financing

In subsequent years, financing became easier. Bank reluctance to loan in Bay Village appeared to diminish with indications that there were to be extensive public improvements. Certainly the households interviewed who bought property in Bay Village from 1963 onward did not have too much difficulty.

Gentrification: Stage Four (Post–1972)

The metamorphosis of Bay Village was almost complete. Renovation of almost every residential structure had been undertaken, with demand sufficiently strong to encourage the conversion of several nonresidential properties into high-rental apartment units. The disorder accompanying public-works improvements was gone, with the restored character of the streets now reinforcing the physical harmony of the renovated houses. This wholesale transformation of Bay Village removed any lingering questions about risk; buyers were happy to pay top dollar and lending institutions eager to approve mortgages in Bay Village.

The home buyer was still primarily professional or managerial (65 percent) or almost exclusively white collar (85 percent). The trend toward younger buyers was continuing, with 63 percent between the ages of twenty-five and thirty-four, and 89 percent under forty-five. The buyer continued to be drawn from the city, with two-thirds of these people having rented previously in Bay Village itself. That there was no recirculation to the same extent within the neighborhood prior to this stage suggests that some people were consciously or unconsciously testing the neighborhood prior to purchase. The most significant change in newcomers during this final stage was among the rental population, changes in this group having been largely difficult to discern in previous stages. For the first time, a greater number of people arriving in Bay Village as renters were from out of state and from elsewhere in Massachusetts, including the suburbs, than from the city itself. This shift in origin among renters gives substance to speculation about a back-to-the-city movement.

In other words, once the neighborhood was fully upgraded—that is, most houses had been renovated and the extensive public efforts had improved the area's physical appearance—it became attractive to an entirely different type of person. The disenchanted suburbanite interested in an urban life style found in Bay Village an attractive alternative to a modern high-rise apartment.

One variable in Stage Four is unique to Bay Village and must be mentioned, since it accounts for much of the neighborhood's sense of community at the time. Two bars on the edge of Bay Village not taken as part of the BRA's land assembly caused considerable disruption to the neighborhood. Noise was far less of a problem than was street safety, with most feeling physically threatened. Half-a-dozen bar-related homicides over several years and alleged retaliatory action by bar owners against residents who lodged complaints forced the neighborhood to organize itself in 1971 under the aegis of the neighborhood association. Skillful use of the media and political pressure by the neighborhood's white, middle-class professionals eventually won the day. Their campaign to close the bars took five years but the organizing, fund-raising, and petition signing involved served to create strong bonds within the neighborhood that have yet to be untied.

Conclusion

The purpose of this chapter has been to review the process of gentrification in a particular neighborhood. To draw some useful conclusions about the process in general, it is instructive to incorporate findings from another case study conducted simultaneously with that of Bay Village. The other study—of a neighborhood in West Cambridge—traced for the same period the impact of a higher socioeconomic class on a working-class neighborhood that had developed as a so-called streetcar suburb with rather eclectic architectural styles. In contrast to Bay Village, West Cambridge experienced a much slower rate of turnover, due largely to the entrenchment of the incumbent population. Vacancies occurred primarily through death, there was no displacement, and there were no particular actions on the part of either the public or real-estate sectors.

Despite differences in experience, the two case studies clearly suggest some common trends. First, some general conclusions can be made about people buying in both neighborhoods across the entire period examined. Second, and more important, both studies serve to point out that within aggregate newcomer statistics and characteristics, there are clearly different persons arriving at different stages in the process of neighborhood reinvestment.

The Young-Professional Home Buyer

Home buyers attracted to both neighborhoods were identified as predominantly professional in occupation—approximately 55 percent in both instances, with no significant differences between stages. In Bay Village, the remainder were drawn almost entirely from other white-collar occupations. In West Cambridge, blue-collar workers constituted one-quarter of all new buyers—reflecting that the neighborhood had not yet lost its working-class identity and that the gentrification process was far more gradual. Buyers in both neighborhoods were also primarily below the age of forty-five. Together these findings give substance to the hitherto largely heuristically derived image of the young professional looking for housing in older urban neighborhoods.

Back to the City

Emerging from both case studies is the fact that buyers did not conform to a back-to-the-city pattern, as had been assumed popularly. This finding concurs with other neighborhood case studies (Gale 1976; 1977). The back-to-the-city label is evidently a misnomer in terms of people's most recent movement patterns. While illuminating, this finding is nevertheless hardly surprising, given that the typical buyer selecting these older city neighborhoods has been seen to be relatively young and, by dint of occupation, to have achieved a high educational level. While many such people may have been raised in the suburbs (no data was available on this), their typical post-high-school experience included college with student housing and a first job with an apartment—both, more often than not, in the city. In other words, by the time many households were ready to purchase their first home, they were already seasoned urbanites enjoying life in the city and its various amenities. Rather than quit their apartment for a house in the suburbs, they opted instead for a central-city location. The back-to-the-city movement as publicized by the media is perhaps an interpretation of a general disaffection with suburban life, a sentiment expressed throughout interviews.

Different People Arrive at Different Stages

Both case studies point to the seminal role played by one particular group. In neither instance would the gentrification process have begun without the activity of a first wave of pioneers. In Bay Village, the original catalysts of change were predominantly gay. In West Cambridge, the pioneering role belonged to architects.

As noted earlier, the experience of the two neighborhoods was quite different—in their relative stability and physical health at the outset of the gentrification process, in the subsequent rate of property turnover, and in the roles of both public and real-estate sectors. Neverthless, pioneers played a common role in both by altering the market perception of the neighborhood. Wittingly or unwittingly, these people demonstrated the neighborhoods' potential to a later round of newcomers. The promotional effort of a realtor notwithstanding, the people looking for a cheaper version of Beacon Hill appear to have been persuaded of Bay Village's future largely on the basis of renovation work already accomplished there. Similarly, the presence of professionals—that is, recent graduates from architectural school—and their remodeling efforts brought the attention of other professions to West Cambridge. The architects were demonstrating both the potential for converting somewhat-unlikely-looking housing to suit individual tastes and life styles and also the feasibility of living comfortably among others socioeconomically different from themselves.

What motivates these pioneers? Whether rehabilitating a house in a clearly declining, predominantly transient neighborhood or penetrating what had hitherto been a solid enclave of working-class, ethnic families, the persons involved are motivated differently from those who succeed or later join them. In the case of Bay Village, gays with limited incomes were "simply wanting a place to live," as one resident asserted. Specifically, these people were seeking a residential environment where they would not encounter an atmosphere of social alienation—hence Bay Village, where at the time the population was essentially transient. In West Cambridge, the architects were anxious to combine the testing of new-found skills against the challenge of an older, unretouched property with the opportunity to send their children to a public school with a good reputation. In the case of the architects, these motives clearly outweighed any fears they might have had of rejection from the community they were, in fact, invading.

It is apparent that the type of pioneer who triggers gentrification may well differ between neighborhoods. This difference may simply be a function of a neighborhood's well being at the time the pioneer makes his initial foray into the area. For example, would the architects who pioneered West Cambridge have pioneered the rehabilitation of Bay Village, given its heavily deteriorated state?

It is suggested here that all prospective home buyers in urban neighborhoods have different perceptions of the risk involved with their purchase. Risk is understood here to mean either: (1) whether there will be an adequate return on investment given the neighborhood's uncertain direction or (2) whether newcomers will win acceptance within the community they are invading. Figure 5–1 represents a continuum along which all buyers fit in terms of their risk perception. Each section of the continuum is associated with one of the first three stages of gentrification outlined earlier for Bay Village. In the final period, Stage Four, the neighborhood is a healthy and thriving entity with no need for any consideration of risk.

The *risk oblivious* have reasons for not conforming to behavioral norms. They are outside the socioeconomic mainstream and their needs are different. These people might include not just gays—as in the case of Bay Village—but also, by way of example, artists, interracial couples and couples with transracially adopted children—people anxious to find a place to live in an atmosphere that allows for self-expression or non-rejection. Accordingly, they are likely to select a substantially deteriorated neighborhood that offers this environment, and they are minimally concerned with risk in terms of financial investment. Indeed, their incomes may well be limited and their rehabilitation efforts reflect an investment of their own time rather than any capital outlay.

The next group along the continuum are *risk prone*. These people may succeed the risk oblivious, as in Bay Village, or they may themselves be pioneers in cases where the neighborhood is not especially deteriorated from the outset—such as West Cambridge. They evaluate risk prior to purchase but, conscious of both risk and gain, they decide to gamble. To them, the potential risk is outweighed by the prospect of obtaining a bargain—in Bay Village a poor man's Beacon Hill and in West Cambridge an inexpensive house that represents a remodeling challenge to newly acquired architectural skills.

Those who follow may be termed *risk averse,* willing to invest in a

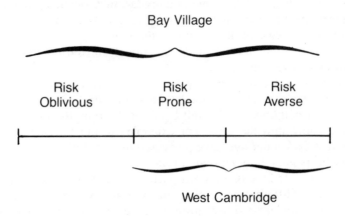

Figure 5–1. Risk Continuum

neighborhood once the perceived risk has been assumed by their predecessors or when they receive other signals that their entry into the neighborhood is secure. To be sure of their investment, they are prepared to
wait and to pay considerably more, if necessary. In Bay Village, the risk
averse were those who selected the neighborhood once it was clear that
public-infrastructure improvements were going to consolidate earlier private efforts. Some attempted to assess the risk by first renting in the
neighborhood. In West Cambridge, the risk averse were those who waited
to see how others of similar socioeconomic status would be accepted in
a working-class, strongly ethnic community.

The seminal reinvestment role played by artists in SoHo in Manhattan
and by gays both in certain Philadelphia neighborhoods and extensively
in San Francisco has been noted by some observers. It is reasonable to
assume that successive waves of in-migrants into these neighborhoods
follow the pattern documented in Bay Village. Today, urban living has
become very fashionable among the middle class. Reinvestment has occurred not only in most major U.S. cities but also in numerous neighborhoods within any given city. This mounting momentum has
undoubtedly served to create both a sense of security in numbers and a
sense of urgency in the need to be able still to acquire a bargain. In so
doing, it has helped alleviate some degree of perceived risk and accelerate
the gentrification process in many instances. Thus, the experience of Bay
Village with its discrete stages is today more likely to be replicated within
a much shorter time span.

Note

1. The Bay Village case study is drawn from an unpublished mas-
ter's thesis; ''The Process of Upgrading and Gentrification: An Examination of Two Neighborhoods in the Boston Metropolitan Area,''
Massachusetts Institute of Technology, June 1977. The analysis combined statistical data from both resident lists and real-estate records with
results from a series of detailed interviews with new and old residents,
realtors, planning officials, and bankers. The Bay Village analysis was
conducted in conjunction with a similar investigation of a neighborhood
in West Cambridge, to which reference is made in the concluding section
of this chapter. The Bay Village case itself is presented here in an ab-
breviated form.

References

Black, J. Thomas. 1975. Private-market housing renovation in central
cities: a ULI Survey. *Urban Land* 34 (November):3–9.

Clay, Phillip L. 1978. *Neighborhood revitalization: the recent experience in large American cities*. Cambridge, Mass.: Massachusetts Institute of Technology.

Gale, Dennis E. 1977. *The back-to-the-city movement revisited: a survey of recent homebuyers in the Capitol Hill neighborhood of Washington, D.C.* Washington, D.C.: George Washington University, Department of Urban and Regional Planning.

————. 1976. *The back-to-the-city movement . . . or is it?: a survey of recent homeowners in the Mount Pleasant Neighborhood of Washington D.C.* Washington, D.C.: George Washington University, Department of Urban and Regional Planning.

6

Some Policy Implications of Theories of Neighborhood Change

Robert Kolodny

Life-Cycle and Push-Pull Theories of Neighborhood Change

It is inevitable that policies for preserving, conserving, and/or stabilizing inner-city neighborhoods will reflect some underlying theory about the patterns of growth and decline in urban residential districts. But few policy documents are explicit about such basic assumptions, and they usually remain unexamined. Indeed it would be naïve to assume that policies always or usually are based on a coherent or consistent analysis of the underlying problems they are supposed to address.

In the case of neighborhood change and decline, however, there are two general propositions that appear to command fairly wide allegiance and provide at least a rough rationale for the set of efforts that currently dominates public policy. The first is that neighborhoods develop through a fairly predictable life cycle and that decline is part of that cycle. (There is some disagreement, as we shall see, whether neighborhood change is natural, and in some sense predestined, or whether decline is set in motion by a series of events that, while commonplace, are nevertheless avoidable or at least reversible.) The second proposition is that neighborhood shifts are set in motion by the behavior of individual households in response to certain *pulls* and/or *pushes* affecting their residential preferences. Household decisions are understood to be the primary instigator.

This chapter examines these two propositions, as they are reflected in several important treatments of neighborhood evolution and change. The purpose is to see what policy implications naturally emerge from these theories of neighborhood change and to explore some alternate views. At the outset, it will probably be helpful to clarify the key concept: *change*.

This chapter was originally prepared for Columbia University School of Architecture and Planning, *Papers in Planning* 5, 1978.

The Meaning of Change

The neighborhood policies we are concerned with are those designed to respond to undesirable change, threatened or in process, in what were felt previously to be stable and satisfactory residential districts. One problem that dogs discussion of transitional or changing neighborhoods is the lack of clarity about what kind of change is problematic and therefore a legitimate focus of public policy. *Change* in this context can refer to:

1. Change in *population*—not simply normal turnover in which like replaces like or the inevitable aging of households that remain in place but population succession that changes a neighborhood's racial and/or class composition;
2. Change in *neighborhood conditions*—objective deterioration in the physical and/or social climate;
3. Change in *attitudes and long-term expectations* concerning the neighborhood, particularly as they affect prices and values in the housing market—loss of confidence based on perceptions that may or may not accurately reflect the extent or effect of other changes.

Indeed, many discussions somewhat indiscriminately blend the demographic, physical-social, and attitudinal transformations and assume, not surprisingly, that one is somehow the direct antecedent or consequence of the other. In the current era, the sine qua non in terms of understanding neighborhood change is thought to be population succession, specifically the replacement of white residents by significant numbers of nonwhite or Hispanic households (Aldrich 1975). (In earlier eras, it more typically involved the succession of white ethnic and religious minorities into majority communities.)

The classic pattern of *population change* begins with an all-white neighborhood, followed by replacement of some members of the majority by middle-class or at least working-class minority residents, followed by the in-migration of lower-income minority residents (Cressey 1938). That the intermediate stage exists is clear from a number of analyses of specific cases, though it tends to be less obvious because only a small number of minority middle class in-migrate, and their presence apparently facilitates the rapid in-movement of lower-class residents. In the classic case, population shifts and neighborhood change occur at the margins of already-changed areas, a pattern that seems intuitively correct to us because it is so familiar and can be explained by theories of market behavior and social psychology (Molotch 1972, p. 17).

The essential point is that change in the racial and class composition of the population is often perceived as synonymous with physical decline, and, therefore, the source of a justifiable change in attitude regarding the neighborhood's future. Observation confirms that there are powerful links among the three, but having made that observation is a far cry from claiming or assuming a simple causal relationship. While deterioration in physical and social conditions generally is identified as the *problem*, the focus of attention is usually on population change. This blurring of an important distinction frequently results in the conclusion that the way to stabilize neighborhood conditions is to manipulate population composition, either by changing the attitudes of current and potential residents or through restricting the entry of certain groups.

The Pushes and Pulls Inducing Population Shifts

While the tendency is to focus on population composition, the complex interrelationship between demographic shifts and neighborhood conditions often makes it uncertain which comes first. One result in the literature and in everyday discussion has been the development of complementary explanations for the same phenomenon, one emphasizing the *pull* of other opportunities that cause population shifts, the other the push of an existing or anticipated set of neighborhood conditions that has the same results. A preliminary survey of the literature uncovers no systematic statement of the composite push-pull model, but its elements are encountered frequently and can be summarized in outline. (See table 6–1.) The major forces operating on neighborhoods are seen to be metropolitan, regional, and even national in scope, which helps to explain the similarities in pattern from city to city and the widespread nature of the change phenomenon.

Once these larger forces are in operation and beginning to have a real or anticipated effect in a given neighborhood, more local manifestations emerge. These are understood to be both the unfortunate consequences of change and, at the same time, a set of pushes that helps create it:

1. Physical decline due to loss of local purchasing power (especially for housing services) as a result of lower aggregate-income flows and/or lower per-capita assets of the incoming population.
2. Commercial decline due to loss of markets by specialized retail and service establishments.
3. Institutional decline due to loss of adherents, membership, or clientele.

Table 6–1
Composite Push-Pull Model

Pull		Push
The rapid pace of upward mobility for large fractions of the society (fueled by rising real incomes) giving rise to changes in consumer expectations and preferences with regard to residences and residential environments.	versus	The aging, obsolescence, and deterioration of the standing housing stock, community facilities and the physical infrastructure of urban residential neighborhoods.
The attractiveness of single-use and lower-density residential districts in more recently developed areas.	versus	The encroachment of so-called hostile, nonresidential land uses and/or increases in residential densities in older districts.
A voluntary preference for residential homogeneity based on race, ethnicity, or class.	versus	Fear of and/or hostility toward minority and lower-status groups; discrimination and enforced segregation that give rise to the operation of a *dual housing market* with its distortion of normal market processes and patterns of mobility.
Decline in transport costs leading to shifts in the location of employers (particularly industrial) and jobs; concomitant increases in accessibility to metropolitan employment opportunities widening the locational options of households.	versus	Attrition in employment opportunities as a result of increased costs of doing business in developed areas; changing economies of scale and obsolescence of existing facilities; costs of redevelopment or expansion on developed sites.
Predisposition of Americans in favor of the new; a tradition of mobility.	versus	A culturally based antiurbanism; lack of attachment to place based both on lack of control over local conditions and weak sources of political-ethical or sentimental allegiance.

4. Redlining by financial institutions, affecting the cost and/or availability of capital to investor-owners as well as individual home buyers.
5. Disinvestment by owners of income properties (both residential and commercial).
6. Blockbusting and racial steering—tactics employed by real-estate-market intermediaries that exploit resident concerns about population change and may either deliberately or incidentally bring it about.
7. Emergence of intergroup (as defined by race, ethnicity, or class) antagonism and conflict.
8. Loss of political power and influence relative to other neighborhoods and a concomitant loss of access to public resources.
9. A real or perceived reduction in the quantity and quality of public services (especially education) and municipal housekeeping.
10. A real or perceived increase in threats to public order, personal safety, and property security.

11. Public intervention that, it is claimed, inadvertently induces population change (that is, so-called welfare dumping, construction of subsidized housing developments, school busing).
12. The apparently self-perpetuating process of change itself.

What the relative strength of pull is as opposed to push, and at what point, if any, the balance shifts are not known. But because the push factors are more concrete and identifiable and become more prominent as change develops, they tend to get the most attention, as signified by the capsule theories of the change process embodied in the concepts *white flight* and *tipping point*. In fact, however, a strong argument can be made that the key sources of neighborhood change are pulls having extralocal origins. The first theory of change we will examine adopts this point of view.

Neighborhood Change as an Evolutionary Process

Implicit or explicit in much of the literature on urban growth is an assumption that patterns of neighborhood change are somehow natural or inevitable. The suggestion that the process is natural is built into the very organic metaphors the Chicago school of urban ecologists borrowed from natural science to describe urban spatial arrangements (Park 1936, p. 9; Johnston 1972, ch. 3). What is more, according to some systems of accounting that take the long view, the shifting of population progressively outward from the center delivers a net social benefit and therefore ought not be viewed as a negative process.

In a seminal article in the *Journal of the American Institute of Planners*, David Birch (1971) endeavors to develop a general theory relating physical and environmental change in subsectors of the city to the characteristics of the people migrating through neighborhoods.

> In the stage theory of urban growth proposed here . . . it is hypothesized that each neighborhood changes character over time, following a well-defined sequence. When neighborhoods are aggregated, regional patterns become apparent. When neighborhoods are looked at in detail, the history of human flows through them can be documented and related to the aging process. Thus, it is possible to match physical development against social change and trace the effect of one upon the other (p. 79).

Birch hypothesizes six stages of residential development and then tests them on the basis of 1967 Census pretest data for New Haven. Sure enough, its neighborhoods are seen to follow an evolutionary course. Starting as low-density *Rural* areas (Stage 1), they experience the *First*

Wave of Development (Stage 2), become *Fully Developed High-Quality Residential* (Stage 3), undergo *Packing* (Stage 4: typified by aging structures, overcrowding, low-income immigration), then *Thinning* (Stage 5) where population declines and the housing further deteriorates, and finally reach Stage 6 (the last, which Birch hopefully designates *Recapture* on the assumption that once a neighborhood reaches bottom, it will be renewed).

Age and density are the key factors that differentiate areas from each other and distinguish among their respective populations. The poorest population lives in the oldest areas, furthest along the sequence of stages to decline. The richest live in the newest areas. The upwardly mobile can be seen to escape areas in Stages 5 and 4 and move to those in Stages 3 and 2. Birch shows the tendency for neighborhoods to move through this progression of stages as uniform, remarkably regular, and apparently quite predictable.

Birch is not concerned primarily with the policy implications of his findings, but he does draw some interesting conclusions. For example, see figure 6–1. Traced hypothetically are the fortunes of a household, in terms of the quality of residential neighborhood it enjoys, over its lifetime. By virtue of its mobility, the household is seen to experience an improvement in its residential situation in spite of the paradox that all the city's neighborhoods are declining around it. Built into figure 6–1, however, are a number of assumptions that deserve to be examined. For one thing, the rate of decline portrayed is gradual and even. The picture might look substantially different if Neighborhood B were to experience a rapid and precipitous decline (such as that experienced in the late 1960s and early 1970s by those central-city areas now considered abandoned) after the family had graduated to it. Figure 6–1 conveniently represents the family's trajectory as staying ahead of decline; that is, even at Neighborhood B's lowest point it is never as deteriorated as Neighborhood A was when the family first entered it; similarly with Neighborhood C.

Moreover, the illustration pays little attention to the family's experience during most of its existence. One possible way of viewing it is as a household chronically caught in a declining environment. Nor is the possibility noted that the periodic moves might be seen by the family not as positive upward mobility but rather as relocations forced by deteriorating circumstances that its members would have preferred to avoid, along with the financial and emotional costs. Finally, there is the implicit assumption of upward mobility. One wonders, for example, how representative is a forty-seven-year-old household (whose male head can hardly be younger than sixty-five) that is willing and financially capable of making the critical move from Neighborhood B to C. Barring that

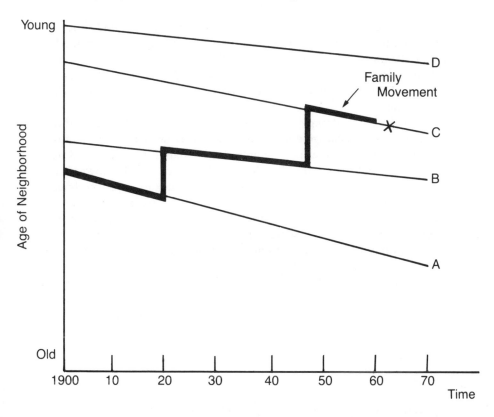

A family enters the area in Neighborhood A in 1900. The family's resources grow while Neighborhoods A and B decline. (The straight-line rates of decline in the fringe are simplified for illustration.) Finally, the jump from A to B is possible, and it is made. In the same fashion, the family moves to Neighborhood C, where it remains until the death of the family head. To an outside observer, or to a family rooted in Neighborhood A, or frequently to the mayor, Neighborhood A and the city as a whole are declining. Our family, however, is experiencing, on the average, continuous upward mobility. The region is serving its needs very well. The fact that certain parts of the region—most notably the older sections of the central city—are suffering in the process is of little consequence to the family.

Source: Birch, David. L., "Toward a Stage Theory of Urban Growth." *Journal of American Institute of Planners* 37, 3(March 1975):83.

Figure 6–1. An Illustrative Example of Family Movement

move, the household in the illustration would enjoy at the end of its life cycle roughly the same level of environmental quality it had at the beginning. Birch acknowledges the very different perspective of a family *stuck* in Neighborhood A (or, for that matter, C), but its history is not charted and the costs this pattern enforces upon it are generally left out of the account.

While Birch's attempt to establish a stage theory of neighborhood change may seem academic and theoretical, it is not trivial in its policy implications. If the pattern of neighborhood change is understood as a natural one, created by individual-household choice and the upward mobility of the population as a whole, if it clearly leads to improved household welfare overall (even if parts of the city "are suffering in the process"), and if it is in fact shown to be the actual and apparently irreversible case for a representative U.S. city, then one logically might draw the policy conclusion that change ought to be, or must largely be, accepted. That is, it ought to be seen as a natural and inevitable pattern that presents problems for some but opportunities for most. This is not to say that Birch would himself advocate no public attention to declining neighborhoods, but his portrayal of the process tends logically in that direction.

An Equilibrium Theory of Neighborhood Change

It appears possible to take most approaches to understanding neighborhood change and to divide them into two main types: those that see it as an evolutionary process and those that view it as discontinuous. The first group, which includes Birch's stage theory, tends to see it as a natural (almost deterministic) process of change closely related to aging and as the consequence of the multiple decisions of many actors such that no single actor can have any decisive impact. The second set tends to see negative change as the result of some outside event or force intervening and triggering the process of change. This group thus inclined to view it as the consequence of some identifiable factor or agent that might be modified or controlled.

The second picture of neighborhood change to be examined, developed by Public Affairs Counseling (PAC 1975), tends to straddle these two positions: it is an evolutionary model that nevertheless views the results as unnatural. PAC, a division of Real Estate Research Corporation, developed its analysis under contract to HUD's Office of Policy Development and Research and aimed its document at practitioners rather than theorists or researchers. Unlike Birch's article, PAC's *The Dynamics of Neighborhood Change* involved no new research but relied on a synthesis of the existing literature. The picture it draws is a familiar and plausible one, and its publication by HUD, despite the usual disclaimers, has given it a kind of semiofficial imprimatur and wide exposure.

PAC, like Birch, takes a behavioral approach to neighborhood change, seeing individual households as the key actors:

> The real force behind neighborhood change is the impact of people moving in, moving out, deciding to stay or deciding to look elsewhere for housing. The dynamics of the neighborhood change process revolve around *the household decision*. Other people (bankers, brokers) make decision, and they are important and often critical, but it is the change in resident population and the decisions behind that, that fuel the neighborhood change process (emphasis in the original, p. 14).

In the normal course of events, movers-in and movers-out arrive and leave without incident. The critical moving decisions that set change in motion tend to be set off by some new or special circumstances.

> Spontaneous events, such as rapid racial change or highway building or the closing of a local employment center (a hospital or shipyard) can lead to accelerated downward movement. Equally, the renewal of a business district or a new transportation access can make a neighborhood suddenly competitive or even "fashionable" and lead to spontaneous revitalization (p. 10).

In contrast to Birch, PAC's version of the neighborhood's life cycle spells out only the downward trajectory. It consists of five stages: (1) *Healthy*, (2) *Incipient Decline*, (3) *Clearly Declining*, (4) *Accelerating Decline*, (5) *Abandoned*. Despite the resemblance between a neighborhood's course and the human life cycle, it differs in one fundamental way: "the trend towards decline and demolition can be reversed, and, in certain circumstances, neighborhoods can be revitalized" (p. 8). According to PAC, maintaining a neighborhood in the healthy phase is a delicate affair. Indeed, from PAC's description of the sources of neighborhood health it becomes apparent that this is an equilibrium theory of neighborhoods and that where homeostasis can be achieved, the evolutionary cycle can be evaded or forestalled. The problem is that many of the factors that trigger decline are outside of local control; that is, the creation of new housing and the decline of other residential neighborhoods in the metropolitan area.

The result is a theory that recommends public and private intervention to maintain or restore equilibrium in a situation where decline is portrayed as virtually inevitable (because it is beyond the control of those PAC is addressing). What is more, despite the emphasis on the interrelationship among housing markets, there is no clear acknowledgment of the consequence that restoration of equilibrium in District A must result in taking the threats that confronted A and displacing them to Districts B and C.

The equilibrium that can be sought in such settings essentially involves maintenance of the status quo, if one can judge from the descriptions of key characteristics of areas at each stage. The key indicator of a healthy neighborhood is the homogeneity of its residents: they are "much like one another in terms of race, income, status, education and job" (p. 23). (In incipient decline areas, by contrast, "the people moving into a neighborhood . . . differ from the people moving out," reducing "the previous homogeneity of residents" [p. 24].) What is more, a healthy neighborhood has residents "who are family oriented, exhibit pride in their home and neighborhood," and are predominantly home owners (p. 23).

The extent to which these are merely *de*scriptions instead of *pre*scriptions is not clear, but the ambiguity itself is suggestive. In any case, they tend to raise and then beg the question of whether any neighborhood initially lacking or having lost these characteristics can be considered healthy. Can a neighborhood that is mixed in socioeconomic or racial and ethnic composition be stabilized? How about a neighborhood solely occupied by low-income residents of whatever race? Indeed, it would appear, although it is not directly stated, that the success of an effort to restore health is heavily dependent on changing the decisions of the so-called right people to move and of other right people not to reject the neighborhood as a potential place of residence. It is acknowledged that the shift from healthy (Stage 1) to incipient decline (Stage 2) is useful, in that it provides newcomers "decent housing at prices that people can afford" (p. 12). But the rest of the analysis suggests that this is only temporary and already represents a condition of disequilibrium.

PAC draws one other important lesson from this equilibrium theory: early action has a much higher likelihood of success (and not incidentally a lower cost) than action initiated only after Stage 3 or 4 has been reached. (Indeed, this observation is made with sufficient force as to set up discouraging overtones with regard to attempting anything useful past the point of incipiency.) PAC's change theory diverges substantially on this point from Birch's. Whereas he sees change as a very gradually continuous historical process, PAC sees it as pathological and discontinuous once some threshold has been crossed. Thus the distinct impression is left that there is a before and an after (though the dividing line is not clear). One either stops change before it takes hold, or it is too expensive, or just plain too late. The logic of the model of change means that scant attention is paid the possibility that something useful can be done for neighborhoods where change and decline are already well underway.

Policy Implications of the Change Theories

We have, then, several ways of analyzing or understanding the process of neighborhood change and decline. They appear to lead basically to three policy options, each of them focused on the population definition of change. The first is to *accept change*. For one thing, it is built into the natural order of things and is probably not reversible. For another, it is primarily the result of households bettering themselves, seizing the opportunity to improve their residential circumstances. Looked at from the perspective of a whole chain of households, each one moving up, the results are positive.

A second policy option is to attempt to *stop change*. Since neighborhood decline is understood as basically a consequence of household decisions—of some not to stay and of others not to enter—the strategy tends to focus on stopping population shifts as a mechanism for forestalling the various undesirable results that are evoked by the phrase *a changing neighborhood*.

The third option, which can be seen as a compromise between the desire to stop change and acknowledgment that it is fueled by so-called natural forces and market preferences, is to endeavor to *slow change*. Again, the focus is on the rate of population turnover. This strategy is based on the premise that if only the pace can be slowed, change can be better controlled or inhibited and will not have so devastating an effect. This approach may be advocated on the grounds that change along race and class lines is inevitable—leading to ultimate resegregation—but that time will give people a better chance to cope. Alternately, it may be assumed that if change is allowed to take its unimpeded course, wholesale transition is inevitable; but if it can be slowed, it may be possible ultimately to stabilize an area with a racially mixed (if not socioeconomically mixed) population.

The Varying Meaning of Change for Different Groups of Households

It is in some ways paradoxical that while both Birch and PAC anchor their understanding of the neighborhood-change process in the behavior of individual households, neither attempts any comprehensive analysis of the range of households potentially involved. Neither their respective roles in the process nor the consequences for them are explored seriously. In fact, neighborhood change typically involves five conceptually separate household groups. They can be distinguished as follows.

1. *The Involuntary Out-Movers*. These are households who have

moved or are contemplating moving because their neighborhood is changing in ways they consider unsatisfactory. They may have considered moving from time to time in the past and may have seen some advantages in it, but they would not ordinarily be acting apart from the changes developing or anticipated in their districts. They are the implicit focus of attention in the PAC analysis (that there might be involuntary participants is barely acknowledged in Birch's treatment) and the explicit focus of many efforts to stop, or slow, change.

2. *The Voluntary Out-Movers.* The voluntary out-movers are those who move for various circumstantial reasons (job, health, retirement, divorce, death) that are specific to a household or because of the lure of other opportunities (more space, ownership, and so on). They are more pulled than pushed. (For Birch, they are the primary household type, embracing both the outgoers and the newcomers.) While as a practical matter it might be difficult to distinguish them from the *involuntary* out-movers, conceptually they are people whose primary reasons for moving have nothing to do with the neighborhood. According to some studies of the change process (Molotch 1972; Rapkin and Grigsby 1960), it is the otherwise routine turnover created by this group that sets the stage for population change, along with the unwillingness of the next group, the *would-be in-movers*, to replace them as had been the customary pattern.

3. *The Would-Be In-Movers.* These are the most ephemeral of the categories to be considered, consisting of those majority households (including newly formed households with one or both partners raised in the neighborhood) that might have considered the area a potential residence but are discouraged by fears or signs of change and/or pulled by what they perceive as better opportunities elsewhere. They are typically the focus of attention where established residents are bent on defending their areas, but there is considerable question about the practicality of a strategy designed to transform them into in-movers.

4. *The Unwilling Stayers.* This group consists of households that in ethnic and class terms are like the involuntary out-movers but lack the resources and/or psychic and physical energy to move in response to the push they feel from changing conditions. A high proportion of the unwilling stayers are likely to be elderly. Among them is a subgroup that might more accurately be termed the *unhappy but unbudgeable stayers.* Social workers and organizers in some changing neighborhoods report that significant numbers of the elderly will not consider leaving their homes (of decades in some cases) even if they had or were given the resources and virtually irrespective of the extent to which the neighbor-

hood has declined in their eyes. The stayers are not frequently a focus of attention in analysis or policy development and are not acknowledged directly by either Birch or PAC.

5. *The In-Movers.* These are households who as a rule are seeking alternate and, usually, better housing accommodations and environments. Predominantly, in the cases we are interested in, they are racial minorities. In many cases the in-movers arrive in phases—moderate or middle income and more upwardly mobile first, followed by lower-income families, and eventually by households receiving public assistance. Thus, depending on the extent of population change, in-movers can be further broken down (according to the stage of demographic transformation reached at the time they entered, which will tend to coincide with differences in socioeconomic status). The in-movers are the other household grouping identified by Birch, but he treats them as just another group of voluntary out-movers, albeit from a neighborhood lower on the ladder (older in stage). PAC sees them implicitly as the source of the problem, if not the initiator of the process.

Preserving Neighborhoods for Whom?

This declension of the household types with a stake in changing neighborhoods sheds a somewhat different light on the policy choices described earlier. One can see, in fact, that the alternate policies tend to favor certain categories of household over others; and, in fact, the theories themselves reflect certain underlying predispositions in terms of whose interests are to be affected and preserved as policies are adopted to deal with the change process.

An approach that basically *accepts change* tends inevitably to endorse the existing distribution of benefits that attach to residential location, if it does not indeed reinforce them. It acknowledges the interests of the voluntary out-movers and at least the first wave of in-movers. It essentially ignores the consequences for the involuntary out-movers and the stayers.

In policies that attempt to *stop change*, the focus tends to be on the interests of those who would otherwise be what we have termed involuntary out-movers, or on the social capital represented by the physical neighborhood itself and the significance of preserving it intact for the city (that is, protecting the tax base). Inadvertently there may be some protection of the interests of the unwilling stayers as well, but they are clearly not the primary focus of attention. The in-movers are discriminated against effectively in this approach, although it may take the form of indirect discrimination in the sense of encouragement and assistance for people already there to stay (or the attraction of would-be in-movers as replacements) rather than direct prohibition of entry by others. The complicating factor is, of course, that there are likely to be voluntary out-movers in any such neighborhood, and the key to success is likely to be the filling of these voluntarily created slots by households similar in race and class to the current occupants.

One paradox that attends efforts to implement this strategy is that any upgrading or improvement tends to make an area that much more attractive to minority households seeking accommodations—not only to current occupants or to potential white replacement households. Where the pool of potential minority residents is significantly larger than the equivalent pool of whites, market factors are likely to be determining unless minorities are actively discouraged (typically through coercive means).

A policy designed to slow change would seem the most benign in terms of which class of residents or would-be residents is served. Its focus of attention would appear to be fairly equally distributed among the groups, although insofar as it is successful, it is likely to inhibit the succession of in-movers to more desirable areas. Moreover, to slow the change, it is probable that special efforts, incentives, and resources would have to be aimed at those who would otherwise be involuntary out-movers and that ultimately they would become the chief beneficiaries, at least in the short term. The unwilling stayers would benefit indirectly. There is, of course, the plausible argument that the in-movers would benefit eventually by virtue of the healthier conditions a slowdown might help to preserve.

The essential problem with this approach is that it is not yet explicit regarding on whose behalf public resources and energies are to be expended. Whatever is going to happen must be made to happen more gradually, and the assumption is that this *in and of itself* will result in some generally desirable end. The focus is on the means—moderating the rate—rather than on the end—preserving the neighborhood for whom?

One complaint about the *stop* and *slow-change* strategies, then, is that they are inequitable in terms of the incidence of costs and benefits; they either ignore or are content with the distributional implications of the preceding analysis. A second complaint is that they are not practical—they ignore the very principles embedded in both the evolutionary and equilibrium theories of neighborhood change and in the push-pull model. Insofar as pull is a significant factor in population change in neighborhoods, strategies concentrating on the push factors are not likely to succeed in a large number of districts (the problem becomes not simply retaining existing households but attracting new ones of like description—a considerably more difficult task). They may have some results in those neighborhoods sometimes termed *urban villages*, where ethnic or class identity creates a potentially countervailing pull that can be built upon, or in areas with housing stock of measurably superior original quality or having unusual local amenity (that is, the brownstone districts). But even where such efforts are successful in one case, they are likely to displace the problem, siphoning off those would-be in-movers who can be persuaded to settle and intensifying demand among minority inmovers for other areas that are not as attractive but nevertheless a notch or more above their present neighborhoods in quality.

In sum, these two approaches underestimate the power of the forces currently operating to induce population change in older, urban residential districts. At the same time, they may well underestimate the possibilities for effective action during and after population change has occurred to sustain neighborhood quality. (The PAC argument for early action is posed in terms of cost effectiveness, but it carries the implication that once a neighborhood has declined, it is no longer a good public investment.)

A Fourth Policy Approach: Managing Change
on Behalf of the Stayers and In-Movers

Alternate policy approaches are clearly possible, even within the framework of a life-cycle theory of neighborhood change and the push-pull model of its dynamics. For example, policy could focus explicitly on neighborhood conditions rather than on population composition, the goal being to sustain to the maximum possible extent the quality of the residential and local commercial services it offers, irrespective of who will be consuming them. Such an approach would reject the proposition that there is a *before* and *after*, and would attempt to treat neighborhoods regardless of the extent of their decline. Thus it would acknowledge that choosing among areas by stage means choosing among the households whose interests are tied to them at various points in their trajectory.

The emphasis would be on the management of the physical and social consequences of population and attitudinal changes so as to mitigate as much as possible their ill effects, rather than on attempts to influence the ebb and flow of particular types of households. Such an approach to managing change assumes that it is not appropriate for the public directly to try to modify or inhibit population movement. Moreover, it assumes that, except in isolated or fairly unique circumstances, it is not possible to inhibit population movement to any significant degree, even where considerable public and private efforts are brought to bear. Thus this strategy can be embraced from considerations either of equity or of practicality.

A premise of this approach is that it ought to be possible to attend to the needs of each of the household groups with some equity, but to do so without damaging the interests of those in most critical need of public support and attention—the *in*-movers and the stayers. This strategy might very well emphasize attempts to modulate and moderate change and to assist households that otherwise might move to stay on. Thus it would not always be distinguishable programmatically from the other strategies. But it would avoid the potential distortions that lurk in the wings where the goal is simply to *slow* change rather than to mitigate its ill effects through creating a more orderly transitional process. In some cases the creation of a more orderly process might lead to an *acceleration* of population change. For example the provision of mortgage finance and public support for an orderly property market could make it easier for involuntary out-movers to sell their properties and leave. Similarly one might attempt directly to facilitate, not discourage, the orderly transfer of ownership of residences, small enterprises (rental housing and local businesses), and neighborhood institutions from those with short-term horizons to those with longer-term expectations for the neighborhood. In many respects, this approach is closer to the evolutionary model of neighborhood change, but it rejects the laissez faire implications of Birch and the resignation of those who argue for planned shrinkage.

Concluding Note: The Limitations of a Behavioral Theory of Neighborhood Change and of Local Strategies for Dealing with It

Both Birch and PAC assert the primacy of the choices made by individual households in determining the patterns that prevail. For Birch the *pulls* are key: a desire for "low density living, . . . more space, better schools for children, and a basic American instinct for privacy," following the analysis of Hoover and Vernon (1962). PAC gives more emphasis to the *pushes*: the erosion of values, confidence, stability, and amenity that cause initial and then accelerated withdrawal from an area. The response of the intermediaries—lenders, real-estate brokers, insurers, shopkeepers, public officials, and service providers—once activated by household withdrawal, further encourages that withdrawal.

One fundamental problem with the push-pull model may be that it is founded on such an atomistic interpretation of social phenomena. If neighborhoods change because of the relatively free and individual choices of so many primary and secondary actors, then it becomes obvious that altering only some portion of them can have but a limited impact on the outcome. Moreover, as the PAC analysis notes but does not fully acknowledge, the pulls that soften housing markets and create opportunities for population shifts are ordinarily beyond the influence of the local policymakers whom they are addressing (and indeed beyond the reach of most neighborhood-preservation efforts that have emerged as emphatically a local, rather than federal, activity).

The behavioral approach to neighborhood change can be contrasted to a more structural approach that would view the scope of household decisions as being defined and narrowed by other factors, particularly the location of economic activity within metropolitan areas and among regions and the institutionalized legacy of discrimination against blacks and other minority groups. Such structural factors, produced over time by a combination of public and private policies and practices, can be seen as introducing incentives and inducements that may be independent of inherent differences in the desirability of residential neighborhoods, considered in and of themselves.

This view would argue, yes, that neighborhood decline is inevitable, but not because it is part of some natural order of things. It is inevitable as long as there are (1) wide disparities in economic and other resources (decline is bound to follow racial change as long as minorities are at the lower end of the economic and social ladder) and (2) such unbalanced patterns of growth among the political subdivisions of metropolitan areas and among regions.

The policy conclusion of such a view is that no purely local or solely neighborhood-focused strategy can succeed in more than, perhaps, managing change and mitigating in some measure its most deleterious effects. Thus the *management approach* just outlined may be the only practical and justifiable one in the short term but is ultimately only a stopgap. The patterns of population movement in and out of neighborhoods are only the symptom of wider and more systemic problems. From this perspective, the only logical neighborhood-preservation strategy is a long-term one that deals with the more fundamental problems of inequality in income, educational achievement, job opportunity, and political power and meanwhile creates opportunities for minority and low-income households elsewhere than in the central cities. And beyond that, it would have to confront the city-versus-suburb and region-versus-region disparities that set up large-scale incentives for the relocation of economic activity and concomitant population shifts.

References

Ahlbrandt, Roger S., Jr.; and Brophy, Paul C. 1975. *Neighborhood revitalization*. Lexington: D.C. Heath and Co., Lexington Books.
Aldrich, Howard. 1975. "Ecological succession in racially changing

neighborhoods: a review of the literature.'' *Urban Affairs Quarterly* 10, 3:327–348.

Birch, David L. 1971. ''Toward a stage theory of urban growth.'' *Journal of American Institute of Planners* 37, 2:78–87.

Cressey, Paul F. 1938. ''Population succession in Chicago.'' *American Journal of Sociology* 44 (July):59–69.

Ginsberg, Yona. 1975. *Jews in a changing neighborhood*. New York: Free Press.

Hoover, Edgar M.; and Vernon, Raymond. 1962. *Anatomy of a metropolis*. Cambridge, Mass.: Harvard University Press.

Hoyt, Homer. 1939. *The structure and growth of residential neighborhoods in American cities*. Washington, D.C.: Federal Housing Administration.

Johnston, R.J. 1972. *Urban residential patterns*. New York: Praeger Publishers.

Molotch, Harvey. 1972. *Managed integration*. Berkeley: University of California Press.

Park, Robert E. 1936. ''Human ecology.'' *American Journal of Sociology* 42 (July):1–15.

Public Affairs Counseling. 1975. *The dynamics of neighborhood change*. Washington, D.C.: Office of Policy Development and Research, Department of Housing and Urban Development, December.

Rapkin, Chester; and Grigsby, William G. 1960. *The demand for housing in racially mixed areas*. Berkeley: University of California Press.

Part III
The Neighborhood Context

Part III discusses the neighborhood as a particular kind of social organization, the demographic dynamics that underlie the neighborhood structure and function, and the attitudes residents hold about neighborhoods and city living. We also look at the community-based organization as the aggregation and instrumental expression of neighborhood preferences and goals. Part of the difficulty planners and policymakers have had in the past in dealing with the neighborhood issue is that there has been little understanding of how neighborhoods shift in the metropolitan hierarchy. We can be sure that the region is an economic unit, that the city (and suburbs and counties) is a political construct. We also know there is a large social element to the neighborhood, but we are unsure about the political and economic aspects of neighborhoods. This part of the book seeks to disentangle these relationships.

Chapter 7, by Dowell Myers, analyzes recent demographic trends as well as important trends in life-style (marriage, divorce, and fertility patterns) that affect the locational decisions of urban households, the dynamics of neighborhood change, and the meaning of different demographic variables for important policy variables. Myers argues that present theories of neighborhood change give insufficient attention to population factors. He makes a compelling case for neighborhood planners, as well as others, to pay more attention to demographic variables and outlines the key elements of a population framework for analyzing neighborhood policies.

In chapter 8 Rachel Bratt critically reviews major surveys and research about the attitudes of citizens toward neighborhoods, concepts of the ideal neighborhood, the latest evidence on propensity to move and priorities of public actions as viewed by citizens, and the assessment of the performance of public and private actors. These are all areas in which there have been substantial recent data that has not been pulled together and bear critically on how we can understand and use popular perceptions in program design and analysis. One of the lessons we learned from the

1960s is that these perceptions are critical to stimulating private action and to calibrating public intervention.

Neighborhood organizations have come to play a variety of roles in urban communities and are gaining widespread recognition as being essential to community infrastructure. Neil Mayer's chapter reviews the traditional roles that neighborhood organizations have played and identifies some of the major changes in these roles that have emerged in recent years. The chapter points to the heightened understanding that residents have of the power their organizations can have to achieve both the expressive and also the instrumental goals of residents in urban communities. Mayer presents a very practical catalog of some of the capacities of these organizations and gives the planner and policymaker some idea of the appropriate ways to involve residents formally in the hierarchy of intervention to improve neighborhoods.

The chapters in this part, taken together, provide an improved basis for understanding the policy toward neighborhoods that is explored more systematically in the concluding part of the book.

7 Population Processes and Neighborhoods

Dowell Myers

This chapter is founded on the premise that a cataloging of population changes (such as one often sees) is of little value for planning if it does not lead expressly to insights about the processes that are generating the patterns we observe. Far from being a comprehensive treatment of urban-population trends, this chapter is intended to provide the reader with a conceptual grasp of the population processes that currently are most responsible for neighborhood changes. In the present chapter four sets of observations are discussed, each leading to a general principle that will enable better planning.

The first of these principles is that *net* population changes disguise much larger actual population movements. For effective intervention it is desirable to address the gross behaviors that underlie the net changes. Second, population analysis demonstrates that the number of people in different age groups is at least as important as the total population size. Because many behaviors change markedly with age, shifts in the age composition of local populations can have major consequences. Third, the number of nonmovers in neighborhoods is at least as important as the number of movers. Although it is generally recognized that movers are the principal actors affecting change in neighborhoods, nonmovers restrict the number of vacancies available to movers. At the same time that they contribute to social continuity and economic stability, nonmovers generate a different sort of social change through the aging of their own family members.

The final principle is that the future impacts of the large baby-boom generation cannot be projected directly from past age patterns of behavior. The simultaneous changes in family formation, female labor-force participation, and home ownership foreclose simple extrapolations. Instead, what is required is more careful monitoring and analysis of housing and neighborhood choices as this giant generation continues to mature.

Net Changes and Underlying Behavior

Net changes are utilized widely to describe populations because they are handy summary statistics. Unfortunately their analytical value is restricted because consequences cannot be inferred simply by taking the difference between two opposing changes. For example, natural increase is a net change calculated by subtracting deaths from births. A positive value (excess of births over deaths) indicates a growing population, and vice versa. Of course, the persons who are dying and the persons who are being born are quite different sorts of people with very different social roles. The net change between births and deaths has no necessary relationship to next year's demand for either caskets or baby carriages. Only where the comers and goers are similar sorts of people does net change have analytic value.

Studies of interurban migration have revealed two outstanding patterns that underlie net changes in population. The rate of in-movement and out-movement varies substantially from area to area, but the two streams are approximately counterbalancing. As a consequence the net change is but a fraction (near one-tenth) of the average of the two gross flows (Birch et al. 1975). It is not certain what accounts for this phenomenon of counterbalancing flows, although the most likely explanation has to do with the repeated migration of so-called chronic movers (Morrison 1971). Many persons move between cities but stay only a short interval before moving back. Thus, the volume of out-movers is nearly proportional to the volume of in-movers. An important observation is that although two cities may have identical net changes due to migration, the city with larger gross flows will be characterized by greater transience. A continuing flow of short-term residents requires an appropriate volume of annual rental vacancies, special services (public or private) for establishing new lives in the city, and an adequate number of suitable job openings. Perhaps it is not a coincidence that the volume of in-movers matches that of out-movers, since the new residents generally will occupy the same housing and job slots as the leavers. In this respect measurement of net change provides valuable information on the relative excess or deficit of persons demanding the slots that have been vacated by out-movers.

In most cases the behavior of in-movers and out-movers is so radically different that separate strategies of intervention are required even if the goal is simply to alter their combined effect on the net change. Migration analysts have discovered the puzzling fact that flows of out-movers do not respond much to the economic climate of a city. A negative net change is produced because the flows of in-movers respond more critically to the relative economic climates of destination cities (Lowry 1966; Rust 1975). The explanation for this difference in response is probably the commonsensical fact that existing residents are more rooted by their families, social networks, and general place familiarity. Potential in-migrants have no such attachment, and hence they behave more rationally. As the flow of in-movers diminishes, the potential supply of out-movers is reduced to only long-term residents who are attached and less likely to move under any economic circumstances.

The implication of these behavioral processes for neighborhood analysis is outlined more clearly in the case of racial integration. white flight has been recognized as a problem in many U.S. cities for at least two decades. The problem is defined in simplest terms as a net increase of black population over white population. More commonly, white flight has been assumed to exist whenever the proportion of whites has declined. In either definition several underlying processes are obscured by a single summary statistic.

In a study of eleven cities with the largest black populations, Long (1975) analyzed changes in the nonwhite percentage between 1950 and 1960, and between 1960 and 1970, in terms of three contributing factors: differences in natural increase, in-migration of nonwhites, and out-migration of whites. Although each of these factors is itself a summary of more specific processes, it is helpful at least to distinguish between the contributions of whites and nonwhites to the rising percentage of nonwhites. Long (1975, p. 260) has concluded that "in both decades white out-migration was generally the single most important factor in raising the percent black. In fact, white out-migration was usually at least twice as important as black in-migration in raising the percent black." Long's methodology is one of statistical decomposition and not causal analysis; nevertheless, he suggests that his findings support strategies for retaining whites as the best means of preventing further increases in the percentage of nonwhites. This, of course, is congruent with the white-flight definition of the racial-change problem.

A different picture emerges when we look at patterns of racial change at the neighborhood level. Molotch (1972) has offerred the hypothesis that white flight from neighborhoods does not exist. Instead, racial change is accounted for by the unwillingness of whites to *move into* an integrated neighborhood. Guest and Zuiches (1971) tested this hypothesis by comparing neighborhoods, as did Molotch, and failed to disprove it. Certainly there are well-known cases where white families most likely have accelerated their out-migration (see Varady [1974] for a careful analysis of one such instance), but most of these cases have not been sufficiently documented. The Molotch hypothesis does not deny such possibilities, rather it treats these as exceptions to the more fundamental process of racial change caused by the diminution of white replacement. In fact, given the evidence on differences in behavior between migration inflows and outflows, it is reasonable to suppose that current white residents of integrating neighborhoods do not react as quickly to increasing integration as do unattached movers searching for new neighborhoods. Current residents might continue to move at normal rates, without replacement by white movers from outside the neighborhood, and as a consequence white flight would appear to occur as the proportion of whites declines. Molotch observes that the correct response to such a situation is not to stop white flight that is proceeding at a normal rate but instead to recruit more white in-movers actively. The problem faced by the community group in Chicago that Molotch studied was that it was economically and organizationally difficult to hold vacancies in anticipation of new white residents when the black demand was so strong. In addition, part of the organizational strategy, which was to make local residents fearful of the racial consequences if they did not cooperate, had the deleterious impact of advertising to potential in-movers that racial change was occurring in the community. In general, the strategy of augmenting white demand in this community was adopted too late for any success to be achieved.

The first population principle for more effective planning is to recognize the limitations of net-change statistics. Net changes disguise actual movements that are many times larger. Moreover, the net difference usually involves a difference between different sorts of people with opposing motivations. To understand or plan for a net change, it is essential to study the gross flows and design policies to address the specific behaviors underlying each gross flow.

The Central Importance of Age

The central variable in population analysis is *age* (Shryock et al. 1976, p. 113). The fundamental demographic events of fertility, mortality, and migration are closely linked with age. More broadly, many social roles, from school child to newly wed to retiree, are largely restricted to particular age groups. As a consequence, the age structure of a population is often times as important as the total size of the population. Because these data are readily available in published census volumes for units as small as census tracts, one of the first tasks in any population analysis is to construct an age pyramid.

Figures 7–1 through 7–4 present the age-sex compositions for some fairly different Boston neighborhoods. Figure 7–1 depicts a census tract located in the West Roxbury section of the city. This population is almost completely white and the majority are owner-occupants. The hour-glass shape of the pyramid indicates that the neighborhood is dominated by middle-aged parents with their teenage children. There is also a fairly high proportion of elderly. Figure 7–2 depicts a contrasting kind of tract. This neighborhood is located in a district proximate to several hospitals and medical-training facilities. There was substantial new construction

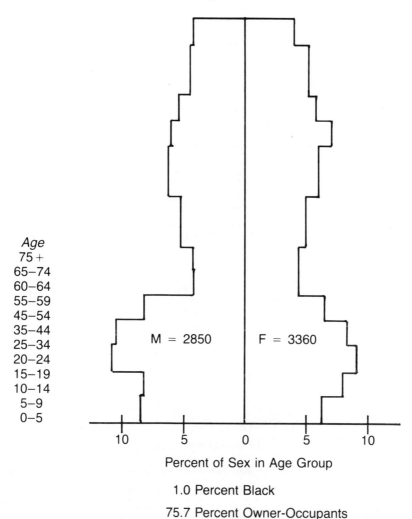

Figure 7–1. 1970 Age Pyramid for Boston Census Tract 1303 (West Roxbury), an Outer-City Family Neighborhood

in the tract just prior to the 1970 census, and as of that date the major share of the housing stock consisted of private rental units. Given this background data the unusual shape of the age pyramid is not surprising. This neighborhood is clearly populated by young adults in the early stages of their careers. In sharp contrast, the older adults in the upper half of the pyramid are likely to have resided in the neighborhood for many years and they have probably witnessed the arrival and departure of countless generations of the young adults.

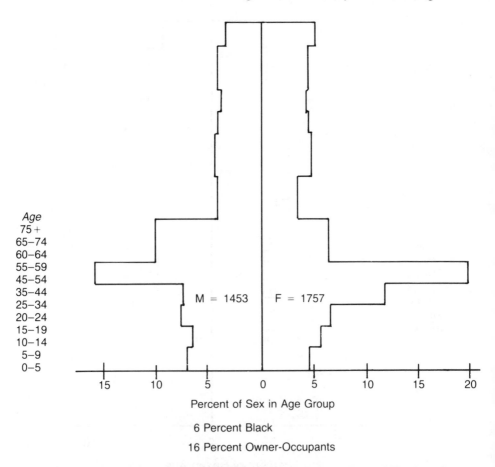

Figure 7–2. 1970 Age Pyramid for Boston Census Tract 809 (Jamaica
Plain), an Inner-City Young-Singles Neighborhood

Figures 7–3 and 7–4 present the age-sex compositions of the same
census tract at different points in time—1960 and 1970. This neighborhood is located in the Dorchester section of Boston, near Franklin Park.
In 1970 the population was almost exclusively black. Nearly one-quarter
were owner-occupants and the shape of the pyramid reveals a heavy
orientation toward child rearing. In 1960 this neighborhood looked substantially different. There were a few more housing units and nearly the
same proportion were owner-occupied, but less than a quarter of the
population was black. The overall profile of the population was one of
aging maturity with a high proportion of the population over age fifty.
The slight flair at the bottom of the pyramid was accounted for largely
by the incoming black families. The upper half of the pyramid consisted
largely of older white adults who had completed their family raising.

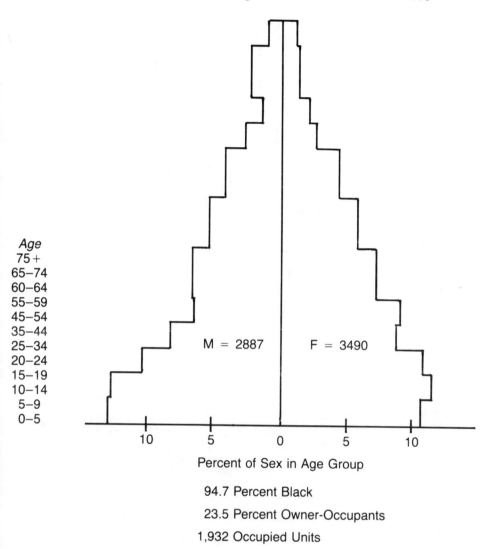

Figure 7–3. 1970 Age Pyramid for Boston Census Tract 901 (Dorchester), a Recently Resegregated Black Family Neighborhood

Perhaps these were individuals described as *frozen* occupants in a later section of this chapter on non-movers. At any rate, over the decade the population was rejuvenated by the arrival of young families. This rejuvenation did not occur by gradual replacement beginning at young ages, rather it was achieved by a wholesale displacement of both older and younger white persons.

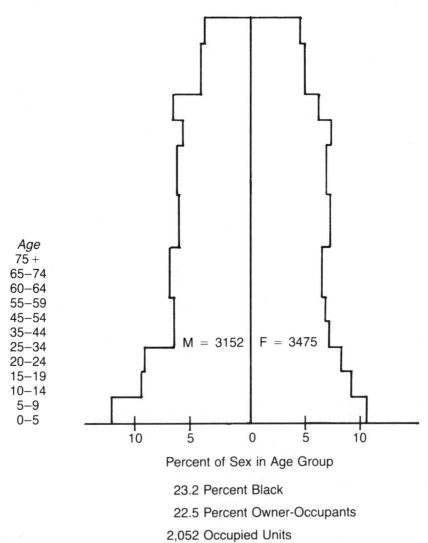

Figure 7–4. 1960 Age Pyramid for Boston Census Tract 901 (Dorchester), at the Beginning of Racial Transition

During such a transition marked conflicts may occur—not simply because of racial prejudice (about which planners can do little in the short run) but because of age differences between the two populations. An examination of the separate white and black age profiles for almost any census tract that is racially mixed will show that the whites are elderly and older middle aged (or perhaps young singles) while the blacks are younger adults and children. When racial transition is sudden the age composition of a neighborhood will shift much more rapidly than is to be expected. And instead of shifting to older ages, as is the tendency over time, it shifts to younger ages. This shift places enormous strain both on formal service systems like public schools and also on informal services and institutions like playground activities and sidewalk recreation. Perhaps an age perspective would enable more sensitive management of racial change. In general, planners are well advised to scrutinize neighborhoods' past and present age profiles for the information they contain about social processes.

There is a distinct age profile to most population changes. One of the fundamental facts of neighborhood population analysis is that residential mobility and migration are highest around age twenty-five and decline sharply thereafter. Table 7–1 presents national data for 1976 showing the percentage of all persons in each age group who have moved into a metropolitan region during the preceding year and showing the percentage of each age group that has changed residences within a metropolitan region during the preceding year. The proportion of residential movers greatly exceeds the proportion of migrants, and moving of either kind declines markedly with age. For neighborhood analysis this suggests that special attention be devoted to younger adults moving from house to house within the same region.

Movers of different ages do not have equal probabilities of settling in particular neighborhoods. There is a clear age pattern to intraurban relocation. Long and Glick (1976) present evidence supporting the view that during the 1960s, as in the 1950s, "many of the metropolitan central cities continue[d] to serve as 'staging areas,' or areas of first residence, for young adults before they move to the suburbs to raise their children" (1976, p. 49). Patterns of net migration by age in central cities typically

Table 7–1

Percentage of Current Residents in Metropolitan Areas Who Changed Residence in the Year Preceding March 1976, by Age

Residents	Total	Age					
		18–24	25–29	30–34	35–44	45–64	65+
Total percentage of recent movers	17.9	34.8	33.9	20.9	13.7	7.8	5.6
Within same Standard Metropolitan Statistical Area	12.5	23.4	24.7	15.0	9.3	5.4	4.0
Entered new Standard Metropolitan Statistical Area	5.4	11.4	9.2	5.9	4.4	2.4	1.6

Source: *Current Population Reports,* Series P–20, no. 305, table 19.

reveal gains (or minimal losses) of white population only in the twenty-to-twenty-nine age range. The thirty-to-thirty-nine age range, in contrast, shows the heaviest out-migration of all the adult years. The pattern in suburban areas is nearly a mirror image of the neighboring central city. The largest net adult in-migration to suburbs is found in the thirty-to-thirty-nine age range and the least is found at ages twenty-to-twenty-four.

Our preceding discussion of the limitations surrounding the usage of net population changes should cause us to interpret cautiously these patterns. Net changes over a decade clearly must mask a great amount of annual in- and out-movement. In addition the staging-area hypothesis explicitly assumes that the motivation of out-movers differs from that of in-movers. Nevertheless, the hypothesis capitalizes on the intrinsic property of age, namely that persons grow older every year. Thus the hypothesis assumes that young persons who enter with one motivation are transformed over time into older persons with the other motivation. The stability of the age pattern over time adds credibility to this dynamic view. That is to say, persons entering a central city at ages twenty-to-twenty-four during the 1950s would be transformed into persons like those leaving at ages thirty-to-thirty-four during the 1960s. In this usage the only shortcoming of the net statistic is that it fails to capture the true volume of movement over the decade.

From the central cities' perspective there is one set of planning strategies that emerges from these population observations. It is clear that people will be coming to and going from the city during the early adult years. It may be fruitless to try to nail them down permanently within the city limits. A better strategy would be to encourage a positive net migration at slightly earlier ages (such as by fostering the establishment of undergraduate colleges or vocational schools). Similarly, policies could be designed to help build positive net migration at slightly older ages; for example twenty-five to thirty-five. The earlier discussion of migration would lead us to stress attracting more in-migrants at these ages. In this case, however, the target age is not one highly prone to interurban migration. Instead, the relevant factors involve residential-location decisions. Given the large bulge of slightly younger population that cities attract, a more effective strategy would be to seek means for retaining these individuals longer; that is, slowing the rate of out-migration to the suburbs. The chief merit of this strategy is that it cooperates with trends that are already beginning spontaneously. In a later section we will review important differences in life styles that recent young adults are exhibiting. Moreover, studies have found that the back-to-the-city movement is not in fact that. It is instead a stay-in-the-city movement (Clay 1979; Hollister et al. 1978).

Aside from the rate of moving, the biggest neighborhood impact of age groups is via differences in housing choices. The major observable difference is with respect to home-ownership acquisition. Table 7–2 shows the percentages of movers in different age groups that are home owners before and after moving. Persons over age thirty-five are the most likely to start as owners, but persons aged twenty-five to thirty-four exhibit the greatest *increase* in ownership. The one-third increase in homeownership for this age group far exceeds that for any other group of movers. In addition, the number of movers in this ten-year age span nearly equals that for all older groups combined. These rapid changes in housing oc-cupancy during the twenty-five-to-thirty-four age span can be character-ized as part of the *family-settlement process*. The decisions on the part of these young households about where to live have pivotal significance for the vitality of neighborhood housing markets.

A final issue of age that impacts heavily on urban analysis concerns the distinction between total population growth and growth of particular age groups. As the population age pyramids (figures 7–1 through 7–4) clearly illustrate, all age groups do not have equal numbers of residents and the levels in each age category do not rise and fall equally over time. The age profile of a population is a historical product of past levels of fertility and of past trends in migration. (At older ages mortality acts to whittle away at the numbers in ever-older age groups.) Because of the inexorable aging process, the future size of an age group is directly related to the number of immediately younger persons.

The U.S. population has an extremely uneven age profile. The na-tionwide event of the prolonged postwar baby boom produced a large bulge of population that has been moving over time into ever-older age groups. As a consequence age groups occupied by this giant generation can experience enormous growth over a few years, even though total

Table 7–2

Percentage of Home Owners among U.S. Households That Moved during 1978 and Retained the Same Head of Household, by Age of Head

		Age				
	Total	Under 25	25–34	35–44	45–64	65 +
Percentage owners before moving	33.8	11.5	30.1	45.3	46.9	48.5
Percentage owners after moving	40.9	19.5	43.3	50.7	47.2	39.0
Total movers (in thousands)	11,272	1,982	4,495	2,031	2,045	718

Source: *Current Housing Reports,* Series H–150–78, Annual Housing Survey: 1978, part D, table A–5.

population growth is very slight. Table 7–3 shows these population changes by age group for five-year intervals between 1970 and 1990. The leading edge of the baby-boom generation is extremely prominent in the pattern of age-group population growth. The thirty-five-to-thirty-nine age group, for example, showed a growth rate over the 1970–1975 interval that was close to the low rate for the whole population (5 percent). In the following two quinquenniums, however, growth of this age group is expected to jump to over 20 percent. This growth is easily predictable because similar large increases have been experienced already in younger age groups that the baby-boom generation has occupied. What makes these large increases so dramatic is that just ten years in front of the baby boom the Depression-era cohorts are so small that net *losses* of population are registered in age groups that they occupy. The transition from declining to exploding age-group demand is so rapid that major perturbations in age-related service systems are to be expected.

The major implication for neighborhood analysis of these changes is that aggregate housing demand will shift rapidly during the next ten years as the large bulge of baby-boom population ages into the stage of family settlement. Hardly had the baby boom been completed than Campbell (1966) was predicting a surge in rental-housing demand for the period around 1970 and a surge in owner-occupied demand for the early 1980s. These projections were based on the persistent association between age

Table 7–3
Projected Quinquennial Percentage Increase of the U.S. Population by Age Group: 1970–1990

Age Group	Time Interval			
	1970–1975	*1975–1980*	*1980–1985*	*1985–1990*
0–4	−7.0	+8.5	+14.6	+1.6
5–9	−13.6	−6.9	+8.4	+14.4
10–14	−2.2	−12.7	−6.8	+8.2
15–19	+9.4	−2.0	−12.6	−6.7
20–24	+19.4	+8.7	−2.0	−12.4
25–29	+26.3	+11.9	+8.7	−2.0
30–34	+22.2	+23.1	+11.9	+8.5
35–39	+4.2	+20.7	+23.0	+11.6
40–44	−6.6	+4.3	+20.6	+22.8
45–49	−2.5	−6.6	+4.4	+20.5
50–54	+8.1	−3.1	−6.4	+4.4
55–59	+5.3	+7.3	−2.8	−6.4
60–64	+6.8	+5.5	+7.5	−2.7
65+	+11.1	+9.8	+8.7	+8.5
Total	+5.0	+4.4	+5.1	+4.7

Source: *Current Population Reports*, P–25, no. 601, Series II projections (1975–1990); 1970 Census of Population *Detailed Characteristics of the Population*, final report, PC(1)–D1 U.S. Summary, table 189.

and housing demand: young adults occupy rental housing and then move to owner-occupancy as they grow older. Marcin (1974), Schafer (1978), and others have pursued Campbell's line of argument more recently. The problem with these forecasts of changes based on *typical* age patterns is that they explicitly assume that the baby-boom generation will follow a housing life cycle similar to its predecessors. This assumption is evaluated more fully in a subsequent section. Nevertheless, the most recent data suggest that the rapid increase of persons in the family-settlement stage is associated with declining residential mobility and with rapid transition to home ownership (see tables 7–1 and 7–2).

Nonmovers and Neighborhoods

The obvious importance of residential choices by movers has led to a relative neglect of the importance of nonmovers for neighborhoods. The dynamic impact of nonmovers is not simply the reciprocal of that for movers. The effects of nonmovers are much more complex and of a very different nature than those of movers. Other things being equal, decisions to either stay or move into a neighborhood both reflect upon the desirability of the neighborhood. But things usually are not equal. As we have seen, movers are concentrated among young people while stayers are predominantly older. Motivations are very different in these two groups. Movers often make carefully reasoned residential choices that are designed to meet their growing family needs, while stayers on the other hand often times remain out of simple inertia.

The principal effect of movers on neighborhoods is to link them with the larger housing market and to provide them with an infusion of young households. A necessary counterbalance to the impact of movers is provided by nonmovers. Households that stay in a neighborhood for a number of years contribute social continuity and they increase neighborhood stability. In particular, the number of stayers limits the number of vacancies available to potential new residents. This has the effect of strengthening property values and of restricting the volume of social change that movers can deliver.

Nevertheless, it is frequently overlooked that nonmovers create social change in a neighborhood that is of a different type than movers create. As time passes, families grow older and predictable changes occur in households. Small children become teenagers and teenagers leave home. If many residents in a neighborhood stay there for over ten years these changes can be quite substantial. At the same time that existing residents are growing older their failure to move prevents young families from moving into the neighborhood and replenishing the younger children and adult age groups.

The number of long-term residents is remarkably large. In 1970 nearly 45 percent of all owners and 14 percent of all renters had lived in the same house for at least ten years. Some of the homes in the remaining 55 percent were relatively new and could not possibly have held occupants for ten years. If we look only at older homes (presumably in older neighborhoods) we find that the proportions of long-term residents are much higher. Within the occupied stock that was more than ten-years old in 1970 fully 60.3 percent of the owners and 17.7 percent of renters had not moved for over ten years. In fact, within the occupied stock that was more than twenty-years old in 1970, 42 percent of the owners and 9.4 percent of the renters had not moved for over twenty years (U.S. Bureau of the Census 1973). These are conservative estimates of neighborhood residency because many households (particularly the renters) are likely to have lived in more than one house within the same neighborhood. Nevertheless, the magnitude of the phenomenon is clearly indicated.

A study in the San Francisco Bay Area found that nonmovers created sharp neighborhood social changes if many of them originally occupied their homes at the same point in time (Myers 1978). This created a neighborhood cohort effect whereby a sizable block of families grew older together and the families' life cycle was writ large in the neighborhood social environment. School enrollments boomed and busted in neighborhoods at different times according to when the nonmovers had first entered the neighborhood. This study pointed out the conflict between empty-nest households filling older neighborhoods and the burgeoning number of young families formed by the leading edge of the baby-boom generation. The problem of large numbers of nonmovers piling up in certain neighborhoods might be termed a *crisis of frozen occupancy*.

In an earlier essay a planning strategy was outlined to address the potential problem of too many nonmovers in one neighborhood (Myers 1978). A first approach is to encourage development of a mix of house types (by size of unit and by cost) in every neighborhood. This mix ensures that persons in different life-cycle stages will be attracted and it also provides the opportunity for older persons to trade down to smaller housing without having to leave the neighborhood. A second objective should be to spread the residential vacancies, particularly in owner-occupied homes, over a longer period of time. Permits for new construction can be phased over a longer time interval, but turnover in existing housing, which is the major source of vacancies in older neighborhoods, is less susceptible to public intervention.

Whatever policies are adopted, it should be recognized that neighborhood stayers are not an unqualified asset. Ideally a neighborhood will have a large number of stayers to provide social continuity and economic stability. But it is also essential to have a small but steady turnover that replenishes the neighborhood each year. This turnover must occur in all sectors of the neighborhood market—not just among the renters, the young, or the minorities but also among the older owners. The desired objectives should be to maintain this steady flow and to prevent the accumulation of blocks of households that might lead to sharp changes later.

The Future Consequences of the Baby Boom

Analysts at all levels of government—federal, state, and city—have begun to warn about the enormous potential impact that the maturing baby-boom generation could have on different housing and neighborhood types (see Marcin 1974; Sanders 1975; Goetze and Colton 1977). These forecasts are based on the assumption that this giant generation will follow the same life cycle as preceding generations. In reality, throughout this century there have been wide variations in the age patterns of family formation and housing acquisition. Many demographers believe, in fact, that the most atypical generation was the parents of the baby-boom cohorts (see Campbell 1973; Westoff 1978; Masnick and McFalls 1976). These demographers believe that young adults today are returning to a family-formation pattern that is more consistent with the century-long trend toward lowered fertility. At the same time, female labor-force participation and housing consumption are shifting toward unprecedented levels. The combination of these life-style dimensions is so unique as to warrant extreme caution in drawing comparisons with the residential choices of preceding generations.

Recent cohorts of young adults have been maturing more slowly in terms of their family formation. That is to say, not as many have married and borne children as did their parents or older siblings by the same age. In 1979 only 51.6 percent of twenty-two-year-old women and 73.2 percent of twenty-five-year-old women had ever been married. These figures contrast with 1970 proportions of 66.5 and 86 percent (U.S. Bureau of the Census, 1980: table B).

The slowdown of family formation is illustrated more dramatically by the declining proportions of women ever bearing children by given ages. Data are presented in Masnick et al. (1978) that show the rate of transition to motherhood has fallen sharply since the mid-1960s. In 1966 71 percent of all women aged twenty-five had borne at least one child.

This fraction fell steadily with the arrival of each new cohort at age twenty-five, so that by 1977 only 54 percent of twenty-five-year-old women had borne a child.

The argument advanced by Masnick and his associates is that this slow start at family formation will lead ultimately to lower levels of parenthood when the baby-boom generation has reached middle age. These analysts emphasize the mounting disparity between young cohorts' stated birth expectations and the actual pattern of fertility that is unfolding. Much of the confusion about the future of the baby-boom generation centers on this problem. The ultimate level of family formation is uncertain, and in the interim the residential behavior of young adults is directed by a mix of vague family expectations and more immediate life-style issues.

Aside from the trend toward reduced parenthood, the most dramatic life-style change involving young adults is reflected by the upsurge in female labor-force participation. In 1960, at the height of both the baby boom and suburbanization, 30.6 percent of all wives were in the labor force. This figure was only 18.6 percent for wives with children under age six. By 1979 the total labor-force-participation rate for wives had risen to 49.4 percent. Although some of this increase can be attributed to reduced parenting, the astounding fact is that the participation rate for wives with children under six had more than doubled to 43.2 percent—a rate much higher than for all wives in 1960 (U.S. Department of Commerce, 1980: table 7/13). In fact, the commitment of U.S. women to the labor force has become so strong that a longitudinal study has reported that many young women now drop out of the labor force for only a few months to have their first child (Mott and Shapiro 1978).

It seems clear that a family life style based on only the husband working, while wife and children are secluded in a safe, family neighborhood, is of declining importance for the maturing cohorts of young adults. Alonso (1977) has suggested that this change will increase the attractiveness of neighborhoods in central metropolitan locations. On average, central locations will minimize the travel time of multiple-earner households, and they provide better access to a wide range of time-saving household services. The family advantages of suburban living will attract fewer households because of the growing incidence of nonparenthood and smaller families among the young-mover households.

At the same time, the growing number of multiple-earner households are relatively rich in per-capita income. This is perhaps the major reason that housing demand has continued to grow despite rising costs and smaller family sizes. The relative attractiveness of inner-metropolitan locations has not curtailed consumption of single-family homes. In fact, there has been an increase among all young-household types in the occupancy of fairly large (five or more rooms), owner-occupied, single-family units.

Data in table 7–4 have been assembled by an ongoing research project on cohort housing consumption directed by John Pitkin at the MIT-Harvard Joint Center for Urban Studies. The cross-sectional pattern depicted, for any single year, is for single-family ownership to increase with age and, within age groups, to increase with the number of children. Yet in 1975 the ownership rate of wives without children was approaching that of wives who were mothers in 1970. Other family types exhibited lesser increases with the entry of new cohorts in 1975. The total ownership rate for all women in the age group increased much less over the time interval because fewer women were joining the high-ownership family types. Nevertheless, these data show that the total demand for single-family ownership by the maturing baby-boom cohorts has exceeded even the expectations that are based on preceding cohorts' family patterns. This demand will remain high unless the trend toward non-marriage and nonparenthood continues to grow or until the ownership rates within family types cease increasing.

It is not certain what has been motivating the increasing housing consumption of small families. We have suggested that in part this increase is due to the greater per-capita income enjoyed by multiple-earner households with few dependents. For many families home ownership is

Table 7–4
Proportion of Selected Family Types Occupying Owned, Single-Family, Five-or-More-Room Houses, by Age of Head and Census Date
(in percentage)

| | *Age of Woman* | | | | | |
| | *25–29* | | | *30–34* | | |
Type	*1960*	*1970*	*1975*	*1960*	*1970*	*1975*
Husband-wife families with:						
No children	23.6	26.9	39.0	32.8	36.5	50.1
One child	33.1	41.0	46.3	44.3	53.1	63.6
Two or three children	43.7	52.3	56.9	57.5	66.3	74.1
Never-married women with:						
No children	0.7	1.3	1.2	2.5	3.2	5.3
Separated or divorced women with:						
One child	4.3	7.0	8.3	8.5	12.9	24.1
Two or three children	8.3	12.8	16.6	13.3	22.7	28.1
All women	31.9	36.4	37.5	45.2	51.9	57.8

Source: Public Use Files of the 1960 and 1970 Censuses and of the 1975 Annual Housing Survey.

considered an investment that is an essential protection against high inflation. In addition, many couples without children may view their home investment as preparatory to later child rearing, but there is no data available to test this supposition.

There is some reason to believe that the younger members of the baby-boom generation will be forced to occupy less desirable neighborhoods and housing types than the older members who are now in their late twenties. Although it is reasonable to suppose that the life-style trends established by these older members will continue to appeal to younger members, the sheer number of would-be participants is certain to overload the number of opportunities. By 1985, when the size of the cohorts in their late twenties will have leveled off, we are likely to see a slower acquisition of home ownership, occupancy of smaller units, more sharing of large units, and residency by middle-class persons in marginal neighborhoods that are not yet gentrified. The competitive pressures on lower-income persons will be much greater then than now.

As a final note on the future of the baby-boom generation, it should be observed that the uncertainties that we have expressed are an asset for planning. Because the family formations, housing choices, and neighborhood impacts are so indeterminate, there is ample room for policy influence. Given the excessively large number of home seekers over the next fifteen years, any shaping of the opportunity structure is certain to elicit response. If we carefully monitor the events as they unfold, we may learn enough about the underlying processes to enable us to achieve publicly desired outcomes.

Conclusions

Population analysis has much to contribute to neighborhood analysis and planning. This chapter has discussed several sets of population processes and four principles useful for planning have been identified. There is a more general advantage to population analysis, however, that should not be left unmentioned. Perhaps the most important asset of the population approach to planning is the dual role played by individuals in the population. They may be treated both as actors shaping the environment for other persons and also as constituents with needs that planners seek to fulfill. It is this dual focus of population analysis that promises to yield the greatest contribution to future policymaking.

References

Alonso, William. 1977. *The population factor and urban structure*. Working paper no. 102. Cambridge, Mass.: Center for Population Studies, Harvard University.

Birch, David L.; Allaman; Peter M; and Martin, Elizabeth A. 1975. *Level and composition of migration streams into and out of metropolitan and rural areas*. Working paper no. 3 of the Inter-Area Migration Project. Cambridge, Mass.: Massachusetts Institute of Technology-Harvard Joint Center for Urban Studies,

Campbell, Arthur A. 1973. "Three generations of parents," *Family Planning Perspectives* 5 (Spring):106–112.

Campbell, Burnham. 1966. *Population change and building cycles*. Urbana: University of Illinois Press.

Clay, Phillip. 1979. *Neighborhood renewal: middle-class resettlement and incumbent upgrading in American neighborhoods*. Lexington, Mass.: D.C. Heath and Co., Lexington Books.

Goetze, Rolf; Colton, Kent; and O'Donnell, V. 1977. *Stabilizing neighborhoods: a fresh approach to housing dynamics and perceptions*. Prepared for HUD, Office of Policy Development and Research, Cambridge, Mass.: Public Systems Evaluation, Inc. and Boston Redevelopment Authority. November.

Guest, Avery M.; and Zuiches, John J. 1971. "Another look at residential turnover in urban neighborhoods." *American Journal of Sociology* 77 (November):457–467.

Hollister, Robert M.; with Auger, Deborah; Walter, Adrian R.; and Pattison, Timothy. 1978. *Measuring neighborhood confidence*. Boston, Mass.: City of Boston, Office of Program Development,

Long, Larry H. 1975. "How the racial composition of cities changes." *Land Economics* 51 (August):258–267.

Long, Larry H.; and Glick, Paul C. 1976. "Family patterns in suburban areas: recent trends," pp. 39–67 in Barry Schwartz, ed., *The changing fact of the suburbs*. Chicago: University of Chicago Press.

Lowry, Ira S. 1966. *Migration and metropolitan growth: two analytical models*. San Francisco: Chandler Publishing Co.

Marcin, Thomas C. 1974. *The effects of declining population growth on the demand for housing*, General Technical Report NC–11. St. Paul, Minn.: U.S. Department of Agriculture Forest Service.

Masnick, George S.; and McFalls, Jr., Joseph A. 1976. "A new perspective on the twentieth century American fertility swing" *Journal of Family History* 1 (Winter):217–244.

Masnick, George S., Wiget, Barbara; Pitkin, John; and Myers, Dowell. 1978. "A life course perspective on the downturn in U.S. fertility." Working paper no. 106. Cambridge, Mass.: Center for Population Studies, Harvard University.

Molotch, Harvey. 1972. *Managed integration*. Berkeley: University of California Press.

Morrison, Peter A. 1971. "Chronic movers and the future redistribution of population: a longitudinal analysis.'' *Demography* 8 (May):171–184.

Mott, Frank L.; and Shapiro, David. 1978. ''Work and motherhood: the dynamics of labor force participation surrounding the first birth.'' *Years for Decision: A Longitudinal Study of the Education and Labor Market Experience of Young Women* 4:65–111. Washington, D.C.: U.S. Department of Labor.

Myers, Dowell. 1978. ''Aging of population and housing.'' *Growth and Change* 9 (January):8–13.

Rust, Edgar. 1975. *No growth: impacts on metropolitan areas.* Lexington, Mass.: D.C. Heath and Co., Lexington Books.

Sanders, Alvin. 1975 ''Expected demographic/geographic shifts in eastern Massachusetts.'' Internal memorandum. Boston, Mass.: Office of State Planning.

Schafer, Robert. 1978. ''Metropolitan form and demographic change.'' *Urban Studies* 15 (February):23–33.

Shryock, Henry S.; Jacob S. Siegel and Associates (1976) *The methods and materials of demography* (condensed edition by Edward G. Stockwell). New York: Academic Press.

Varady, David P. 1974. ''White moving plans in a racially changing middle-class community.'' *Journal of the American Institute of Planners* 40 (September):360–70.

Westoff, Charles F. 1978. ''Marriage and fertility in the developed countries.'' *Scientific America* 239 (December):51–57.

U.S. Bureau of the Census. 1980. *Current population reports.* series P–20 no. 349 Washington, D.C.: U.S. Government Printing Office.

————. 1978. *Current housing reports*, series H–150–76. Annual Housing Survey: 1976, part D. Washington, D.C.: U.S. Government Printing Office.

————. 1973. *Housing characteristics by household composition. Final report HC(7)–1, Washington, D.C.: U.S. Government Printing Office.*

————. 1972a. *Detailed characteristics of the population: 1970.* Final report PC(1)–D1 U.S. Summary. Washington, D.C.: U.S. Government Printing Office.

————. 1972b. *Census tracts.* Final report PHC(1)–29, Boston, Mass. Washington, D.C.: SMSA, U.S. Government Printing Office.

U.S. Department of Commerce. 1980. *Social indicators III.* Washington, D.C.: U.S. Government Printing Office.

8

People and Their Neighborhoods: Attitudes and Policy Implications

Rachel G. Bratt

By the late 1970s, the neighborhood movement had assumed a significant position within this country's overall urban strategy. In 1977 Congress established the National Commission on Neighborhoods and one year later enacted two important pieces of neighborhood-oriented legislation, the Neighborhood Reinvestment Corporation Act and the Neighborhood Self-Help Development Act.

During those years, enthusiasm and commitment to neighborhood issues were at a peak, with support for the movement coming from a variety of diverse groups. After tracing the development of the neighborhood movement briefly, this chapter will examine why and how one tool of neighborhood planning, the citizen survey, has been used. The chapter will review several surveys, primarily based on Boston, as a way of understanding exactly what can be learned from this type of research. Finally, implications of the surveys for policymakers will be discussed.

Actors in the Neighborhood Movement

The most important group that contributed to the growth of the neighborhood movement were the local residents themselves. Neighborhood people were instrumental in calling attention to their concerns through defensive as well as offensive strategies. As a defensive force, visibility and strength were gained by protesting such issues as highway expansion and mortgage unavailability, or redlining. The burgeoning power of neighborhood groups also stemmed from citizen frustration with federal approaches to solving urban problems (for example, urban-renewal and model-cities programs) and out of a deep-grained feeling that neighborhood residents understand their own problems better than Congress, HUD, and even city hall.

The neighborhood movement did not, however, stop at staging protests and lodging complaints. By 1980 it had already demonstrated its potential as a creative, offensive force. Neighborhood groups have been

133

successful, for example, in implementing housing rehabilitation programs (such as the original Neighborhood Housing Services program,
launched by Pittsburgh's Central North Side community), community-
economic-development efforts (such as Brooklyn's Bedford-Stuyvesant
Restoration Corporation), and new subsidized housing developments (such
as those built by Inquilinos Boricuas en Accion in the South End of
Boston).

Urban professionals formed a second group that began to view the
neighborhood as a more manageable unit for understanding problems
rather than viewing the city or urban area as a whole. For example,
planners and policymakers increasingly became aware that there is no
single urban housing market. To understand housing supply and demand,
one must examine a host of markets, or submarkets, all of which have
intricate relationships and interdependencies with each other. These submarkets are defined according to some unique set of characteristics and,
frequently, it is the *neighborhood* that provides the framework for analysis.

Rolf Goetze was influential in popularizing the view that neighborhood dynamics must be carefully understood and that the new challenge
for planners would be to assist communities in their struggle to maintain
or increase levels of confidence. Goetze went so far as to state that "the
confidence of any neighborhood in its future is the decisive factor shaping
housing dynamics. (Further), it is important to gauge accurately, since
housing policy must be tailored to the confidence level if it is to be
effective" (1976, p. 43).

Researchers and the academic community also contributed to the
popularity and acceptance of the neighborhood movement. During the
latter half of the seventies, there was a dramatic shift in the theoretical
conceptualizations of neighborhood dynamics. The old ideas then in good
currency were detailed in "The Dynamics of Neighborhood Change,"
prepared for HUD by the Real Estate Research Corporation. In this mon-
ograph the five stages of neighborhood change was articulated: from
healthy to incipient decline to clearly declining to accelerating decline to
abandoned. This stage process of neighborhood change or decline was
widely held from the late 1960s to the mid-1970s and was a logical
extension of the various notions of the filtering theory—that housing
units decrease in value due to age and obsolescence and that they are
then occupied by successively lower-income groups (Grigsby 1963).
Neighborhoods were not seen as moving upward except after abandonment was well under way: "At the end of this, the shambles that once
was a thriving neighborhood may be razed and rebuilt, re-entering the
cycle of neighborhood change" (HUD 1975). In this context the urban-

showpiece neighborhoods such as the South End in Boston, Society Hill in Philadelphia, and Georgetown in Washington, D.C., were seen as anomalies—they simply did not follow what was viewed as the normal patterns of urban decline.

Thus, by the mid-1970s the concept of neighborhood change was based upon the key assumption that once decline has started, the process is virtually irreversible. As former Columbia University professor Robert Kolodny writes, with specific reference to ''The Dynamics of Neighborhood Change'': ''The logic of the model of change means that scant attention is paid the possibility that something useful can be done for neighborhoods where change and decline are already well underway'' (1978).

But, as described above, by the time of Kolodny's writing, the traditional theories of neighborhood change were already being challenged. Neighborhoods that government officials had been willing to write off as too far gone were proving that viability was an option for these areas. It is now widely acknowledged that upward neighborhood change is both desirable and possible and that the citizens themselves, through their own local initiative and vision, occupy a pivotal position in the process.

Even the rhetoric of the Reagan administration acknowledges both the potentials for neighborhood preservation as well as the importance of local development organizations: ''Because of their commitment to the quality of life of low-income households in rural and urban areas, nonprofit groups are often particularly suited to play an important role in housing and neighborhood improvement efforts'' (Final Report of the President's Commission on Housing 1982). Yet, the actions of the president have undermined neighborhood upgrading through local initiatives.

Thus, there is a sad twist to the current views on neighborhoods. While the potentials of neighborhoods and their citizens seem to be understood and highly acclaimed, there is no federal program for supporting or encouraging this movement. Yet, state and local governments continue to grapple with how to best guide local initiatives and how to provide resources for neighborhood activites. Particularly in view of President Reagan's so-called New Federalism the need for good local decision making and neighborhood planning assumes increased significance.

Whether or not the federal government defines a role for itself in neighborhood issues, lower levels of government will continue to be concerned. Different cities have adopted a host of approaches for staying in touch with their neighborhoods. One strategy that has been used extensively is the citizen survey.

Rationales for Neighborhood-Survey Research

The most important reason for conducting neighborhood surveys is to gauge what is going on. The neighborhood that one lives in not only carries with it an array of services—shopping, transportation, schools, parks, churches—but it also signals a person's socioeconomic status and wealth. The quality of housing and who lives there becomes closely intertwined with the individual's self-perception.

The importance and identification with the neighborhood is so strong, for most people, that the characteristics and desirability of a particular house assume secondary importance when compared to neighborhood quality. For example, in a survey performed by the MIT-Harvard Joint Center for Urban Studies roughly 80 percent of the respondents indicated that the neighborhood was more important than the house in deciding where to live (Coleman, Working paper no. 49, 1978).

This finding suggests that neighborhood research is a key tool for understanding the issues that contribute to a community's sense of well-being and gives insights into what people are looking for in their quest for so-called the good life. Translated into planning jargon, it is clear that citizen surveys are an important way of measuring neighborhood confidence.

A companion objective of citizen polls is to enable policymakers and public officials to become informed of constituent attitudes. If levels of neighborhood confidence can be assessed, it is assumed that someone will be listening and watching. To the extent that local policies may be designed according to confidence levels, surveys supply one type of important information. Thus, surveys are a useful mechanism for people to communicate their concerns and priorities to government; they can provide useful information on what local investments would be most valued as well as an evaluation of ongoing programs. For example, in Dallas an annual survey of residents is conducted: "It measures public assessment of city services and these findings weigh heavily in the City Council's annual budget process. It allows the city staff to determine whether program changes have had their intended effect" (Urban Consortium 1980, p. 21). In view of the utility of citizen surveys, it is now appropriate to examine what, exactly, they tell us.

The Surveys

Surveys on resident attitudes are plentiful. "From city hall to the Oval Office, public opinion polling in this country is becoming almost commonplace" (Kunde and Kasoff 1978). Partly for this reason—because the number of surveys is virtually endless—and partly to sharpen the focus of this chapter, Boston was chosen as the primary area for investigating neighborhood attitudes. Five Boston-based surveys, undertaken between 1970 and 1981, were reviewed along with three surveys with a non-Boston focus. Table 8–1 lists and briefly describes the surveys discussed in this chapter.

Strengths and Weaknesses of Urban Neighborhoods

Surveys of resident attitudes reveal three major themes that are of concern to people in their living situation. Low crime, friendly and desirable

Table 8–1
Surveys of Resident Attitudes in Boston and Selected Other Cities

Area	Survey Name	Scope	Number of Interviews	Date
Boston	Boston Urban Observatory (BUO)	Boston, citywide	507	July 1–September 15, 1970
	Cambridge Marketing Group for the Boston Redevelopment Authority (BRA)	Boston, citywide	500	March 24–27, 1973
	Hart Hollister et al.	Boston, citywide Dorchester, Roxbury, Jamaica Plain, only	2,555 376, plus 40 in-depth	April–May, 1977 July 18–August 31, 1977
	Floyd J. Fowler, Jr., for the Boston Committee	Boston, citywide	900	May 1981
Non-Boston	Richard P. Coleman for the Joint Center for Urban Studies of Massachusetts Institute of Technology and Harvard	Metropolitan Houston, Dayton, and Rochester	900 (300 in each area)	late summer-early fall, 1976
	Gallup for the Charles F. Kettering Foundation and Charles Stewart Mott Foundation	National (cities with 50,000 or more residents)	3,242	October–December, 1977
	Louis Harris and Associates under contract to the Department of Housing and Urban Development.	Nationwide cities, suburbs, town and rural areas. (The findings reported in this chapter are based only on the interviews conducted in cities.)	7,074 (3,298)	December 1977–January, 1978

people, and good housing emerge as the variables that determine overall neighborhood satisfaction. Because each survey asked questions in a slightly different way, aggregating responses is not possible. Instead, similar questions from the surveys, which highlight positive and negative attributes, are examined together. Table 8–2 provides examples of the types of responses made to specific questions in the different surveys concerning strengths and weaknesses of neighborhoods.

In survey after survey the need to reduce crime and/or to be assured of good police protection emerges as the most compelling physical requirement of urban residents. For example, the Boston Redevelopment Authority (BRA) survey found that the joint problems of crime, law enforcement, and police protection were considered key by 42 percent of those polled. Similarly, the Hart survey found that crime was considered the most important neighborhood weakness by 26 percent of the residents, while the Gallup poll found that high crime was ranked the most important neighborhood problem by 18 percent of their respondents.

In response to the Boston Urban Observatory (BUO) survey question: "How safe do you feel walking around your neighborhood alone at night?" only 40 percent of respondents indicated that they felt safe or pretty safe. A majority indicated that they felt either pretty unsafe or very unsafe. Eleven years later, the Fowler survey produced similar findings: 44 percent of respondents answered that they either felt very safe or fairly safe in their neighborhood at night.

A more general question included in the Hart survey, "How safe do you feel in your neighborhood?" elicited a very different response. Seventy-four percent indicated that they felt either almost totally safe or fairly safe. Simlarly, 85 percent of respondents in the Fowler survey indicated that they felt very safe or fairly safe during the day. In view of the importance that people place on living in safe neighborhoods, it is noteworthy that during daylight hours a substantial majority of Boston residents feel safe in their own neighborhoods. It is, however, disappointing that so many people still feel unsafe at night and, if anything, the situation may have gotten somewhat worse over the past decade.

The desire to live in neighborhoods that are well maintained and have decent housing is the second most pressing concern of neighborhood residents. Twenty-three percent of the respondents in the Hart survey indicated that well-maintained, quality homes were the most important strength of their neighborhood. Forty-four percent of those surveyed by Gallup responded that poor housing was the major contribution to the image of a bad neighborhood.

Yet, probably the clearest finding of the surveys is that most respondents feel that it is the people themselves that either make or break

Table 8–2
Key Qualities of Strong and Weak Neighborhoods

Question	Response	Percent of Respondents Giving Answer	Order of Answer's Importance within Survey	Survey
Positive Attributes				
Most important factors in deciding where to live?	Safe neighborhood.	40	1	Hart
	Reasonable rents/ housing prices.	26	3	
Strengths of neighborhood?	Close knit community/good neighbors/ similarity of residents. Pride in neighborhood.	57	1	Hart
	Well maintained/ quality of homes.	23	2	
	Safe/good police.	7	3	
	Strong neighborhood feeling/types of neighbors.	36	1	Hart
	Safe neighborhood.	18	3	
Satisfaction with neighborhood characteristics?	Way neighborhood residents get along.	80	1	Fowler
	Way property is kept up.	70	3	
When deciding to move here:	Housing affordability/ characteristics were very important or important.	68	1	Harris
	Neighborhood safety was very important or important.	61	2	
Most critical services/facilities?	Police Protection.	76	1	Boston Re-development Authority
Images of ideal neighborhood?	Friendly people.	45	1	Gallup
	Good housing.	34	2	
	Low crime.	24	3	
Negative Attributes				
Most important problems in neighborhood?	High crime.	18	1	Gallup
	Poor housing.	15	2	
	Unfriendly people.	9	4	
Problems facing residents?	Crime/law enforcement/police protection.	42	1	Boston Re-development Authority

Table 8–2 continued

Question	Response	Percent of Respondents Giving Answer	Order of Answer's Importance within Survey	Survey
Most important problem?	Too much crime and fear/not enough protection.	26	1	Fowler
Crime in this community is a:	Severe problem.	72	1	Harris
Weaknesses of neighborhood?	Undesirable elements/race/lack of cohesion and good neighbors.	40	1	Hart
	Crime.	26	2	
	Deteriorated housing.	15	3	
Public services or facilities in neighborhood in need of improvement?	Police/law enforcement/ protecting citizens.	15	1	Boston Urban Observatory
Any serious ways (other than cost) that house or neighborhood is not a good place to live?		Only 37 percent Yes, of those:		Boston Urban Observatory
	Safety.	11	1	
	Neighborhood property not well maintained.	2	2	
	Specific undesirable group (other than racial) populating area.	3	3	
Threats to their neighborhood?	Crime.	30	1	Gallup
	Poor housing.	21	2	
	Unfriendly, undesirable people.	21	2	
Images of worst neighborhood?	Poor housing.	44	1	Gallup
	High crime.	41	2	
	Unfriendly people.	23	3	
Why want to move from neighbor- hood?	Housing.	30	2	Gallup
	High crime.	17	4	
	Unfriendly people.	14	5	
Primary reason for wanting to move?	Too much crime.	30		Boston Re- development Authority
	Rents too high.	20	2	
	Want more pleasant surroundings.	17	3	

a neighborhood. In describing neighborhood strengths, terms like *close-knit community*, *friendly people*, and *good neighbors* are found again and again throughout the surveys.

The Hart survey provides an interesting interpretation of what constitutes a strong and weak neighborhood. It states that:

> Strong neighborhoods are built upon intangibles—good neighbors, stability, quiet, pride, etc. The weaknesses of a neighborhood are much more tangible—its crime, its robberies, its sanitation, litter and dirt, its boarded-up buildings, its delinquents, and most of all—property is not maintained. People can spot a weak neighborhood—it is there for them to see. Yet making a neighborhood clean or low in crime does not necessarily make the neighborhood strong—that must come from the neighbors themselves.

But what does this statement really mean? It seems quite clear that hidden behind the stated desire to have good neighbors is often the quest for homogeneity. Again, the Hart survey is particularly revealing: "In Boston, people are looking for cultural uniformity rather than diversity. Residents have systematically made their decisions on where to live on this basis."

And, according to Richard Coleman, not only Boston residents strive for similarity in their neighbors; all U.S. citizens want safe and comfortable cities and neighborhoods: "To be 'safe' socially means to be isolated in one's neighborhood from unwanted populations . . . 'Comfortable' in the social sense means to be surrounded by one's own kind in class and/or ancestry . . . and certainly by people who share one's values."

Yet, interesting and somewhat contradictory information on the quest for homogeneity or heterogeneity comes from the Harris survey: "Americans are more likely to prefer living in neighborhoods where the residents have varied incomes, levels of education, political attitudes, and religious affiliations and are of different age groups and ethnic origins than they are to prefer neighborhoods where other people are similar to themselves in these regards."

But when it comes to racial issues the desire for heterogeneity is much less pervasive: "Americans state a preference for racially homogeneous neighborhoods more often than they do for homogeneity in any of the other regards."

Further, Harris reports that: "A majority of the people who live in either all white, or half white and half minority neighborhoods say they prefer the kind of neighborhood in which they now reside." In this case, actions speak as loudly as words. According to Harris, "nine out of every ten white Americans say that they live in predominantly white neighborhoods.'' Thus, while there appears to be a high degree of interest in living in neighborhoods that are heterogeneous along socioeconomic lines, there is less preference for racial integration. Taken together, the surveys make clear that the preference of most urban dwellers (and others) is to live among people with whom they feel, quite literally, most at home. And, while it is encouraging that many people express positive feelings about living with diverse groups, it is sobering that preferences for racially segregated neighborhoods are still so pervasive.

Considerations Involved in Staying or Moving

Ours is a transient population, with the average family moving every four or five years. There are many reasons for this mobility. Moving as a way to improve one's neighborhood and/or housing are only two of the factors involved in making the decision to relocate. Increasingly, families move to seek employment opportunities or because of job transfers.

In reviewing survey data on the issue of moving, three questions are particularly relevant and will provide the framework for the following section:

1. To what extent are people so dissatisfied with their living situation that they are prepared to move?
2. Which groups of people contemplate moves most seriously?
3. What can the city do to retain as much of its population as possible?

Both the Gallup and Hart surveys found that a substantial number of respondents are likely to move from their neighborhoods in the foreseeable future. Gallup found that 62 percent of their interviewees were either almost certain or fairly certain that they would be moving within the following five years. Hart found that 33 percent of their respondents indicated that they were almost certain or fairly certain that they would be moving within the following three years. Thirty-five percent of the central-city respondents in the Harris survey indicated that they would definitely or probably move within the following two years.

Moreover, all three surveys found that those who are most likely to want to leave are young people and those who are still unsettled. In addition, Hart and Harris found that, as one might expect, renters are more likely to be contemplating a move than owners.

Those who feel most attached to Boston and are least likely to be moving are ethnics and elderly people. While 60 percent of Hart's general population responded that a move was not likely, 69 percent of the

Italians; 67 percent of the Irish, and 76 percent of those over sixty-years old said that they were not planning to move.

While one might expect that those with the lowest incomes would have the fewest resources with which to make a move and the least job mobility, this finding was not consistently borne out by the surveys. The Hart poll found that those with incomes of under $15,000 per year indicated roughly the same likelihood of leaving the neighborhood as the general population. However, the Gallup poll did find that those who want to move the least are people from lower socioeconomic groups.

If Gallup is correct, this finding has important implications for the gentrification issue. It indicates that if lower-income neighborhoods become attractive to upper-income groups, many indigenous residents will be displaced against their will.

Concerning the types of changes that would be needed to make potential movers change their minds, 33 percent in the Hart poll and almost 40 percent in the Gallup poll indicated that they would probably move no matter what the city might do—nothing could make them want to stay. Along these lines, it is not surprising that the single largest group of people who plan to leave their neighborhoods (40 percent according to Hart) are seeking a change in life style, with their expected destination both outside Boston and to a different area.

For those people who might be swayed to stay in their neighborhoods if certain changes took place, no single improvement would tip the balance. Rather, as Hart points out, "the city must undertake a series of objectives rather than just one to induce people to remain in their neighborhoods." Yet, certain changes would be particularly significant. Lowering the property tax would have the greatest impact on potential movers. Thirty-six percent would consider staying solely on this basis. It is also noteworthy that of those contemplating leaving:

Thirty-one percent would reconsider if the city set up a program to create more employment opportunities.

Thirty-one percent would reconsider if more police were placed on the beat.

Twenty-eight percent would reconsider if loans to repair housing were provided.

Thus, the themes that emerged in the last section are reinforced when one examines the reasons for staying or moving. Reducing crime, improving housing conditions, and strengthening neighborhood associations surface as persistent concerns of urban residents. While the need for employment opportunities is also important, this element has less to do with a specific neighborhood and more to do with the general economic well-being of the city or region.

Policy Implications

What, then, is the message that these surveys communicate to federal, state, and local politicians and policymakers? One of the clearest findings of the surveys has no precise policy implications. The notion that the people themselves are what make a good neighborhood is practically a dead end for policymakers. As the Hart survey points out: "There is nothing that the city can do to make people good neighbors" (other than setting) "a tone and direction which creates a spirit of good will." Perhaps the only course that a city can pursue to promote neighborliness involves programs that are specifically aimed at improving neighborhood morale and interpersonal relations. Boston has launched two such efforts. The Neighborhood Confidence Project was created in 1977 "to stimulate positive self-fulfilling prophecies" (Hollister et al. 1978) in selected neighborhoods. The strategy pursued by Boston planners was to identify strengths of local residential districts and to communicate them to present and prospective residents, and to institutional representatives. Thus increasing reliance on survey research by local officials was accompanied by efforts to directly influence the attitudinal dimensions of neighborhood change.

A second local initiative was the formation of the Boston Committee in 1980. Following several race-related incidents and in response to a general perception that racial tensions in Boston are a serious problem, a prominent group of citizens joined together "to direct an integrated effort to address the problems that contribute to racial tension and conflict" (Fowler 1982). Trustees of the committee include businessmen, clergy, a union official, educators, neighborhood representatives, and the media.

While these efforts are helpful, there is also an awareness of how difficult it to to change well-ingrained stereotypes of areas of a city as well as to reverse prejudicial attitudes. Yet, these types of support programs have been helpful in opening lines of communication between the public and private sectors and neighborhood residents.

Another important finding of the surveys is that for people to want to stay in their neighborhoods and to indicate high levels of satisfaction with them, they need to feel safe from bodily harm and theft. A large proportion of public resources must still go toward crime prevention and police protection. Most large cities are already heavily involved with programs of this type and the cry for law and order, particularly popular around election time, appears to be what people want to hear. Along these lines, efforts by the media to downplay crime in the cities, rather than to sensationalize it, would also go a long way toward improving people's perceptions of the cities. Finally, more experimentation is needed in devising crime-prevention and law-enforcement programs that pair city police departments with neighborhood agencies or organizations. Efforts by the U.S. Department of Justice have already demonstrated the efficacy of this approach.

The preference for racial homogeneity disclosed in the surveys has some disturbing implications. Indeed, if this attitude were to be embraced as a public policy, we would be back in the dark ages of civil rights, long before the passage of the Civil Rights Act of 1968 and the concept of Equal Housing Opportunity. The full implications of this approach are racist and unimaginable. Yet, it may be quite possible to pursue more positive policies that may, in fact, be at the heart of what residents really hope for when they speak of homogeneity. Some of the qualities embodied in descriptions of homogenous neighborhoods, such as pride, stability, and comfort (in the social sense) can certainly be achieved by following well-accepted, nonracist routes.

For example, increasing homeownership opportunities, initiating and expanding housing-rehabilitation programs, and supporting community-based development through neighborhood associations are three policy directions that would promote neighborhood confidence and presumably encourage and enable existing residents to stay in their neighborhoods. These will be discussed briefly in the context of what we know about the effectiveness of these policies as well as the present thinking in Washington.

Federal Urban Neighborhood Policy and Resident Attitudes

The three policy directions mentioned above—which would have the greatest likelihood of delivering to neighborhood residents what they want and which would have the greatest impact on stabilizing neighborhoods—do not enjoy strong support by the Reagan administration, in spite of their apparent effectiveness.

Urban Home Ownership Opportunities

Ever since George Sternlieb found that owner-occupied multifamily dwellings were better maintained than absentee-owned buildings (1966), the notion that ownership is a key determinant of property maintenance has been well accepted and confirmed by other research. Rates of home ownership have not only been positively correlated with maintenance and property improvement, but owner-occupancy has also been shown to be "the most important determinant of neighborhood confidence." This finding has important implications for public policy. As Hollister et al. state: "encouraging owner-occupancy may be a more effective public strategy for building confidence than financing housing rehabilitation . . . efforts to improve physical conditions should be coupled with encouragement of owner-occupancy" (1978).

Furthermore, the experience of home ownership programs for low- and moderate-income people has been positive. Although there was much negative publicity about the Section 235 program and while there were numerous reasons why homebuyers had less than an optimal chance of having a successful experience, almost 80 percent of those who participated have managed to hold onto their homes.

Other small-scale home-ownership programs have also proved successful. Some local initiatives, such as the one operated by Homeowner's Rehab, Inc., in Cambridge, Massachusetts, have utilized the sweat-equity technique. In this way, lower-income families have been able to trade their own labor for cash down payments thereby making home ownership a reality. However, groups such as Homeowners Rehab are scarce and the total number of people they are able to assist is few.

Additional home ownership opportunities for lower-income people have evolved through a handful of demonstration programs. For example, the Equity Transfer Assistance Program, which operates in Brookline, Massachusetts, is aimed at providing subsidies to low- and moderate-income people whose buildings are being converted to condominiums and who, otherwise, would be facing displacement. But, again, this program is extremely small and does not exist nationwide.

In spite of the exciting possibilities of urban home-ownership programs, the federal response is almost nonexistent. Since the moratorium on the Section 235 Program in 1973, a subsidy program for lower-income families to purchase homes has not been an item on the federal agenda. The revised 235 Program has provided interest-rate subsidies to only about thirty thousand households. To the extent that there is any interest in home ownership, the focus is on issues of affordability for middle- and upper-income people who are being squeezed out of the housing market. Urban homesteading programs, which recycle HUD-foreclosed or city-owned houses, are not aimed at the lower-income, first-time homebuyer. Instead, clients of such programs tend to be more affluent, upwardly mobile members of the middle class and, in fact, are often able to outbid community residents.

While the federal government has been overlooking the home-purchase needs and desires of lower-income people, pressure on urban housing markets has been increasing due to the back-to-the-city movement. In addition, skyrocketing housing costs, which are closely intertwined with inflationary forces, keep driving prices beyond the reach of renting families who have no equity in a house. The convergence of these three trends—the middle class showing a new interest in urban housing, no supports for lower-income people to purchase homes, plus the overall inflationary atmosphere—will increasingly mean that home ownership will be for the well-to-do only. And, to make matters even more problematic for urban residents, the dramatic increase in conversions to condominiums in many urban housing markets is producing even more pressure on low-income residents. All of this points to the likelihood of gentrification becoming more and more of a threat to lower-income residents of urban neighborhoods.

Housing Rehabilitation

People investing money to repair or renovate their homes is one of the most overt signs that a neighborhood is on the upswing. Yet, similar to the federal government's attitude toward subsidized home-ownership programs, housing rehabilitation has not enjoyed much support. Current thinking on the subject is that localities may design and implement their own housing-rehabilitation programs, using Community Development Block Grant allocations, if they so choose. But while many cities have successfully launched their own rehabilitation programs, funding usually lags far behind demand and need for assistance.

At the federal level, two types of housing-rehabilitation programs exist. Section 312 provides low-interest loans for housing rehabilitation, but the total outlay for this program is low and is dependent solely on payments on old loans.

A second federally sponsored rehabilitation program is the Neighborhood Housing Services program, operated by the Neighborhood Reinvestment Corporation. But while this program has enjoyed a great deal of success, even its sponsors admit that it is not the right approach for very poor neighborhoods and areas where there are low rates of home ownership. What is lacking are sufficiently "deep" subsidies that would make rehabilitation affordable by lower-income and elderly homeowners and incentives for owners of rental properties to repair their homes, without passing rent increases on to their tenants.

Community-Based Development through Neighborhood
Associations

Although people seem to care about what is going on in their neighborhoods, few people are actually involved. The Hart survey found that 78 percent of respondents are not involved at all with neighborhood affairs. Even in the neighborhoods in which the most activity takes place, only 30 percent are involved. But whether or not people actually participate themselves, Hollister et al. found that people value the existence of a local neighborhood group and view it as a major stabilizing force. For example, in describing the growing sense of confidence . . . in the stability of their neighborhood expressed by residents of the Neponset section of Dorchester, the report states that: "The source of this confidence lies in the positive activities of local neighborhood associations . . . The effect is a renewed sense of optimism which strengthens the commitment of area residents."

Interest in neighborhood associations and actual federal dollars to support them peaked during the latter half of the Carter administration. In 1978, Congress passed the Neighborhood Self-Help Development Act (NSHD), which provided funds to directly support local development initiatives sponsored by community groups. The enthusiasm and confidence in this program was extremely high. In announcing the first round of funding under NSHD in the spring of 1980, Geno C. Baroni, assistant secretary for Neighborhoods, Voluntary Associations, and Consumer Protection, emphasized the rationale for supporting locally-based initiatives: "We know these projects will have a major impact on their communities because they were conceived and initiated by the people in the neighborhoods they will serve. These groups are deeply rooted in their neighborhoods and they are uniquely capable of developing projects to meet the needs of their own areas" (HUD 1980). But in spite of the logic, appeal and even positive outcomes under this program, NSHD was one of the first programs to fall victim to the Reagan cutbacks. After a brief funding period, and a total allocation of about fourteen million dollars the promise and potential of NSHD as a direct way of supporting neighborhood groups faded into history.

Conclusion

The results of the surveys discussed here are not really surprising. People are looking for safety, comfort, and stability in their neighborhoods.

Based upon this conclusion, the types of programs that must be pursued and adequately funded include homeownership opportunities for a broad range of income levels, rehabilitation programs, and supports for activities sponsored by neighborhood associations. What this says is that although each new generation of urbanists and policymakers may feel some pressure to create new tools and approaches for tackling our urban neighborhood problems, old tools may only need minor modifications and retuning to be appropriate. Perhaps there is not much new under the urban neighborhood sun. What would be novel, however, would be for the federal government to make a commitment to a comprehensive urban-neighborhood policy and for this commitment to be seen through to a successful ending.

References

Boston Urban Observatory. 1972. "Life with Boston: citizens' assessment of services." Prepared by Bradbury Seasholes, Tufts University. University.

Cambridge Marketing Group, Inc. 1973. "A study of current residential life styles and expectations among publics in selected Boston communities."

Coleman, Richard P. 1978. "Attitudes toward neighborhoods: how Americans choose to live." Working paper no. 49. Massachusetts Institute of Technology-Harvard Joint Center for Urban Studies.

Fowler, Floyd., Jr. 1982. "Black and white perceptions of quality of life in Boston." Prepared for the Boston Committee, Inc., by the Center for Survey Research.

Gallup Organization. 1977. "State of the cities survey."

Goetze, Rolf. 1976. *Building neighborhood confidence.* Cambridge, Mass.: Ballinger Publishing Company.

Grigsby, William G. 1963. *Housing markets and public policy.* Philadelphia: University of Pennsylvania Press.

Harris, Louis, and Associates. 1978. "The 1978 HUD survey on the quality of urban life." Prepared under contract to the U.S. Department of Housing and Urban Development. Washington, D.C.: U.S. Government Printing Office.

Peter D. Hart Research Associates. 1977. "A survey of attitudes toward the City of Boston and its neighborhoods."

Hollister, Robert M., with Auger, Deborah; Walter, Adrian Ruth; and Pattison, Timothy. 1978. "Measuring neighborhood confidence." Prepared for the City of Boston.

Kolodny, Robert. 1978. ''Some policy implications of theories of neighborhood change,'' *Papers in Planning*, 5.

Kunde, James E.; and Kasoff, Mark. 1978. ''Public opinion and public policy.'' *Nation's Cities*. November.

President's Commission on Housing. 1982. *Final Report of the President's Commission on Housing*.

Sternlieb, George. 1966. *The tenement landlord*. New Brunswick: Rutgers University Press.

U.S. Department of Housing and Urban Development. 1975. ''The dynamics of neighborhood change.'' Prepared by the Office of Policy Development and Research by Real Estate Research Corporation.

U.S. Department of Housing and Urban Development. 1980. News release, HUD No. 80–152. May 7.

Urban Consortium for Technology Initiatives. 1980. ''Dividing the pie: resource allocation to urban neighborhoods.''

9 How Neighborhood Development Organizations Succeed and Grow: A Summary

Neil S. Mayer

Background and Objectives

In recent years, neighborhood organizations have played a growing role in generating revitalization projects in their communities. These organizations have worked to build and renovate housing, create jobs and businesses, provide commercial goods and services, train workers, and conserve energy. Particularly in seriously troubled neighborhoods, but in many others as well, nonprofit citizen organizations have stepped in to carry out community development activities that traditional private and public actors are unwilling or unable to conduct.

The extent of work by neighborhood-development organizations (NDOs)—neighborhood groups undertaking housing, economic development, and energy projects rather than playing advocacy or social service roles alone—is substantial. Hundreds of organizations have carried out a wide array of projects. The largest NDOs have multimillion-dollar budgets, a hundred or more employees, and a dozen or more development projects under their belts. Many smaller groups were born and made great strides toward effective development work during the 1970s.

But the resources available to NDOs for their critically important work have always been limited, and recent declining federal support repeats and accentuates past patterns of interruption in funds flowing to them. At the same time NDOs differ greatly in their capabilities to carry out revitalization work, with or without aid. The organizations' own varying levels of skill and maturity have major impacts on what work they can do effectively and what type of assistance they need. With levels of NDO support sharply restricted by federal cutbacks, recession, and high interest rates, it is now doubly important to match assistance to NDOs' needs and abilities.

We conducted a study at the Urban Institute to examine how NDOs become successful in community-development work. Key results of that

The research on which this chapter is based was supported by the U.S. Department of Housing and Urban Development. Jennifer L. Blake assisted the author in its conduct.

study are summarized very briefly in this chapter.[1] We hope that the findings are of use both to NDOs working consciously to develop their own capacities and successful projects and to current and potential sources of assistance to them trying to shape their support effectively.

The study addressed four related questions:

1. What specific organizational characteristics are essential to NDOs' success in carrying out community development projects?
2. How can NDOs' differing levels of capacity to carry out such projects best be categorized and described?
3. What forms of technical and financial assistance are appropriate for NDOs at various stages of growth, both to help them carry out projects and to increase their capacity to do such work in the future?
4. How can NDOs' effectiveness in carrying out projects and using assistance be measured?

Answering the first two questions is necessary to any systematic effort to support NDO development. The building of project competence and success—whether undertaken by an NDO alone or with sources of outside aid—must be shaped by understanding: (1) the capabilities that are most important for an NDO to develop and (2) an organization's current status in developing them. Recognizing what assistance is most valuable under various conditions (question 3) contributes directly to outsiders' ability to aid NDO growth. And properly measuring NDOs' project accomplishments and use of assistance (question 4) provides feedback that can help direct future aid. Careful answers to the four questions can help guide support for the growth of NDOs' project activities and of their skills and capabilities.

To meet our study objectives we first reviewed existing literature on NDOs and interviewed recognized experts in NDO activity and development. Using that groundwork to form study hypotheses, we then visited twelve NDO sites where we talked to people working directly within, or along with, the NDOs themselves. Their views and the inferences we drew from observing NDO characteristics and successes or failures form the basis for our conclusions about how NDOs succeed and grow.

Key Characteristics for Success

The factors we found of major influence in successful NDO community-development work can be divided into three groups: characteristics internal to an organization—its staffing, management, and structure—an NDO's relations with its community and with other actors in the private

and public sector; and the economic, social, and political environment
in which an organization operates.

Internal Characteristics

The nine internal characteristics that helped determine NDO project capability include:

Leadership by an Effective Executive Director. Systematically, credible,
committed, and confident leaders are key to NDOs' success in carrying
out projects. They need not possess technical skills in development themselves, but they must have the ability to identify opportunities, initiate
plans to pursue them, and recognize requirements for expert staff and
outside assistance.

Paid, Full-Time Staff with Development Expertise. Generating and especially expanding NDO success in development work is strongly tied
to the full-time availability of at least one skilled and experienced de-
veloper/manager with major project responsibilities. The individual needs
a broad understanding of the development process, knowledge of the
specific steps in carrying out projects, actual experience in project planning and implementation, a sense of entrepreneurial opportunity, and a
firm commitment to the community.

Control of Work Levels for Key Staff. Protecting key staff members,
and particularly executive directors, from being continuously overloaded
with tasks is important to short- and particularly long-run effectiveness
in NDO neighborhood-revitalization efforts. Overload interferes with the
careful work needed to earn funding, burns out valuable staff, and limits
opportunities to plan future work.

Doing Homework. Carrying out the detailed work of making and fol-
lowing-up funding applications, project design, cost estimation, progress
reporting, and related tasks is crucial in attracting and retaining funder
and political support for NDO projects. Outsiders regularly report looking
for these signs of competence in considering their own participation in
NDO work, and though their performance is generally good some NDOs
have yet to realize how much homework matters to others.

Flexible, Resourceful Planning. One-time planning efforts resulting in
comprehensive, written long-term plans are usually of very limited value
to NDOs, who face shifting environments and opportunities. Informal,

continuing planning processes—often largely a series of discussions among key staff and board members, producing consensus on the focus of project work and identifying targets of opportunity—proved far more useful.

Board/Staff Relations: Defined Roles and Shared Objectives. A clear, internally agreed-upon definition of the separate roles of board members and staff is important to NDOs, to reduce conflict, smooth internal administration, and increase productive work by the board. In addition, staff and board members must develop a common conception of an NDO's desired role in development (for example, whether it is the organization's primary work) to avoid repeated fighting of old battles.

NDO Control over Any Development and/or For-Profit Spin Off. Close control by the parent nonprofit-over-spin-off organizations in the same lines of work yields several advantages. It makes NDOs better able to exploit available opportunities by smoothly shifting resources among organizational components, avoid internal conflicts (that is, over salary levels or division of responsibilities), and keep project activities in line with community desires by drawing on the parent's long-time processes for neighborhood input and control.

Competent Financial Record Keeping. While most NDOs handle bookkeeping adequately for project needs, a few have their very survival threatened by inattention to this area. Being unable to demonstrate clearly how funds were used can be deadly to NDOs if their honesty is challenged by outsiders fighting with them over other issues.

Track Record of Success. While a track record of effective development work is a result produced by other capabilities, it also has value of its own, once established. That value is especially apparent in attracting funding and generating grassroots support for NDO work; and some NDOs craftily design their stream of projects to show at least some visible, early results upon which further work can be built.

The key internal characteristics are in general a mixture of factors important to for-profit businesses of similar scale and other features unique to NDOs' nature as community-based and controlled institutions. For example, NDOs' need for in-house, technical-staff capability is certainly shared with private business. On the other hand, special care and talent are required to build this capability without damaging the community roots that enable NDOs to succeed under conditions where others (both private and public actors) fail. Technical expertise is often available only by recruiting outside an NDO's immediate community and paying relatively high salaries. And long-time NDO participants are often wary of losing control over policymaking to high-powered staff. Assuring continued community control over policy is a key to preventing internal disputes that often arise over outside hiring. Such assurances are also necessary to retain wide community support. Creating adequate means of assurance requires other internal capabilities including clearly defined board and staff roles and the exercise of special leadership skills by the executive director. Business practices and skills alone do not suffice.

Relations with the Community and Outsiders

NDOs operate in neighborhoods whose residents have very limited financial resources and often lack technical training and experience, and where private investment and enterprise and sometimes public action have been in short supply. Obtaining assistance and cooperation from a variety of external sources, combined with community support, is critical to NDO success.

Important aspects of NDO relationships to community and outsiders we identified include:

Roots in the Community. The strength of an NDO's support in its own community and staff and board commitment to the community are significant in many ways. In our study, this importance was most clearly manifested in such areas as identifying and properly designing projects to meet resident needs, attracting neighborhood participation in NDO projects, showing potential funders a community base, and protecting the organization when it was attacked.

Conflicts and Harmony within the Community. NDOs in long-running disagreements with other community actors can suffer serious drains in energy—time spent lobbying, counterattacking, and defending—even if they are winning battles. Unfortunately, NDOs generally cannot prevent the fights, over such matters as so-called rights to resources or NDO hiring and firing choices; but they do sometimes offset the costs, by raising their credibility with outsiders through successful work in the face of acrimony.

Political Clout. NDOs' political influence and power (electoral and otherwise) clearly have significant impact on their ability to attract and maintain funding, obtain other services and cooperation from local government, and protect themselves from outside attack.

Working Relationships with Local Business People (for Applicable Projects). One of the reasons NDOs find commercial-revitalization projects more difficult than housing projects is that they have inadequate links to and project participation from potentially affected merchants and service providers. Involving business people very early on in designing projects, and in NDOs themselves, is key to getting their agreement to invest in storefront improvements, make joint marketing efforts, and take other necessary actions.

Working with Private-Project Developers. Sharing a project with an experienced private-development group often helps an NDO attract funding and may help implement a project smoothly, substituting for an NDO's own experience where it is as yet limited. For long-term success, however, NDOs need to work consciously at internalizing the skills and reputation the partner brings.

Outside Relations with Other Private Actors. Key friendly individuals in major private foundations and businesses have been at times very useful in linking NDOs to sources of investment finance, technical advice, tenants for commercial/industrial buildings, or customers/markets for the products of NDO ventures. NDOs typically have difficulty establishing relationships with these people and do well to take advantage of the access one individual, often initially at a foundation, can provide to others.

Sources of Flexible Administrative and Venture Funds. Flexible funds allow hiring good core staff, upgrading management capabilities (for example, in accounting), planning future work, and making timely investments in NDO's priority projects that may not match individual funders' priorities. Advanced NDOs can use flexible funds to undertake backlogs of work their records prepare them for or to break into new lines of work, while relative newcomers can purchase such "luxuries" as staff stability and adequate technical expertise.

Early Aid from Private Risk Takers. Assistance early in an NDO's history of work—in the form of direct funding, technical assistance, volunteer staff, meeting places, and so on—is critical to eventual success. Churches and foundations who most often take these risks make possible the building of track records and contacts that lead to support from others.

Access to Technical Assistance. Technical assistance in a host of areas, listed later in this chapter, is a significant element of the work of nearly any successful NDO. Most organizations are too limited in scale and expertise to have all needed skills on staff, especially early in organizational life.

Characteristics of the Economic, Social, and Political Environment

The difficult environmental conditions NDOs face severely constrain their performance in neighborhood revitalization. This is no surprise, since many of the same environmental factors were important in producing the conditions to which NDOs now react. Six major types of conditions we found influential were:

Housing and Economic Market Conditions. Major aspects of housing and economic market conditions significantly influence NDO project success in much the same way they affect projects by private entrepreneurs. Neighborhood market factors, especially declining resident incomes, were central in producing deteriorated housing or depressed commercial strips and cannot be offset easily or inexpensively. National economic conditions—high interest rates, slowed business expansion, unemployment—buffet NDOs' already-marginal neighborhoods and projects especially hard.

Project Cost Factors. Very simply, some NDOs face significantly higher direct project costs than others, affecting project feasibility and requiring compensating funds. Straightforward examples include high land and building costs for some NDOs fighting displacement in strong markets and high energy costs in cold climates.

Reluctance by Private Lenders to Lend Funds. Even before recent periods of tight money and high interest rates, NDO projects were limited or stymied by difficulty in obtaining loan capital from private institutions. The problem is still especially acute in minority neighborhoods and requires continued use of risk-reducing "carrots" and regulatory "sticks."

Racism and Sexism. Minority organizations in our study suffered special disadvantages in obtaining not only private loans but other outside support for their projects—some government grants, placement of their trained workers, or major customers for their ventures. The signs of discrimination on the basis of race, sex, and simply low income were sharply apparent even in our brief on-site visits, though the translation into specific-project impacts was more subtle.

Political Attitudes. In a minority of cases, a form of political conservatism opposing support for active neighborhood-based self-help efforts presents a barrier to NDOs. In particular, it blocks attempts to establish working relations with the local government for funding, technical assistance, linkages to other outsiders, and provision of supporting services/goods for its projects, although at times painting a very business-oriented face on NDO work can moderate the impacts.

Timing of Political Events. Many political occurrences beyond NDO influence affect their program options. During much of our study, expanded Community Development Block Grants (CDBG) and Comprehensive Employment and Training Act (CETA) programs were reflected in NDO growth—as the more recent decline in public funding is now reflected in current NDO retrenchment. While these powerful effects are easily apparent, they deserve careful attention in assessing NDO performance and in NDOs' own planning for perhaps more diversified and self-sustaining future funding.

How NDOs react and adjust to these environmental conditions is extremely important for success. For example, successful NDOs carefully selected projects to correspond to the specific opportunities that housing and economic markets provided or allowed; battled high project costs through such advance-planning means as land banking; and took full advantage of nonfinancial aid from lenders. These NDOs also used the spectre of citizen action and new regulation to encourage lending and pressed administrators of new government programs to make these programs workable for community-based organizations. Since every NDO confronts powerful constraints because of its environment, resourcefulness in recognizing opportunities and minimizing limitations is crucial to project success.

At the same time, it is necessary to understand that the extreme external difficulties NDOs face can overwhelm even NDOs with very good internal capabilities and links to others, if the resources to offset such conditions are not provided.

Stages of Development

How NDOs develop the capacity to undertake revitalization projects is very complex. The process is not divisible into neatly defined stages. Organizations with differing beginnings, neighborhood problems, initial activities, sources of support, and other characteristics take very different paths to maturity.

Realistically, we can describe NDO growth patterns in two ways. First, NDOs pass through a series of common processes at *some* time in their lives that lead to more successful revitalization-project development. Each process involves multiple changes in outlook, knowledge, experience, and a range of specific capabilities. NDOs work through the processes in different sequences, but those that have worked through more processes, more completely, appear notably more adept in project activities. We identified the following significant processes:

Formally establishing an organization. Informal organizations do productive work in planning and pressing for solutions to community problems. But formalizing, by establishing a clear identity to out-siders, qualifying for funds, creating policy-setting mechanisms, and designating staff, is necessary early preparation for taking on development projects.

Deciding to carry out programs and to create institutions. Many NDOs do not initially assume they will themselves undertake pro-grams and projects. Finding others unwilling or unable to meet needs they identify, some move—often with significant internal debate—to take on the work themselves.

Confronting the difficulties of early neighborhood-revitalization projects. First development projects involve learning to establish realistic expectations, to identify needed capabilities, to recognize the key steps in project work, and to anticipate some likely problems.

Becoming competent in specific-project work. NDOs follow up recognition of the difficulties of project work by consciously building required capacity and further learning by doing.

Developing a network of relations with outsiders. NDOs learn where and how to find a broader and longer list of sources of potential assistance and establish working relations with them.

Building a diverse range of projects. NDOs expand beyond a single line of development work, building new project-type-specific capabilities and drawing on past successful work to create new opportunities.

Institutionalizing expanded project competence. To fit their expanded operations and maintain capacity once developed, NDOs delegate responsibilities, assign staff members more specific areas of work, reorganize boards of directors into working committees along functional lines, and so on.

While the order of the above processes appears to represent a logical time progression, in fact we observe many variations. Within our set of twelve study NDOs, even two of very similar and substantial longevity and success followed very distinct paths of organizational development. One formalized and started projects almost simultaneously and stayed in a single line of work until well established. The other created an external network early on in advocacy work, formalized later, did no development work for several more years, and then moved into several areas simultaneously.

A second way to describe growth in NDO capability is to examine the development of individual key characteristics of capacity, particularly internal capabilities and relations to outsiders listed earlier. The characteristics again need not develop in consistent time sequences or particular combinations. Whatever the order of growth in specific elements of capacity, NDOs with many of these well-developed characteristics are relatively advanced in ability to take on projects.

We found that our study-site observations did reveal a clear development pattern for a significant subset of key characteristics. These include—among NDO characteristics—staff technical expertise, track record, leadership by the executive director, record of doing homework, and good board/staff relations; and—among relations to outsiders—roots in the community, political clout (a less clear growth process), relations with private lenders, and use of technical assistance. Describing the growth process of these characteristics provides numerous implications for actions by both NDOs and external actors to help develop the capabilities. For example, the best relations with private lenders clearly resulted from NDOs' conscious, deliberate actions to create them. Since these relations have long-run importance for project work, the strong suggestion is that NDOs must plan and implement strategies to establish them. NDOs can also benefit from technical assistance in designing proposals attractive to lenders and use their own contacts with other key actors to get access to lending officials.

Funding Support and Technical Assistance

Obviously NDOs need operating and investment funds from outside sources to carry out significant community-development projects and to survive as organizations doing programming more generally. But certain kinds of funding, or their creative use by NDOs, can be especially valuable. Specific funding may affect organizational survival, development of key projects, capacity growth, or ability to raise or productively use other funds. The importance of particular funds may lie in their timing in relation to NDO or project development or in the general level of difficulty in obtaining money for certain purposes. Significant aspects of funding and fund use fall into seven groups, the first two of which were discussed already under factors on success:

Early funding, before an NDO's track record is established.

Sources of flexible and continuing funds.

Important substitutes for flexible funds: If general funds are not adequately available, special-purpose funds for planning and preparation of specific projects, real-estate loan pools available in advance for quick action, short-term loans to deal with cash-flow problems, and internally generated surpluses can be important substitutes.

Major increases in funding scale or scope: NDOs need to be well positioned in terms of key capacities discussed above to take full advantage of expanded funding levels when such opportunities arise. The scope and scale of funding need to be matched to ability to use it.

Leveraging funds: NDOs need to be clever and skilled at using the availability of one cash or in-kind resource to pin down commitments from other reluctant or slower-moving funders.

Recycling financial resources within the community: Advanced NDOs especially have been conscious of the potential to retain more of the funds in or coming to a community within its boundaries—an oft-noted problem in low-income neighborhoods. An example is development of housing ownership and management programs by NDOs involved in rehabilitation.

Adequate project funding levels: NDO projects are frequently underfunded from the outset by their sources of support. More realistic funding would relieve NDOs of the need to use up general funds for project purposes and give projects a chance to be self-sustaining in the long run.

Many forms of hands-on technical assistance prove valuable to NDOs. Important areas of aid include:

Proposal writing.

Project packaging.

Special professional services in architecture, engineering, and such.

Legal assistance.

Accounting.

Assistance with relations to outsiders, especially funding sources.

Defining board and staff roles and training board members in development.

Organizational structuring and design, including board composition and structure and spin offs.

Multipurpose project and organizational counsel.

Two broad issues are critical to NDOs' effective use of technical assistance. First NDOs must learn to control the use of outside technical aid. Technical assistance is generally most valuable when an NDO itself has identified, carefully defined, and contracted for specific technical services. NDO staff must have the confidence and knowledge to insist, throughout the contract, that technical-assistance providers deliver the specific products promised and operate within the stated guidelines of community goals. NDOs usually learn the importance of such control through their own unsuccessful experiences or the advice of sources of technical assistance with long NDO experience.

Second, many types of technical assistance must be designed for gradual elimination. Successful, mature NDOs perform much or all of their proposal writing, day-to-day project implementation, fund-raising strategizing, and other tasks in-house, although these NDOs formerly may have received a great deal of technical aid. NDOs must structure the delivery of early technical assistance to result in the training of their own staffs (and sometimes board membership) and find aid sources who are willing and able to contribute to that process.

Performance Measures

Measuring the effectiveness of NDOs in carrying out their projects and in using financial, technical, and other aid can play a valuable role in encouraging NDO growth. Such assessment provides feedback on current NDO support efforts that can help to direct future assistance, and it can provide the basis for assuring policymakers that aid to NDOs is a productive use of neighborhood revitalization resources.

Identifying appropriate measures of NDO performance is a difficult and sensitive task. One difficulty is taking into account the full range of impacts that NDO projects may have. Measured project benefits need to include not only primary direct outputs (that is, houses rehabilitated in a home-repair project) but also other direct outputs (that is, training neighborhood youth to do the repairs) that may be among NDO objectives but not those of other actors undertaking similar projects. The income (and other socioeconomic) distribution of project benefits must also be evaluated, because serving low- and moderate-income and other disadvantaged people is generally a principal NDO goal and can certainly involve added costs and complications. In addition, NDOs' own project efforts and aid from outsiders are often intended to produce not only successful projects but increased NDO capacity for similar future work. The very complex task of measuring improved capability is thus a necessary one.

A second, but related, type of measurement difficulty is to establish reasonable standards against which to compare NDO performance. One useful standard is the level of direct accomplishments originally proposed by an NDO. That standard is especially relevant because sources of assistance are presumably providing aid on the assumption that expected results are worth the requested support. Another potentially useful standard is past performance by other actors in similar projects. But truly equivalent activity may be very difficult to find, given the difficult conditions in which NDOs operate. Adjusting performance measures for differences in many environmental conditions is imprecise at best and often infeasible. It is important not to establish standards so insufficiently comparable that differences between NDO and other actors' project outcomes actually represent differences in project activities and environment rather than differences in true performance.

A final major area of complexibility in measuring NDO performance is in properly attributing observed neighborhood change to NDO work. Certainly NDO projects will have indirect impacts, as other people take actions in response to the organizations' project activities (that is, increased home repair by neighbors of NDO-rehabilitated structures). But attempts to separate out reaction to NDO work from the impacts of other events will face the severe difficulties that plague analysis of any neighborhood-program intervention. In addition, policymakers are sometimes interested in measuring broad community outcomes, to see whether major changes in neighborhood unemployment, housing deficiency, and other problems have resulted from NDO work. We believe that NDOs, and certainly single NDO projects, cannot be held accountable for outcomes so buffeted by larger external forces. Direct and indirect NDO impacts that correspond to community problems (for example, job creation or housing improvement) are much more appropriate measures of NDO performance and use of assistance than are overall community outcomes.

Further Directions

The findings of our research are based in significant part on one-time visits to each of a sample of twelve NDOs, in addition to interviews with recognized experts in the NDO field. It is clearly desirable to make further observations of NDOs' project activities and growth processes to substantiate and extend our results. The Urban Institute is completing a study of nearly one hundred NDOs over two years that provides verification and challenge to the findings reported here. It, and hopefully similar future studies, will also allow a more complete understanding of NDO diversity and of the needs and possibilities for tailoring approaches to capacity-building and external assistance to those variations. A critical further line for inquiry is how best to structure the project work of NDOs and other interested actors into successful strategies for true overall revitalization of distressed neighborhoods.

Note

1. A full description of findings is contained in Neil S. Mayer, with Jennifer Blake, *Keys to the Growth of Neighborhood Development Organizations* (The Urban Institue, 1981).

Part IV
Neighborhood Policy and Planning

The present period affords a great opportunity to accomplish lasting improvements in urban neighborhoods and also to advance the knowledge of neighborhood dynamics and to strengthen professional methods of planning at the neighborhood scale. But unless we can perceive more clearly which features and dimensions of neighborhood development are generic, rather than purely contemporary, professional concepts and tools will not have progressed. The debates about neighborhood policy that are most salient in the late 1970s and early 1980s are important in their own right. In addition, they represent a chance to deal more fundamentally with the underlying and timeless dilemmas they represent—dilemmas about what are the most appropriate and efficacious roles for federal and local government in guiding neighborhood development, for the private sector (including both business firms and the burgeoning nonprofit sector at the grassroots).

The first chapter in this final part criticizes the protriage approach to neighborhood policy that has gained a certain amount of support in recent years. The pro- and antitriage debate crystallizes major dimensions of policy choice. Subsequent chapters advance major proposals for changing federal policy toward neighborhoods. The book concludes with a chapter by the editors that advocates making neighborhood planning a distinct field of professional work and outlines major working principles to guide neighborhood planning.

Conrad Weiler, in "Urban Euthanasia for Fun and Profit," responds directly to the increasing advocacy of triage. Weiler rebuts that approach, arguing that it implicitly and inevitably disadvantages the most needy, that it misreads present trends in the most physically deteriorated areas and distorts the impact and the prospects of present and proposed programs.

In this era of serious attention to national policy toward neighborhoods, the book includes two sharply contrasting perspectives on national policy. Geno Baroni, in "The Neighborhood Movement in the United States," explains the evolution of neighborhood movements in terms of the consequences of federal programs and changing political and economic conditions. He documents the emergence of strong and increasingly effective community groups, organizing around a broad range of local issues, and their coming together nationally to advocate their common interests. Baroni forcefully advocates a strong federal-government role in support of the self-help initiatives of local neighborhood organizations. As an assistant secretary of the U.S. Department of Housing and Urban Development during the Carter administration, he helped to design and to implement that kind of federal role.

Robert Hawkins's chapter argues a fundamentally different approach to governmental policy. He takes issue with the dominant approach that he characterizes as "conceptualizing neighborhoods as merely administrative cogs in the federal system." He presents a case for viewing neighborhoods "as limited yet independent actors in the federal system." This would mean federal policies that decrease the amount of federal control and that maximize opportunities for neighborhood self-government.

The concluding chapter by Phillip Clay and Robert Hollister, "Toward the Practice of Neighborhood Planning," argues that present and future needs, plus the direction of major societal trends, requires a new focus by urban professionals on planning for neighborhoods. The authors highlight key public issues and explain why each requires a neighborhood-planning focus. The chapter discusses major elements and dimensions of any effective approach to neighborhood planning: goalsetting, population mix, private/public interface, information, citizen involvement, regulatory strategy, resource allocation, and public management.

10 Urban Euthanasia for Fun and Profit

Conrad Weiler

In the mid-1970s it became fashionable in academic and policy circles to speak of planned abandonment, triage, planned shrinkage, and even planned death of urban neighborhoods. To be sure, the imagery of dying cities had been current since the sixties and certainly the idea of dying neighborhoods was an active assumption underlying much urban-renewal planning even in the 1950s. What was important about the new fashion of neighborhood death in the mid-1970s was that it often emanated from liberal sources reluctantly concluding that liberal programs from the 1950s and 1960s designed to prevent neighborhood and city death had failed, leaving no humane choice except to actively *plan* for the urban death that now seemed inevitable in the light of liberal-policy failure.

It is our contention that the advocacy of planned neighborhood death or triage was (and is) not only in itself unnecessary and destructive but also contributed in the 1970s to concealing patterns of inner-city reinvestment that threatened and displaced existing working-class and poor residents while reclaiming their neighborhoods for well-to-do newcomers.

The New Fashion of Neighborhood Death

The new fashion of neighborhood death grew from several sources. There were the various articles and speeches by Roger Starr in and about New York City, particularly an article in the 14 November 1976 *New York Times Magazine*, entitled "Making New York Smaller."[1] There were Anthony Downs's observations on dispersal and triage in *Opening Up the Suburbs* and elsewhere.[2] Then there was the article, "On the Death of Cities" by William Baer, in the Fall 1976 issue of the *Public Interest*.[3] These major sources in turn were reflected in countless other less-known and local discussions. While the intellectual sources of the triage or neighborhood-death arguments actually are shared by most mainstream U.S. urban social science in the more vague shape of the neighborhood life-cycle and filtering concepts, the discussion in the mid-1970s was a very immediate, active, policy-advocacy discussion. The triage discussion of the 1970s was not simply projecting the eventual death of cities

167

and neighborhoods, it was actively, openly, and immediately proposing it as a matter of good public policy. Thus triage and its synonyms of planned shrinkage, planned abandonment, planned death, and such are terms of overt, active public policy; they are not terms of abstract urban sociological theory. For simplicity we refer to all terms that actively and immediately propose a public policy of neighborhood death as *triage*. The argument for triage (as developed in the 1970s) generally reduces itself to the following:

1. Urban or neighborhood death or decline is defined as the growth of so-called slums, and the tendency toward physical deterioration, housing abandonment, and out-migration of population, leading to a nearly, or totally, inevitable final state of disorganization and inutility.
2. Most authorities shy from recognizing or admitting the inevitability of city and neighborhood death, for political or (misguided) humanitarian reasons.
3. Most or all policies to prevent urban decline and death are failures or are at best delaying actions, and even historic restoration and gentrification now occuring in some urban cores are no real alternative to urban death but are instead merely a postponement or minor deviation from the norm, or at best a limited phenomenon.
4. The only sensible and humane policy is therefore to try to reduce the human and economic costs of urban and neighborhood death by planning for it, helping it along where appropriate, confronting it frankly, and dealing responsibly with its side effects in a policy of triage, planned abandonment, planned shrinkage, or so-called urban euthanasia. This spares the victims from even worse suffering and allows government to efficiently use its resources under conditions of decline.

The Definition of Urban Death

On the one hand it makes eminently good sense to see slums, deterioration, abandonment, and flight to the suburbs as unfavorable developments from the point of view of the city or neighborhood suffering them.

On the other hand, the images of urban decline—and particularly of urban death—often convey an anthropomorphic analogy of physical death of living, biological organisms, which may be stimulating but hardly is very scientific. Regardless of the connotations of terms such as *urban death*, the assumption on which the triage model is based is that urban or neighborhood decline is nearly or completely inevitable and thus unavoidable. In fact, if this assumption is granted, the triage argument does make sense. The problem, however, is that while much urban distress is clearly evident, as Baer admits,[4] few neighborhoods of the total and no cities actually have died. Thus, the triage argument rests on the fact of urban problems projected forward often through powerful imagery toward a vision of inevitable urban entropy, not on scientific evidence. The policy scientist as well as the practitioner is in reality asked to make a "leap of faith" that the facts of urban ills are part of a negative developmental sequence leading to urban death, when what *should* be asked is whether in fact such a developmental sequence exists in part or at all—and what can be done to change it if it does exist.

Discovery of the Inevitability of Urban Death

The frequent posture of triage advocates of reluctantly forcing us to confront the new reality of urban death in reality merely revives one of the oldest and most powerful myths in U.S. political culture generally and urban policy in particular. Was it not Jefferson, after all, who practically called for urban death in 1800, writing to Philadelphia's Dr. Benjamin Rush during a yellow-fever epidemic that, "The yellow fever will discourage the growth of great cities in our nation, and I view great cities as pestilential to the morals, the health and the liberties of man."[5] Throughout the nineteenth and twentieth centuries, from the Know-Nothings of the 1820s to the attacks on urban immigrants by the Progressives at the turn of the century to the urban-renewal planners of the 1950s, the death or decline of cities has been an antiurban theme throughout the United States and a central consideration of urban policy. In recent years, the literature of the social sciences, as well as the popular press and the media since the Watts riot, has been dominated if not overwhelmed by questions such as, Are our cities dying? Can cities survive? and on ad nauseam if not ad absurdam.

Triage advocates in the 1970s thus created a dangerous straw man. By bemoaning the apparent squeamishness of urban experts in avoiding the prospect of urban death, they created the sense that urban death was not a central, or even an important, assumption of U.S. political culture or of urban policy. Thus, triage advocates attracted attention by seeming to point to an ignored, but emerging, hard reality previously avoided— when in fact urban death or decline is, and for two centuries has been, in one fashion or another *the* central fixation, not to say goal, of American thought on the city. The straw man of the discovery of the "inevitability" of urban death is not only the result of ignoring the history of the city in U.S. culture, but it is actually a strident reaffirmation of that very tradition.

Beyond that, the discovery of the inevitability of urban death is psychologically and logically necessary to sustain the third triage proposition (also a straw man), which is that that thirty years or so of liberal policies to save the city have unfortunately failed or at best merely postponed the death of the city.

That is, if triage advocates were to argue: "For 200 years Americans have predicted, called for, and occasionally planned urban and neighborhood death," the concluding argument to adopt a *new* policy of triage and planned death would become weak—not to say silly. Triage advocates would have been in the unenviable position of proposing a renewed attack on a strangely indestructible foe, rather than creating a new policy breakthrough. They would, in short, be themselves defending an idea, if not a policy, that has historically failed—the decline or death of cities—rather than attacking failed policies to save cities. Thus, given the conclusion of the triage argument—to kill neighborhoods—we speculate that it is probably logically or psychologically necessary for the triage argument to claim that killing cities and neighborhoods previously has been avoided and never advocated by thinkers and policymakers, although in fact the opposite is true. Far from being a new policy, triage is the banal and most recent expression of a centuries old U.S. antagonism toward the city and its less fortunate inhabitants.

The Alleged Failures of Urban Policy

The central assumption of the triage argument here is the idea that policies to prevent urban death have failed because they have not eliminated out-migration, slums, deterioration, and disinvestment. But the fact is that urban renewal as legislated and, certainly, as applied was at best only marginally a welfare program and was nearly always aimed at and used for strategic reconstruction of the central business district of large central cities *to reattract the middle class.*[6] This reconstruction of the downtown was *strategic* because it sought a long-term change in the basic forces affecting the city qua city—not the city measured by the improvement of its poor, the justice of its rule, or the vitality of its individual neighborhoods. City qua city meant (and means) an increase of business, service-sector jobs and taxable (middle-class) incomes, and residence and a decline in the number of welfare-dependent people and slums in the city (à la Forrester).[7] While liberals have often objected that urban renewal and other urban policies based on the central municipalities of large metropolitan areas have often displaced, rather than eliminated, poverty and slums, many of these same observers have missed the basic loopholes in all these programs: no federal program based on a large municipality contains an effective safeguard against core cities using these programs to play the same basic population-movement game (with federal help) against the suburbs that the suburbs played and play (with federal help) against the city. A careful look at central-city demographic maps from the 1950s to the 1980s will show in most large cities that the pattern of movement of slums and the poor as well as the movement of upper-middle-class and service-sector jobs is by no means random but instead forms two great vectors: the first—the movement of slums, man-ufacturing, and the poor and working class—is inexorably *outward*, eventually to the suburbs (there is virtually no known example of slums, factories, and working-class residence spreading *closer* to the down-town); the second vector shows the movement of service-sector jobs and upper- and middle-class persons ahead of the poor and the slums to the outer suburbs then *back to the expanding downtown*.

The wholesale indictment of urban policies, especially urban re-newal, as a failure, therefore conceals and confuses more than it reveals. Urban renewal and related policies at the highest levels have long defined their goals as returning the middle class to the city—not primarily as helping the poor. The tactics of achieving this strategic goal involved the careful and systematic redistribution outward of slums and poor peo-ple; so that the apparent failures, of thirty years of urban policy may be in fact actually the short-run transitional phase of a strategically suc-cessful long-range program to reverse the direction and geopolitical ad-vantages of intrametropolitan job and population migration back to the central cities.

Neighborhood Death for Fun and Profit

In most of our big cities, it was obvious by the early 1970s that some of the middle and upper-middle class were returning to old neighborhoods in and around the downtown; preserving and restoring old houses; cre-ating new artist quarters and attractive and often avant-garde shopping areas; staging city festivals; helping to revive ethnic pride; serving as community organizers to fight crimes or superhighways, to organize green-lining campaigns, or to build basement trout tanks. While the extent of this redevelopment and resettlement of old city neighborhoods may still be in dispute by urban-policy analysts, anyone who actually lives in old city neighborhoods or looks around Boston, Philadelphia, Baltimore, Washington, or dozens of other cities knows it has been happening.[8]

This return to the city—spurred by the baby boom, gasoline shortage, disillusionment with suburban life, residential taste changes, increasing density and aging of suburban housing, rising cost of new housing, service-sector growth in downtowns, city locational advantages and many other factors—is a small but continuing trend of metropolitan political life.

As the neighborhood redevelops several things happen. There is an increase in private investment, sometimes preceded but usually followed by an increase in public investment. Property values suddenly increase, often dramatically. Abandoned, "bombed-out" buildings suddenly become "shells for restoration by urban pioneers." New people move into the neighborhood and these new people are typically artists or middle- or upper-class professionals. At first, they move into empty buildings or ones being sold in the normal neighborhood process of real-estate turnover. Often these newcomers establish or attract new businesses and give new life to old ones. They become active and actually may help to improve the neighborhoods. Typically, they value the diversity of the neighborhood highly and moved to the neighborhood originally because they believed in a diverse, urban-neighborhood life style. Up to this point, neighborhood economic, and possibly racial, diversity has increased as a result of recycling.

Unfortunately, the diverse recycling or redeveloping neighborhood is often merely at a temporary midpoint between what might have been a largely poor or working-class homogeneity and an emerging upper-middle-class homogeneity. Just as racial stability in a neighborhood cynically, but perhaps accurately, has been called: the time between the first blacks moving in and the last white moving out, so diversity in the redeveloping neighborhood might be defined as: the time between the first upper-middle-class professional moving in to restore an old house and the last old timer being moved out by rising property taxes, rising rentals, and changes in neighborhood life styles.

The result of historical preservation in inner-city areas, and other actions going far beyond mere historic restoration, has been to restructure market preferences and investment parameters so that the private investor now has a new and potentially vast market of old-city housing to exploit with virtually no adequate public-policy controls to preserve such values as social and economic diversity or to protect those who never left the neighborhood.

It is therefore very curious that just as inner-city residential reinvestment and redevelopment was becoming widespread in the early 1970s, the triage arguments emerged, often actually denying or downplaying the significance of this new development. Baer, for example, dismissed historic preservation as having any real influence on the approaching death of cities.[9] Even more curious is that some urban-dispersal and triage advocates were dismissing inner-city reinvestment as having no policy importance at the same time they themselves were recognizing or promoting it in other quarters.

Downs, who in 1976 was recommending triage of badly deteriorated areas and dispersal of the poor, in 1975 published a study for HUD documenting historic preservation and neighborhood redevelopment in many cities, along with actual displacement of existing low- and moderate-income residents from the neighborhoods.[10] Sternlieb, whose grim prognostications about the future of cities as early as the late 1960s certainly contributed to the triage argument, in 1975 chaired a panel for the Federal National Mortgage Association that advocated taking advantage of the abandonment process as a means of promoting middle-income housing in the inner city.[11]

How to explain these seeming inconsistencies? Without speculating further on how the individuals involved resolved them, it seems clear that there was from the beginning a hidden agenda to the triage argument, one that is there if one looks very carefully. Roger Starr, for example, wrote that after closing down deteriorated neighborhoods, the land would "lie fallow until a change in economic and demographic assumptions makes the land useful once again."[12] Downs himself states, "Eventually, after the very deteriorated areas are almost totally vacant, they may be redeveloped with wholly different uses."[13]

Triage, then, as it was argued in the mid-1970s, was in reality far more than a simple statement of despair about the future of cities and neighborhoods. Triage as a policy recommendation was in reality inextricably connected not with the inevitability of urban death, but with the emergent fact of urban revival. Triage was not so much the closing down of deteriorated neighborhoods for the sake of their unfortunate residents, who might humanely be guided and relocated to so-called better housing and economic opportunities in the outer city or suburban areas, as it was a process of acquiring inner-city land for some *future* use and dispersing its unneeded inhabitants. What this future use would be was already apparent in the mid-1970s—housing and other spaces for upper-middle-class workers in downtown service-sector jobs.

The triage argument is thus both disingenuous and backwards: backwards because triage as a policy arose historically not (as stated) because of the failure of urban policy and the death of cities but precisely because of the possibility of the revival of cities and the imminent success of urban policy in beginning the recapture of the middle class back to the city centers; disingenuous because triage was advocated primarily to acquire land and buildings that were to be used to house the recaptured middle class not, as stated, primarily because cities were dying, or to help the poor.

Interestingly enough, the triage argument has recently been revived and adapted to accomodate the fact of upper-middle-class resettlement of inner cities. Professor Michael Lang's book, *Gentrification Amid Urban Decline*, accepts the resettlement of inner-city areas by the affluent, a possibility dismissed by most triage advocates in the 1970s, and proposes triage as a way to clear out in an orderly fashion those lower-income residents who will inevitably be displaced by inner-city redevelopment.[14] Thus, in the 1980s the mask is finally off the triage argument—the repossession of valuable inner-city land—no matter what effort was made in the 1970s to conceal it.

The Banality of Triage

Viewed from geopolitical and historical perspectives, the final outcome of the triage argument and the recommendations of the neighborhood-death advocates are suddenly reduced to near banality; far from being something new, they are actually restatements of old arguments. Though claiming to be toughly realistic, the triage argument usually was made with a hidden agenda.

In essence the triage argument really amounts to the following: inner-city land close to the downtown is or soon will be very valuable both to city governments and to private developers; let us systematically use government to clear it through triage for future private development and at the same time move its present occupants outward to outer-city or suburban locations where it may be argued they will be better off but in any case they will cost the city less than in their present location.

For those whose view of U.S. society includes the idea that people have a right not to be forced from their homes by government for the benefit of the rich and the idea that cities should be made up of stable, relatively self-sufficient neighborhoods each comprising diverse income and racial groupings, a policy radically different from that of neighborhood death is desirable.

This alternative would be a policy that actually challenges the root values causing our problems rather than merely perpetuating them in new guises. Such a policy would encourage reinvestment and redevelopment but prevent displacement; it would promote economic and social diversity instead of homogeneity and create successful neighborhoods that are integrated socioeconomic and political organs instead of cities that manipulate populations and economic activities to maximize taxes and minimize costly populations. Such a policy would especially not advocate municipal government extracting taxes from neighborhoods from which public services and people are being forcibly removed—and certainly not then use residents' taxes to kill the neighborhoods in order to "save" the city by later moving in the rich.

Notes

1. Roger Starr, "Making New York Smaller," *New York Times Magazine*, 14 November 1976.

2. See, for example, Anthony Downs, "Alternative Futures for the American Ghetto," ch. 2 of *Urban Problems and Prospects* (Chicago: Markham, 1970) pp. 27–74; Downs, *Opening Up the Suburbs*, (New Haven: Yale University Press, 1973); and Downs, "Using the Lessons of Experience to Allocate Resources in the CD Program," in *Recommendation for Community Development Planning* (Chicago: Real Estate Research Corporation, 1976).

3. William Baer, "On the Death of Cities," *Public Interest* 45 (Fall, 1976).

4. Ibid., p. 4.

5. Quoted in Charles N. Glaab and A. Theodore Brown, *A History of Urban America* (Toronto: The MacMillan Company, 1970), p. 55.

6. See, for example, Conrad Weiler, "Urban Planning and Redevelopment," ch. 7 of *Philadelphia: Neighborhood, Authority and the Urban Crisis*, (New York: Praeger, 1975), pp. 128–154.

7. Jay Forrester, *Urban Dynamics* (Cambridge, Mass.: MIT Press, 1969).

8. See, for example, Shirley B. Laska and Daphne Spain, eds., *Back to the City: Issues in Neighborhood Renovation*, (New York: Pergamon, 1980); and Conrad Weiler, "Achieving Social and Economic Diversity in Inner City Neighborhoods Through Increased Demand for City Housing by Middle Income Persons," paper delivered to the Fifth Annual Back to the City Conference, (Hartford, Conn., 8 October 1978).

9. Baer, *Death of Cities*, pp. 12–13.,

10. U.S. Department of Housing and Urban Development, *Neighborhood Preservation: A Catalogue of Local Programs* (Washington, D.C.: USGPO, 1975).

11. Federal National Mortgage Association, *Forum Two: The Changing Market for Middle Income City Housing* (Washington, D.C.: Federal National Mortgage Association, 1975), pp. 44–56.

12. Starr, *Making New York Smaller*, p. 105.

13. Downs, "Using the Lessons of Experience", pp. 18–19.

14. Michael H. Lang, *Gentrification Amid Urban Decline: Strategies for America's Older Cities*, (Cambridge, Mass.: Ballinger, 1982).

11 The Neighborhood Movement in the United States: From the 1960s to the Present

Geno Baroni

In the tragic aftermath of President Kennedy's assassination, President Johnson, true to his populist instincts and emboldened by congenial economic conditions, committed his administration to a program that his predecessor had conceived—a comprehensive war on poverty. The principal instrument for what would become the most dramatic assault upon economic and social inequality since the New Deal was to be the community organization. Utilizing local communities to treat economic dislocation was not a new idea; it had been tried during the New Deal but largely in connection with stricken rural communities. The centerpiece of the 1965 Economic Opportunity Act was the Community Action Program, and this time both urban and rural communities would be included.

Soon after the community-action agencies were formed, however, a controversy arose over the meaning of language calling for "maximum feasible participation of residents of the areas and members of the groups" involved in the local programs. Community activists in the field and some members of the Office of Economic Opportunity contended that the wording articulated one of the program's major goals—empowering people at the grassroots. Poverty was not merely a condition of economic deprivation; it also was marked by powerlessness, by the inability of poor people to shape decisions that keenly affected them. Through community organizations then, they were to participate in the formation and administration of policy.

Many congressmen and urban analysts involved in the program's design disagreed. Its principal goal was to deliver social services and other forms of assistance to the nation's most destitute citizens. The term *maximum feasible participation* of the poor, they argued, was not employed with the idea in mind of community empowerment. According to one insider, the provision was "intended to do more than insure that persons excluded from the political process in the South and elsewhere would nonetheless participate in the benefits of the community-action programs."[1]

The merits of the Great Society legislation are still the subject of hot debate. The poverty program in particular has been severely criticized:

177

Most of the programs produced modest results at best because the problems they were designed to treat were not properly defined.

Too many were badly administered due to the lack of experienced personnel.

The various programs deemed components of a comprehensive strategy were poorly coordinated, frequently overlapped, and were wasteful.

The target population often lost interest because the people running the programs promised more than they could deliver.

Supporters of the poverty program, who perceived it as a means to empower the poor, have argued on the other hand that the Vietnam War coopted funds that could have been used effectively in reducing poverty, that citizen participation was never really given a chance, and that, in those cases where poor people achieved some measure of political influence, local officials pressured Washington to cut off funds to them.

Still other commentators not identified with either faction have observed that the community-action programs failed on some fronts but succeeded on others:

In spite of serious budget cutbacks, many community organizations formed in poor neighborhoods have survived and today represent the only viable local institutions in those neighborhoods.

Thousands of people acquired leadership and political skills contributing to the dramatic rise in the number of elected officials from black and Hispanic communities over the past decade and an awareness on the part of politicians everywhere that minority voters cannot be ignored.

An even larger number of minority-group Americans acquired job skills previously denied them and today enjoy important positions in the public and private sectors.

The success of community-owned and -controlled credit unions proved that even low-income neighborhoods can generate financial resources to strengthen local economies.

The Community Action Program also produced some important insights into the nature and scope of the urban crisis and the limitations of government:

Many policymakers were shocked when they discovered that some of the programs they had designed to improve the quality of life in the city—urban renewal and expressway construction—actually destroyed more housing than they built and devastated entire neighborhoods.

The infusion of money channeled to poor neighborhoods through a host of different programs often created chaos, produced dependency on the part of the local people and forced them to accept the priorities of decision makers in Washington.

Finally, many activists and others involved in the Community Action Program began to recognize that people lived in neighborhoods not cities—and that their conservation was vital to the reclamation of depressed urban areas.

The Neighborhood Movement during the Early 1970s

In 1968 Richard Nixon, a man who was ideologically opposed to government playing a major role in revitalizing the cities, was elected president. His favorite urbanologist, Edward Banfield, provided the intellectual rationale for reducing the flow of federal dollars to the cities during what some writers have called eight years of benign neglect:

> Most of the problems that are generally supposed to constitute "the urban crisis" could not conceivably lead to disaster. They are—some of them—important in the sense that a bad cold is important, but they are not serious in the sense that a cancer is serious.[2]

The urban crisis, in other words, was a myth manufactured by well-meaning but naïve do-gooders.

This was bad news for the poor but also for residents of working-class and lower-middle-class neighborhoods that were faced with many of the same problems afflicting their less-affluent neighbors. By the late 1960s they were in desperate need of help too, and when assistance was not forthcoming from government they set about organizing their communities largely through private funding. In less than a decade they would grow in number and quality and provide much of the impetus for what would become known as the neighborhood movement of the 1970s. To provide a proper backdrop for this phenomenon, we must say a few words about recent urban history in the United States.

With the return of millions of GIs after World War II, a trend toward suburbanization, which had gathered steam in the 1920s only to be checked by the Great Depression and the war, resumed in the late 1940s. Growing families, the scarcity of urban housing, the allure of suburban life (which in the minds of many Americans was a sign of "making it"), and the desire to escape racial strife, congestion, declining services, and soaring taxes accounted for one of the most massive migrations in the nation's history. Millions of urbanites, with the help of government housing and transportation legislation, struck out for the suburbs. Many of their old neighborhoods henceforth became home for poor, black, and Hispanic Americans who had been uprooted by the mechanization of agriculture (in the United States and Latin America) and sought work and a brighter future for their children in the cities. Most of their neighborhoods would become targets of the Community Action Program.

A significant number of working-class and lower-middle-class minority urbanites, however, were excluded from such programs. In many cities they lived close to or in the same neighborhoods with white ethnic Americans—the descendants of European immigrants who arrived in massive numbers from the late 1880s to the mid-1920s. In contrast to earlier migrations, most of these newcomers were Roman and Eastern Rite Catholics and Jews from eastern and southern Europe. In search of jobs they congregated primarily in industrial northern cities. Their neighborhoods intrigued the founding fathers of urban sociology at the University of Chicago early in this century.

Like their former teachers in Germany and France, the scholars at Chicago believed that urbanization was destructive of viable communities, breeding alienation and social disorganization. Immigrant neighborhoods were different: most displayed a strong sense of community solidarity, in large part because the residents shared cultural values sustained more or less intact by tight-knit families, ethnic fraternal and welfare societies, and by the trinity of urban ethnic power—the church, the political machine, and the labor union. This situation was also true of those black and Hispanic communities that could count on strong local institutions to mediate between them and the centers of power that operated in the metropolis.

For many years neighborhood political organizations tied to the machine downtown provided access to city hall, served as quasi-welfare agencies, and offered a source of economic mobility. But even at their height the urban machines that practiced the old politics of patronage functioned largely on behalf of individuals and not collectives. The old politics provided divisible benefits—jobs, contracts, and assorted favors—but failed to provide indivisible rewards necessary to check massive housing speculation, the construction of expressways, and urban-renewal schemes.

With the onset of the New Deal and the passage of welfare legislation after World War II, federal agencies henceforth controlled jobs, contracts, and favors that were the urban political machine's lifeline. As the federal government's involvement in urban affairs grew, coalitions involving public administrators and private business enterprises and labor organizations developed. Political scientists have labeled them *functional fiefdoms*, suggesting that their stake in health, housing, education, and other functional areas is a strong common bond that enables them to dominate public policies in their respective areas of interest. In many places residents discovered that the new centers of power were often less sensitive to the needs of their neighborhoods than the old politicians.

To a significant degree, many neighborhoods began to deteriorate when the local political organizations declined. At the same time, suburbanization reduced the power of the churches and local labor organizations whose members were trekking to these new areas in search of homes and jobs.

It was against this backdrop that residents of low-to-moderate-income neighborhoods sought to organize new local institutions to check the threats to their communities, later developed programs to revitalize them, and still later built coalitions with neighborhood organizations across the country to influence national policy. The examples below suggest what has been occurring throughout the United States over the past decade.

Organizing Residents of an Endangered Neighborhood: The Birmingham Neighborhood Coalition, Toledo, Ohio

By the mid-1950s the residents of the predominantly Hungarian-American neighborhood of Birmingham in Toledo, Ohio, began to witness the harm being done to their community by the city's neglect and suburban competition. Some improvements became spotty, the housing stock declined, younger families were forced to purchase homes elsewhere because conventional loans were difficult to secure, and suburban competition hurt local retail businesses. Despite numerous fraternal organizations, church-related associations, and social and political clubs, the neighborhood did not wield much clout at city hall.

In the spring of 1974 the community—led by a loose coalition of residents—successfully fought the closing of the neighborhood's public library. The victory had a bracing effect on the people because it was vivid proof that the neighborhood was not entirely powerless, that by working together Birmingham's residents and local organizations could once again wield power. The community was still celebrating the victory when it was announced that the city intended to build a four-lane overpass across a string of railroad tracks dividing the neighborhood. The city's plans were deeply disturbing for two reasons. First, for over twenty-five years neighborhood spokesmen had urged the city to build a two-lane overpass to facilitate traffic movement to the suburban community of Oregon, where industrial development was on the rise. Secondly, now that the city was prepared to act, it was talking in terms of a four-lane overpass, signifying that the planners intended to widen Consaul Street, perhaps making it a four-lane road. This prospect was especially disconcerting since three of the neighborhood's four churches were located on the street, along with a renowned Hungarian restaurant that attracted customers from all over the city, a lumberyard, the Veterans of Foreign Wars and Knights of Columbus, and a significant number of small businesses and homes. It was estimated that one-third to one-half of the structures on the street would be destroyed, dealing the neighborhood a devastating blow.

This threat prompted local religious and lay leaders representing all segments of the community to form the Birmingham Neighborhood Coalition to fight the overpass. The coalition mobilized a significant portion of the community around the issue and recruited help from former neighborhood residents and unions such as the United Auto Workers and the Teamsters, forcing the city to back down and build the overpass elsewhere.

The decision to build the overpass and make Consual Street a four-lane street made sense to the city's engineers. But their plan demonstrated that, like many urban decision makers, they did not understand the importance of a viable residential neighborhood to the urban system. Preoccupied with engineering and economic criteria, they were prepared to take an action that eventually would destroy a healthy neighborhood, compelling residents and businessmen to relocate elsewhere—most likely outside the city's corporate limits. In the long run Birmingham's destruction would not only have dire social consequences for Toledo, but it would have profound economic implications, too, for the taxes generated by the home owners, residents, and businessmen there were considerable.

The site finally selected to construct the overpass and expressway was in Ironville, one of the first urban-renewal projects undertaken by Toledo. Typically, after the community had been bulldozed and new streets and sewer lines constructed, a significant portion of the cleared land was never developed. The new site meant that the alternative route had to be one-tenth of a mile longer and the overpass itself had to be twice as long as the original one. The cost of the project was somewhat higher, but not one home or business would be destroyed. This site is where the construction should have been planned in the first place. If it had not been for organized grassroots protest, the city would have gone along with the original plan at great cost to the residents of Birmingham and to the city at large.

Moving from Community Organization to Community Development: The Southeast Community Organization, Baltimore, Maryland

The establishment of a viable community organization is a necessary first step in the process of stabilizing a neighborhood and providing a setting where ordinary people, through collective action, can influence decisions affecting their lives. But over time the residents want more than a veto over destructive initiatives; they want to take positive measures that will enable them to revitalize their neighborhood. It is in this connection that the experience of the Southeast Community Organization (SECO) is worthy of examination.

About ninety thousand people live in a six-square-mile quadrant of southeast Baltimore; most of them are white ethnics although a small number are blacks, Indians, and whites from rural Maryland. By the mid-1960s this predominantly blue-collar area was losing industry, small neighborhood businesses, and jobs. The percentage of absentee-owned buildings was rising, as were the number of abandoned dwellings and the area's schools were in advanced stages of neglect. To make matters worse, the city planned to construct an expressway right through the heart of the area. Under these circumstances, many long-time residents and businesses were leaving.

The spectre of the expressway in particular prompted community leaders—clergymen, social workers, and labor leaders—to start working toward the formation of a federation of community groups. An organizer was hired toward that end, and he discovered that despite its numerous problems southeast Baltimore had many strengths. Absentee landlordism was spreading, but over 50 percent of the residents owned their own homes and many who earned middle-class incomes wished to remain in the city even though they had the means to relocate. This attachment to the neighborhood was a plus that could be the basis for community organization. While the traditional institutions were declining, a decision was made to restore or restructure them and bring them together under the umbrella of the proposed federation.

In April 1971 a founding congress was held with seventy local organizations participating and the Southeast Community Organization was born. While SECO received considerable publicity, it had not as yet demonstrated its credibility with the city. This, after all, was at a time when community organizations funded largely with the help of the Office of Economic Opportunity (OEO) were collapsing. There was no reason to believe that SECO, which did not enjoy massive government funding, would fare any better.

Through a series of successful confrontations with local authorities marked by comprehensive research and skilled, determined leadership, SECO gained the respect of city hall and the business community. But, while the ability to muster community power was a necessary first step toward neighborhood stabilization, it was not a sufficient condition for revitalization, involving programs that would reverse the tide of blight that threatened southeast Baltimore's neighborhoods.

SECO's leaders were struck by their inability to move in this direction when on one occasion a landlord who had refused to maintain his buildings offered to give them to SECO. The offer was refused because SECO possessed neither the resources nor the expertise to refurbish the dwellings. On another occasion a community health program SECO had helped develop collapsed when the doctor who owned the facility decided to pull out of the enterprise.

It was with these and similar experiences in mind that SECO concluded it had to develop a programmatic capacity of its own and the means to cooperate with public agencies and private enterprises to secure new investments and more responsive social-service delivery systems for the community. Something had to be done about the decline of decent housing and the flight of small local businesses in particular.

In November 1973, SECO received a $100,000 grant from the Ford Foundation to conduct a community-planning survey. Extensive citizen participation in the survey was a basic requirement of the grant. As expected, one of the problems most often mentioned was the difficulty of securing mortgage and rehabilitation money, which was linked to the decline of formerly strong indigenous savings and loan institutions (S&Ls) and the failure of lending institutions to provide loans to the community.

The urgency to move on this front resulted in SECO's helping to organize the Neighborhood Housing Service (NHS) of Baltimore, a non-profit neighborhood-based corporation, in 1974. With the assistance of the Urban Reinvestment Task Force (a coalition of five federal agencies) the program became operational in 1975 and the Patterson Park community was selected as the pilot neighborhood. During the program's first three years of operation, it achieved the result shown in table 11–1.

Table 11–1
Source and Volume of Loans, Baltimore Neighborhood Housing Service

Source of Loans	Number of Loans	Aggregate Amount
NHS revolving fund	140	$ 608,000
City of Baltimore	62	796,000
Savings and Loan Associations	297	2,552,000
Total loans	499	$3,956,000

In making residential rehabilitation loans, NHS not only provides financial assistance but also helps with the preparation of job specifications and monitors and inspects all work in progress.

Since ownership is viewed as essential to neighborhood stability, NHS has also concentrated on assisting tenants to purchase their homes and attracting new home owners to the Patterson Park area. Through the Homeownership Promotion Program, NHS bought, rehabilitated, and sold seventy-six vacant homes and assisted 245 families to buy homes in the area as of January 1978.

Not wanting to confine its development activities to residential rehabilitation, SECO established Southeast Development, Inc. (SDI), in 1975. SDI is a nonprofit community-development corporation, funded by grants from the Economic Development Administration and the Office of Minority Business Enterprise. Through a number of spin-off corporations, SDI is engaged in a truly comprehensive program of neighborhood revitalization including land banking, health care, commercial revitalization, home maintenance, youth services, and cottage industries. Most of SDI's activities involve creative partnerships between community residents, local government, private lenders, and federal agencies.

Mobilizing Grassroots Organizations to Influence
National Policy: National People's Action

At a time when political pundits in Washington were blaming government programs for contributing to the urban crisis, community activists began to express concern about lending institutions redlining their neighborhoods—that is, refusing to provide mortgage or rehabilitation money to home owners, landlords, and small businessmen in low-to-moderate-income neighborhoods.

In Chicago, a multiracial coalition of community groups operating under the umbrella of the Metropolitan Area Housing Alliance (MAHA), with the assistance of the National Training and Information Center, conducted a survey of lending practices in the city. It revealed that redlining was part of a larger, more insidious enterprise—disinvestment—leading to the eventual destruction of entire neighborhoods. It involved the premeditated transfer of funds from older low-to-moderate-income neighborhoods to more affluent communities elsewhere in the city or in the suburbs or outside the region, in violation of the charters of the savings and loan associations.

The survey indicated that from July 1972 to June 1973 many older neighborhoods received less than three cents in conventional mortgage and rehabilitation money for each dollar they deposited in local S & Ls. During the same period outlying suburbs received over thirty-one cents for every dollar they had on deposit in Chicago S & Ls. A hearing conducted by the Illinois Legislative Investigating Commission found one S & L that offered either FHA or conventional mortgages with 50-percent down payment in its main service area, but offered conventional mortgages with only 10-percent down in suburban communities. Research conducted by neighborhood organizations in a host of cities—Rochester, Baltimore, Cleveland, Washington, D.C.—revealed similar examples of disinvestment.

The outcome of disinvestment is predictable: those who can leave redlined neighborhoods often do so before things get even worse. The people who replace them are primarily poor and minority Americans who cannot afford housing elsewhere or who, denied a suburban residence, get deteriorated housing at grossly inflated prices. Even those who are lucky enough to purchase a sound dwelling are not spared; the presence of abandoned and/or run-down buildings—inevitable components of disinvestment—helps legitimize disinvestment practices. In many cities, for example, insurance companies will not provide protection to home owners or businessmen next door to an abandoned building.

In 1972, 300 community organizations from 110 cities representing white, black, and Hispanic neighborhoods formed the National People's Action (NPA) to carry the fight for neighborhood conservation and revitalization to the national level. NPA, with the assistance of the National Center for Urban Ethnic Affairs bombarded Congress with data supporting the charge that disinvestment was a national practice responsible for the decline of countless neighborhoods. As a result of this effort the Home Mortgage Disclosure Act of 1976, requiring lending institutions, among other things, to provide information pertinent to their lending practices, was enacted.

The men and women in what was to be dubbed the neighborhood movement of the 1970s urged elected officials, policymakers, and urbanologists in and out of academia to recognize that the conservation and revitalization of residential neighborhoods were vital to the larger task of reclaiming the nation's older cities. They pointed out that, with the decline of center-city residential neighborhoods, a host of predictably grim consequences are set into motion.

> Neighborhoods bonded by a sense of community, of sharing and caring, are lost, along with jobs, business revenues, and property taxes, denying local jurisdictions funds needed to care for disadvantaged residents and to provide services other citizens expect and deserve.

> In areas where they serve as buffer zones protecting more affluent communities from urban blight, middle-class residents flee to what they think are safe harbors distant from the disease, leaving in their wake neighborhoods manipulated by speculators. Home owners in the old neighborhood, meanwhile, are frightened into selling their homes at deflated prices—and even less fortunate persons purchasing them at inflated prices often have to default; in a few short years they become unfit for human habitation.

> In many cities and close suburbs the presence of endangered neighborhoods fosters a climate of despair causing industry, retail businesses, lending institutions, and home owners who may be far from the afflicted areas to leave because the community has no future.

> For all the preceding reasons, public and private reclamation programs in the pipeline or under consideration are put in grave jeopardy, often making certain that funds for housing, education, health, and other vital needs will be wasted, poorly utilized, or only serve as temporary solutions to deep-seated problems.

Although the media, policymakers, and the informed public began to speak favorably about neighborhoods and the need to conserve and revitalize them in the last years of the Nixon and Ford administrations, there were many commentators in both major political parties who dismissed ambitious neighborhood programs. The basis for this position was that the older cities were no longer economically viable and to plug their declining neighborhoods into federal life-support systems was an unconscionable act prolonging the pain of a terminal patient.

The Carter Administration and the Neighborhood Movement

In 1978, for the first time, President Carter provided a comprehensive set of policies to guide federal actions and programs for urban areas in the United States. It is noteworthy that he titled his draft describing his proposed urban policy, "A New Partnership To Conserve America's Communities," clearly signifying in his own words that "It represents a long-term commitment to the revitalization of America's communities." Indeed, one of the administration's nine urban-policy objectives was to "stimulate greater involvement by neighborhood organizations and voluntary associations" in all stages of the urban policymaking process.

The New Partnership alluded to reflects the fact that government cannot solve all of the nation's problems. It is based upon the conviction that local business, labor, and neighborhood and voluntary associations, in conjunction with public agencies, must work together to eliminate unemployment, crime, physical blight, and other problems afflicting communities throughout the United States.

It was with this objective in mind that the president formed a new agency in the Department of Housing and Urban Development—the Office of Neighborhood Voluntary Associations and Consumer Protection. Its mission was to work with local suburban and rural self-help organizations, not just center-city neighborhoods. Many commentators continue to speak of the urban crisis exclusively in terms of center cities, but it has begun to dawn on an increasing number of suburbanites and residents of rural areas that the problems they have associated with the inner city have reached them.

Residents of close-in suburbs and small rural towns are encountering physical blight, rising crime rates, declining services, and the destruction of commercial strips. To their dismay they also are discovering that they are powerless to do anything about the decline of their communities. The taxpayers' revolt presently preoccupying the media in the United States suggests that things are not going well in the most distant and affluent suburban subdivisions either. The absence of focused, coherent planning and the capacity of strategically placed private interests to dominate what has served a land-use policy have contributed to suburban sprawl—the symptoms of which include ecological deterioration, wasteful duplication of services, and soaring taxes to pay for roads and utility hook-ups over a widely disperse area.

The new Neighborhood Office's mission was to serve as an advocate for community organizations and other self-help associations within the federal government and to encourage agencies to revise, coordinate, and expand their programs to assist them. The office worked closely with state and local government to coordinate intergovernmental neighborhood-conservation activities. Another vital function was to provide technical assistance directly to neighborhood organizations so they could better utilize their resources and take advantage of public programs.

Finally, the Office of Neighborhood Voluntary Associations and Consumer Protection functioned as a clearinghouse for information pertinent to local self-help organizations, to provide data and models that can be used by them and by government agencies throughout the United States.

In addition to HUD, other federal agencies were involved in building local neighborhood organizations. To mention only a sample:

ACTION, through its urban volunteer program, placed volunteers in communities to help them conduct research, take surveys, and perform other tasks that neighborhood groups with slim budgets need done.

Another neighborhood-oriented effort at ACTION was its minigrant program, which provided modest funding to local communities to cover the costs of tools, supplies, materials, and administrative support to carry out voluntary projects.

A third federal program, designed specifically to deal with disinvestment, is administered by the Neighborhood Reinvestment Corporation. It is conducting a survey of community organizations to develop models that neighborhoods, along with local lending institutions, can employ to reinvest in communities that have been stricken by redlining.

These are just a few examples of the actions the Carter administration took to build viable neighborhoods in cooperation with state and local governments and private enterprises and institutions. In 1977 the president appointed a National Commission on Neighborhoods comprised of community activists, elected officials, scholars, and businessmen. It was charged with the job of undertaking ''a comprehensive study and investigation of the factors contributing to the decline of city neighborhoods and of the factors necessary to neighborhood survival and revitalization.'' The commissioners traveled to neighborhoods throughout the country consulting with local leaders, residents, businessmen, and elected officials and conducted in-depth research on all aspects of neighborhood decline and measures that can be taken to reverse that trend. The commission's findings published in 1979 remain an important agenda for action, still largely unimplemented.

The Carter administration's conviction that neighborhoods must be a centerpiece of national urban policy was both a matter of pragmatism and principle. At present, there are an estimated fifteen thousand community organizations in urban, suburban, and rural communities throughout the United States. Some are merely block clubs representing a handful of families who have joined together to keep the areas around their homes and apartments clean, to fight crime, or to complain to local officials with the power of a collective voice. At the other end of the spectrum are community-development corporations with million-dollar budgets, large well-trained staffs, and sophisticated long-range plans. They are involved in inducing development, the restoration of neighborhood business strips, the construction and rehabilitation of housing, job training, and other programs that are components of comprehensive community-controlled and operated enterprises. By way of their numbers alone, government cannot ignore them.

Another practical feature of their existence is that they have produced impressive results. For example, nongovernmental cooperatives and other privately funded community enterprises in New York City have constructed and refurbished more homes than the city has since the end of World War II. Local organizations are now conducting health-care, job-training, senior-citizen, and many other programs that are desperately needed in fiscally strapped cities. Recent experiences with community organizations also demonstrate that they are essential to the design and implementation of viable public policies. The site selected by the neighborhood organization in Toledo for the construction of an overpass proved to be a much better choice than the one local officials had favored. In Newark, New Jersey, a Puerto Rican community was encouraged by the city to construct a park reflecting the residents' Hispanic heritage. When finished it closely resembled the kind of plaza one would find in Puerto Rico rather than the United States. In communities throughout the United States, such local input will greatly improve public planning.

Neighborhood Organizations and Citizen Participation in Advanced Industrial Societies

In addition to the preceding practical considerations, the Carter administration was committed to empowering people in their communities as a matter of principle. The grassroots movement in the United States and its counterpart in western Europe are a reaction to the centralization of political and economic power peculiar to all advanced industrial societies. When they were relatively small and predominantly agricultural, the family and community performed many functions—educating and training the young, protecting members against economic hard times and ill health, and serving as instruments of social control—that the state largely performs today. To avoid devastating economic crises and to manage a massive, complex economy, the state also has had to perform functions that were previously the preserve of private economic enterprises. People in western Europe and the United States are attempting to cope with this phenomenon by organizing at the grassroots. The concentration of economic power in the hands of corporate Leviathans that dominate many areas of public policy is another important motivation for local organizing. What we are observing is an attempt to come to grips with a crisis of accountability; many voters and consumers feel helpless to do anything about political or economic decisions that affect the quality of life. Through grassroots organizations they are searching for new avenues of access to centers of power.

Finally, as Alexis de Tocqueville, one of the most perceptive observers of democratic societies, noted almost 150 years ago, the concept of citizenship is born and nurtured in local communities. At a time when economic difficulties and the stresses and strains of life in the nuclear age are threatening the civic bonds that hold democratic societies together, we must make every effort to strengthen them.

In this connection, Robert Nisbet has observed that the real problem of modern democracies is the failure to "create new contexts of association and moral cohesion within which the smaller allegiances of men will assume both functional and psychological significance."[3] Perhaps grassroots organizations like the ones described in this chapter will provide the mechanisms around which citizens can coalesce and, through collective self-help endeavors, find new social and psychological significance to their lives.

Notes

1. Daniel P. Moynihan, *Maximum Feasible Misunderstanding: Community Action In The War On Poverty* (New York: Vintage, 1967), p. 44.

2. Edward Banfield, *The Unheavenly City Revisited* (Boston: Little, Brown, 1968), p. 6.

3. Robert Nisbet, *Community and Power* (New York: Oxford University Press, 1962), p. 73.

12 Neighborhood Policy: An Alternative to the Dominant Conception of Neighborhoods

Robert B. Hawkins, Jr.

The contents of this chapter were originally presented at a meeting of the University Consortium for Neighborhood Research and Development. As chairman of then-President-elect Reagan's Task Force on Neighborhoods, I had been asked to speak on issues of neighborhoods. Then, as now, I had been a long-time supporter of limited, yet real, neighborhood governance (a proposition that finds little support in the belief systems of academics, policymakers, or neighborhood groups whose survival depends on federal monies). Two years later, this statement seems as sound as it did then. And since it does, it is worth spending some time on the practical reasons why this is so.

While many neighborhood activists will state that the lack of interest displayed by the Reagan administration on neighborhoods merely reflects its ideological bias, the reasons are, of course, much deeper. In fact, one can argue quite strongly that the Reagan philosophy and administration would gain considerable political advantage by pursuing an aggressive policy on neighborhoods. However, the Reagan policy on neighborhoods is an issue for state and local governments and not the federal government. But, the point is even more basic: neighborhoods have never been high on the nation's agenda. When one ranks the perceived importance of neighborhoods against other issues in Washington, even the most ardent neighborhood supporter must accept the low ranking. Notice that the word *perceived* is used for an argument that the health of the nation is, in large part, dependent upon strong and healthy neighborhoods. This is a proposition nearing the status of a self-evident truth. We must take this proposition into account as we deal with the issues of neighborhood governance, citizens' opportunity to invest in themselves at the neighborhood level, and how we think about relationships between neighborhoods and other units of governments.

Anyone reading President Reagan's Neighborhood Task Force recommendations, will be struck by two facts.[1] First, the report clearly recommends a number of policy changes that will increase the opportunities and fiscal resources that citizens in neighborhoods have to invest in themselves and their communities. Clearly, the Task Force was trying to get away from bureaucratic and top-down schemes that have showed so little success in the past. Second, the report is strangely silent on the issue of neighborhood governance. In part this silence is a function of members feeling that governance is a state-local responsibility but also, in part, a function of conventional wisdom. It is precisely this conventional wisdom that requires us to discuss neighborhoods and neighborhood policy in a new and fundamental way; in a way that at least opens the possibility of thinking about neighborhoods as limited, yet viable, political economies. If we are willing to entertain this possibility, then we must also place such concerns within the context of U.S. federalism. For example, we must think in terms of constitutions for neighborhoods and the implications of self-governing institutions on the health and welfare of neighborhoods. The importance of rethinking neighborhoods and neighborhood issues is to be found in the very nature of the policy process in a nation committed to pluralism and self-governing institutions. Policy is about choices and the policy process is about making rational choices. To make choices, citizens or policymakers must be able to assess the capabilities and implement a policy.[2]

Needed: A New Conception of Neighborhoods

If citizens and policymakers are to have choices then we must have an alternative to the dominant conception of neighborhoods. The prevailing conception is one of neighborhoods as voluntary or administrative agencies that work through or with city, state, and federal administrative agencies. Great efforts are made to integrate neighborhoods into what might be called a national system of policy, administration, and grants. There is almost no distinction between governance and policy, an indication of the degree to which managerial concepts dominate our thinking about possible ways of organizing our political societies.[3] Even as one reads through the report of the National Commission on Neighborhoods, he is struck by the relative lack of interest in questions of governance and the overriding interest given to federal policy and how it can be made more responsive and effective.[4]

There is little merit in arguing that there is no federal role because there is a limited role. The role of the federal government can only be addressed when we have some notion of what it is that neighborhoods are about and what role they should play in governing local communities. However, there are real problems with conceptualizing neighborhoods as merely administrative cogs in the federal system. Besides problems of cooptation and administrative coordination, there are very serious political and moral problems. One of the key presumptions of the U.S.

experiment in self-governance is that citizens, through reflection and choice, can create, maintain, and change their governmental institutions.[5] The political presumption is clear: citizens should be involved in the constitutional questions of establishing and abolishing units of government. The moral imperative is one that runs deep in our Western liberal tradition: societies of men have an obligation to be responsible for their own lives and for their collective institutions. It can also be argued that the imperatives of citizenship are developmental ones that must be exercised like any other capacity, through experience. Thus, institutions created and maintained by administrative fiat suffer very serious problems of legitimacy, plus they short-circuit important political processes that create and maintain citizenship. They also short-circuit political processes that can create the needed consensus to implement policy. One of the clear findings from recent studies on implementation is that a necessary ingredient for successful administration is political consensus within a given community.[6] Just as important are the implicit economic implications of citizenship in the above notions. George Borts's definition of a region as "one where citizens will voluntarily accept a low return on capital or labor in order to remain in the region," is clearly a minimal definition of a neighborhood. However, for sustainable political associations to emerge there must be opportunities for citizens to exercise their authority. Thus, we must be clearly cognizant of the opportunity structure needed to allow neighborhoods to become viable entities and for citizens to invest in themselves.

There is also a profound need to rethink the ways units of government in our federal system effect one another. Growing dependence upon federal authority and federal dollars is not a healthy state of affairs. As Norton Long has noted, "a nation of dependent cities cannot be an independent nation."[7] I would argue that the same logic prevails between cities and neighborhoods. Thus, the goal of any national research strategy on neighborhoods should include conceptualizing and thinking about neighborhoods as limited, yet independent, actors in the federal system, and to developing conceptions of neighborhoods that provide information on the capabilities and limitations of different alternatives for neighborhood governance and administration.

Toward a Federal Theory of Neighborhoods

An alternative to the managerial notion of neighborhoods is to be found in the political foundations of U.S. federalism. Daniel J. Elazar has noted that the key principle of federalism is "the distribution of power to a number of quasi-independent centers of authority," while the key operating principle is "self-rule through shared rule."[8] How do we move from this general definition to a justification for limited neighborhood governance? The answer is to be found in the nature of public goods and services and in the limitations of government institutions. For the last fifty years the rational form of governmental organization has been the large, consolidated local government. One capable, at least theoretically, of realizing economies of scale and effective government—and one that is responsive.[9] Likewise, such a unit, it was predicted, could plan rationally, internalize externalities, allocate scarce public resources among competing demands, and minimize the need for state-federal intervention because of its expanded tax base. We cannot go into all of the arguments against this theory; however, we can point out a few examples where there are justifications for some limited neighborhood governance:

> There are few economies of scale in local government services and these generally occur in capital-intensive services.[10]

> Local services, such as police, have many subfunctions, some of which can be produced just as, or more efficiently, at the neighborhood level.[11]

> Government services that are client-centered may well benefit from being produced by institutions that are rooted in local governing institutions.

> Finally, there is a suspicion, backed by some evidence, that especially poor neighborhoods may not get back what they pay for through taxes.

Each of these areas suggests that there are at least rational grounds for consideration of some form of governing structure at the neighborhood level.

The Political Foundations of Neighborhoods

The political foundations of neighborhoods are not to be found in the planner's matrix of traffic flows, spheres of influence, or conjunction of vital services. While these are important factors, they are also the very stuff of administration—allowing administrative factors to define the political. These myriad factors are the primary reason that one can read many articles with different definitions and means of determining the boundaries of a neighborhood. The political method of determining neighborhoods is indeterminate in terms of planner's criteria, yet more determinate in outcome. The foundation of any neighborhood is a function of community expressed through communities of interest. The key question is: How does one aggregate these communities of interest? If one is consistent with the rules that have dominated the formation of self-governing institutions through most of U.S. history then what is needed are political rules that allow citizens to begin the process. Before outlining some of these rules, let me state one important caveat. Since neighborhoods differ on many grounds, the most important being their desire for a particular type of political empowerment, citizens need access to a number of different political instruments if their choice-making process is to be rational and if they are to have any chance of producing a public institution that is responsive to their needs.

The most basic political question is first constitutional: How do neighborhoods constitute themselves as political enterprises? Vincent Ostrom has noted four requisite elements for what he terms the constitution of self-governing public enterprises. They are:

A public good that is shared and of sufficient magnitude to create interdependence among a large number of users produces the necessary interest for the creation of public enterprise.

Public facilities or institutions are subject to use under terms and conditions that are considered by the relevant community to be reasonably designed to meet their common welfare.

A bureaucracy is immediately accountable to the relevant community of interest for which it is acting.

The costs of providing a service are funded by the constituents in proportion to their benefits.[12]

I would add a fifth criterion:

Any public enterprise created through the normal political processes of petition and election, should be relatively free from state or city constraint.

While these criteria suggest the operational principles for neighborhood governance and tests for the emergence of significant interest to warrant their creation, we must still ask the question: By what authority can they be constituted? It is clear that most city charters or state constitutions do not convey the needed authority to undertake such enterprises. And, it is precisely the states, rather than the national government, that become the key political entities in considering questions of neighborhood governance. States determine the rules of the game by which public enterprises are created, maintained, and operated. Through state constitutions and state enabling acts the needed authority to operate, at liberty, is conveyed to citizens or local governments.

Unfortunately, little attention has been paid to this aspect of urban policy. There are numerous reasons for this state of affairs. States have been seen as unresponsive by most groups seeking redress to the problems that plague low-income and minority communities. I think this contention is generally true but for the wrong reasons. States, by and large, have been conditioned by the managerial ethic to see consolidation and hierarchical relationships as most efficient and responsive. They are also, many times, the captives of local-government lobbies that do not want the possible competition of formerly constituted neighborhoods. I would also argue that the tendency of most groups to seek solutions to neighborhood problems in Washington is a direct function of the policy of most states to create monopolies out of local governments. I know of no state today that endorses a policy of a competitive local-government system. As liberty to form and maintain local governments has subsided, we have seen a movement toward solutions based on administrative relationships and court-imposed equity

What are the critical policy questions that need to be addressed to a federal theory of neighborhoods? The overriding question of policy is: How do we develop means by which citizens of neighborhoods see it in their self-interest to form political communities and make investments in themselves? What is ironic about most neighborhood action is that it is voluntary and outside the public realm. Yet most of such activity is inherently public and should, in many cases, be synonymous with a public entity. How one rejoins community and political authority is thus the central question of neighborhood research. I would argue that we must adopt an experimental posture toward meeting this question both in theory and practice. One step in that direction is to create, through state constitutions or enabling acts, a broad range of political and governmental opportunities so that citizens have the ability to choose between alternative forms of governance. If this is the case, then we need information on the following:

What types of political and governmental forms can be utilized by neighborhoods? Here we need to look at experience. Since we have limited experience with neighborhood governance, we should look at the experience and record of special-district governments. District government is particularly relevant since neighborhoods, by definition, will have a limited range of interests and capacities. We need to know the capabilities and limitations of various types of district governments and how they can be adapted to the needs of neighborhoods. Also, we should begin to understand the role of states in drafting, implementing, and changing such enabling acts in light of various weaknesses that appear.

We should also gain a better understanding of the various forms of governance that can and should be used. Since problems, interests, and capabilities differ we should have recourse to a number of enabling acts—from community-service districts providing a broad range of services to the need for single-purpose entities or taxing districts to be understood and designed, or adapted, for use within cities.

Finally, we need to address a range of questions regarding the political capability of neighborhood governments. How should they be formed—by what processes and by what majorities? Further, we must have some idea of how they should be maintained, how they should be financed, and how they can be dissolved. Externally, we must have some idea as to their limitations in relationship to other units of government. Politically, it is clear—the questions of civil rights, discrimination, and the general principles of representative government take precedent over the preferences of neighborhoods. Just as clearly, in an interdependent society, no unit of neighborhood governance can have unilateral authority. How one balances these different interests is a question of policy that cannot be answered in the first instance. Enabling acts are not infallible and we can only adopt a posture of learning that suggests that such acts must be changed as problems arise and unintended consequences occur. Again, experience needs to be assessed to ascertain how these processes can be instituted so that we develop self-correcting processes.

The Neighborhood as a Political Economy: Methods of Fiscal Empowerment

The critical question of neighborhoods as economies is a simple one: How do citizens invest in themselves? An ancillary question is: How do other units of government invest in neighborhoods without the debilitating effects of cooptation and perverse results? To make sound decisions, citizens and policymakers need information that presently does not exist or is not in a form that is usable. Specifically, we need to know:

What is a neighborhood economy and how is it distinguished for a city or regional economy?

What are the economic resources of a neighborhood and how are private and public resources invested in our poor neighborhoods?

What are the tax resources of the neighborhood and how are those resources invested back into the community?

Once we have information on the above, the critical questions of institutional design emerge. Again, we need to have some idea about the capacity and limitations of alternative institutional arrangements for using scarce public resources efficiently and responsively. Key questions are:

What range of institutions can be used, how do they integrate with other institutions, and what are their limitations?

What are the tax resources of neighborhoods and what types of state enabling acts exist or are required to allow neighborhood institutions to use those monies effectively and responsively?

How can financing be provided by city, state, and federal agencies that mitigates many of the problems associated with traditional programmatic methods? Specifically, vehicles such as tax credits, improvement vouchers, and matching of local taxing efforts should be given serious considerations.

**Some Thoughts on Practical Models
for Neighborhood Governance**

Before outlining some practical models or alternative-policies mechanisms for neighborhoods, a few preparatory comments are needed. First, it would be a mistake of the old national-planning perspective to assume that every neighborhood wants some form of neighborhood governing structure or that it needs one. Just as importantly, it would be a mistake to assume that there is one rational model that can fit all neighborhoods. This area points to a second requirement: we need to have multiple options when thinking about the institutional alternatives for neighborhoods. Also, we must keep in mind that we are not trying to recreate the Greek city-state but rather a limited, yet viable, set of institutional mechanisms that will strengthen local neighborhoods while not placing governmental burdens on them that are beyond their capacities.

Finally, there is one last point of design that reflects my bias but that, nonetheless, has important implications of neighborhoods, service delivery, and the need for neighborhood governing mechanisms. One of the reasons there is a strong need for neighborhood governing mechanisms is that most cities are impregnable public monopolies in which city officials and administrative officials do not want to compete for neighborhood groups. If this is a true representation of most large urban areas, then tremendous gains can be made merely by providing citizens with the enabling acts to form neighborhood institutions. In such an institutional setting, one can imagine citizen groups creating negotiating strategies that work on the self-interest of public officials to provide responsive services in return for *not* forming neighborhoods. What occurs when the institutional incentives are changed is a lowering of the trans- action costs that neighborhood citizens must pay to obtain satisfactory responses from their local officials and administrators. In a word, neigh- borhood citizens would no longer be captives, they would be more equal in negotiations with local officials.

Yet there are a number of instances where some form of empower- ment to neighborhoods is required. Here we outline several options that are consistent with our notion. Each of these models is offered to remedy a common set of problems often associated with demands for some form of neighborhood organization.

Municipal-Service District

An often-heard complaint is that either the wrong services are provided to a neighborhood or the wrong levels are provided. Furthermore, the argument is continued to suggest that local officials, administrators, or employee unions will not allow for the proper mix of services to be provided to the neighborhood. The purpose of a *municipal-service district* would be to provide citizens with the necessary authority to change the mix and level of local services.

How would such a district be conceptualized? The simplest and most direct approach would be to give neighborhood citizens the right to form a municipal-service district that would have the right to determine how 10 percent of its total property tax would be spent on services. The monies earmarked by this district would provide a board of directors with the needed revenues to negotiate effectively with city officials. In other words, these monies would provide the critical marginal dollars to affect service allocations significantly over a broad range of functions.

The state enabling act for forming such a district would establish the rules and procedures. It might well follow the rules set down by the California State Legislature for forming municipal-service districts. The process of forming a district would be started by citizens through the circulation of petitions that are then submitted to the respective city for verification. In California a valid petition requires the signatures of 10 percent of the citizens of a proposed district. The petition would contain a description of the services desired or to be changed, the boundaries of the proposed district, and an estimate of the revenues to be generated by the 10-percent allocation.

Upon receipt of the petition, the city would verify the boundaries and estimates and then would hold a public hearing to take testimony on the proposed district. At a specified time, an election would be held to form the district and to select officers. Officers of the district would either be appointed from recognized groups in the areas or through formal election when the district is formed.

The financing of such districts is straightforward. Low-income communities would have increased control over the provision of services into their communities. Federal programs might be directed to such districts through cash grants to city-districts whereby the use of those monies would be negotiated rather than being dictated by administrative regulations or coopted at city hall. Federal policy might also give tax credits or rebates to such districts for the purchase of needed services.

The limitation of such districts is that they are merely mechanisms to change the incentives of existing political and service-delivery coalitions. They would not have the capacity to deliver their own services. However, if we assume that time is a scarce commodity, the most rational use of time by neighborhood citizens might be to negotiate from a position of strength with existing service providers rather than forming their own unit of government.

Limited Neighborhood Government

To increase the effectiveness and negotiating power of the municipal-services district it is important that the citizens have the option of forming a limited-purpose neighborhood government. If one criterion of design is to provide citizens with numerous design options, then the most attractive and existing government structure is what is called, in many states, the *community-services district*. The community-services district has been used in numerous states to allow citizens in unincorporated areas to exercise a wide range of governmental powers and to provide a variety of services. It was first created in California in 1955 and has been used in other states by different names.[13] In Florida, it is called the *improvement district*. These districts are enabled by state statute to provide a broad range of services. In California, they have been empowered to provide almost every municipal service, except general-policy powers; they have no formal powers in areas such as permits, code enforcement, eminent domain, and planning. Yet, the Florida Reddy Creek Improvement District has been granted these powers.

Citizens are empowered and must start the formation process by circulating a petition specifying what services will be performed by the districts, the boundaries of the district, and how the services will be financed. In California, once 10 percent of the citizens in the proposed district have signed the petition, the county board of supervisors must hold a hearing of certification. Assuming that protests are resolved, inclusions and exclusions into the new district are made and the county must call an election to determine the question of formation and to elect officials to the new district. The role of the citizen continues after formation. State law requires that citizens must vote on the addition of new services, and they must vote to increase taxes past a certain limit.

The fiscal capacity of these districts is considerable. They may levy a property tax within limits, levy service charges, issue general obligation and revenue bonds, and may also utilize assessment-bond financing. They are also able to establish zones of benefit so that they can respond to special interests by requiring that they pay for special services.

Community-service districts are also empowered to enter into contracts with other units of government and the private sector. Through contract, they can perform general-policy-power functions of county governmnent; they can contract with a county to grant permits, enforce codes, and they can develop advisory boards to assist the county in planning.

While the powers of such a district are clearly sufficient and they allow for a neighborhood governing institutions to development around one issue or service before taking on other functions, there are clearly political and intergovernmental issues that must be addressed. Clearly such an option will threaten local elected officials and legislators. Regardless of how overtaxed or incapable a local government may be, the political realities will make it difficult to institutionalize neighborhood governance with significant development of the issue, plus active support by state and national leaders. Likewise, issues of coordination and service delivery will have to be addressed, more at the level of actual problems than at the level of theory.

The aforementioned models are merely two general options. One could think of many more. The use of the joint powers of cities and counties could well be used to establish neighborhood-governmental entities with significant authority and financial capability. What is critical is that we begin to work with the notion of how we allocate authority, power, and decision-making capabilities in ways that meet the political needs of diverse communities of interest, while taking into account the very real issues of service delivery and coordination. Yet, for too long administrative needs have dictated how political communities will be represented—this obviously must change.

Conclusion

I argue that what we may need is a national strategy for neighborhoods that denationalizes the neighborhood question. The most important goal must be to provide a sound, local institutional setting for neighborhoods. It must be both political and economic. Citizens in neighborhoods must have access to opportunities that allow them to choose between a range of governmental options—options that include fiscal resources that are, in the first instance, locally generated so that staff and projects have local support. Second, assistance from up-stream governments must be designed so that it does not skew local priorities or create perverse incentives so that local administrations are coopted by state or federal agencies. Only when these conditions are met can we talk about *neighborhood government* rather than *neighborhood administration*. Research can provide critical information needed to make important institutional choice.

The problem we face is within the neighborhood movement. Do we want to base our effort on the goal of self-governance, realizing that it will be a long road, or do we merely want to refine a system that is no longer a system in any meaningful sense of that word? In the words of Alexander Hamilton, "Do we want to base good government on reflection and choice, or do we want our constitutions to be based on accident or force?"

Notes

1. Neighborhood Advisory Group to President-elect Ronald Reagan, "Neighborhood Policy" (Washington, D.C., 1980).

2. Vincent Ostrom, *The Political Theory of a Compound Republic* (Blacksburg, Va.: Center for Public Choice, 1971).

3. Vincent Ostrom, *The Intellectual Crisis of American Public Administration* (Tuscaloosa: University of Alabama Press, 1973).

4. Robert B. Hawkins, Jr., and Charles D. Hobbs, *Alternative Models for Fiscal Empowerment* (Washington, D.C.: National Commission on Neighborhoods, 1978).

5. Alexander Hamilton, "The Federalist No. 1," in *The Federalist*, edited by Jacob E. Cooke. (Middletown, Conn.: Wesleyan University Press, 1961).

6. Aaron Wildavsky and Jeffrey L. Pressman, *Implementation* (Berkeley: University of California Press, 1973).

7. Norton E. Long, *The City as a Political Economy* (St. Louis: Center for Community. Metropolitan Studies, University of Missouri, 1972).

8. Daniel J. Elazar, *American Federalism, a View from the States* (New York: Thomas Y. Crowell Company, 1972).

9. Robert L. Bish and Vincent Ostrom, *Understanding Urban Government: Metropolitan Reform Reconsidered* (Washington, D.C.: American Enterprise Institute, 1972); and Elinor Ostrom, *Scale of Production and the Problems of Service Delivery in a Federal System* (Bloomington: Workshop for Political Theory and Policy Analysis, 1974).

10. Governor's Task Force on Local Government Reform, *Public Benefits from Public Choice* (Bloomington: Workshop in Political Theory and Policy Analysis, 1974).

11. Elinor Ostrom; Roger B. Parks; and Gordon P. Whitaker, "Do We Really Want to Consolidate Urban Policy Forces? A Reappraisal of Some Old Assertions" in *Public Administration Review* (September/October 1973):423–433.

12. Vincent Ostrom, *An Alternative Approach to the Design of Public Organizational Arrangements* (Bloomington: Workshop in Political Theory and Policy Analysis, 1972).

13. West's Annotated California Codes, 1966, Sections 60000–60160, "Taxes Generated in District and Feedback."

13 Toward the Practice of Neighborhood Planning

Phillip L. Clay and
Robert M. Hollister

The preceding chapters have covered various aspects of U.S. neighborhoods. They discuss both new trends and old issues that have been recast to reflect current concerns and social changes. As the chapter by Albert Hunter in part I points out, interest in neighborhoods is not new. At different times in recent decades neighborhoods have received a great deal of intellectual attention and have been of some professional interest. Looked at this way, neighborhood interest might be viewed as an intellectual and professional fad. We might expect that in a few years attention will be directed once again toward the region or the metropolitan area. Instead of calls for neighborhood empowerment we might hear calls as we did in the 1950s for metropolitan government, or the calls of a few years ago for substate regionalism or multistate regional-level planning.

What has emerged in recent years, and is reflected in many ways throughout this book, is the importance of social meaning in public policy—both in physical planning and in institutional planning. U.S. neighborhoods remain vitally important social and political units, and a better understanding of neighborhood dynamics is a powerful contribution to a number of policy dilemmas. While federal policy toward neighborhoods continues to be hotly contested, the past two decades of federal programs have spurred the development of an impressive array of neighborhood-based organizations. These groups—ranging from residents' associations to multiservice centers and community-development corporations—now comprise a vital part of the national infrastructure. Their needs and potential, documented persuasively in the chapter by Neil Mayer, reaffirm the efficacy of planning at the neighborhood level. Moreover, the recent phenomenon of neighborhood revitalization reflects the important role individuals play.[1]

At the level of political symbolism and in the vocabulary of policy debate, the *neighborhood* floats in and out of popularity. It was a cornerstone of the Carter national urban policy, then wholly absent from the Reagan agenda. Yet for the lives of U.S. citizens, neighborhood needs and issues are constant and enduring. Tracing the evolution of public policy from the 1960s to the 1980s, the important policy choices show more similarity than difference.

While planners have tried to do broad-aimed planning for small areas in the past, they have often dealt with a narrow range of issues or only part of the population (that is, capital improvements, housing for the elderly, community services, rehabilitation, and such). The increased discretion granted to local governments through federal grants and the necessity to make comprehensive allocational assessments suggest that planning will have to break out of this narrow mold and replace segmented planning with more comprehensive attention to local needs.

We are further reminded of the experience with the ambitious, multiple-goal urban programs of the 1960s. Through the Model Cities Program and various housing and community-development initiatives, significant efforts were made to improve neighborhoods only to find that after a few years the physical improvements were undone and the social pathology had not been relieved. Programs were designed (in Washington) and services were delivered by intermediaries (that is, developers, social workers, consultants, and so on). The role of the neighborhood and neighborhood residents in the planning process was minimal despite lip service to citizen participation. Since the long-term benefit of certain improvements required that the residents have some sense of feeling for the changes, improvements were often undone by residents who felt no stake in the planning process or the changes that were made.

If the lesson in these experiences is that we should take into account the social and contextual dimension of planning, then we are led to what we will call in this chapter *neighborhood planning*. It is planning that is concerned with generating certain physical changes in small areas through a partnership of the residents (or their organizations), the private sector, and, of course, the public sector.

Contemporary theory offers scant guidance to this emerging notion of neighborhood planning. The purpose of this chapter is to identify and elaborate on some issues in neighborhood planning based on recent documented experience. We do not mean to offer theory here nor are we able to be definitive about paradigms of practice. That must await both more research and more reflection on practice.

Elements of Neighborhood Planning

While it would be premature to call neighborhood planning a fully developed field, the processes of goal-setting and action at the neighborhood level have matured greatly and become quite pervasive and broadly accepted. Therefore it seems appropriate to chart the outlines of neighborhood planning as an emerging field of practice. The major elements of neighborhood planning have been identified from the activities cities actually participate in as part of efforts to plan for neighborhood development. For each of the major practice areas we present some of the major theoretical and analytical issues that are relevant to particular elements of planning practice.

The elements of such a concern include the following, which are discussed in detail below: priority setting and goals, resource allocation, population-change management, models of citizen participation, regulatory policy, and public/private interface.

Priority Setting and Goals

During most of the last two decades, the development activity of cities was focused on the downtown and some central-area nonresidential projects, often results of the urban renewal program. These were aimed at removing blight, improving the tax base, or providing new facilities for government or institutions. While some residential construction and rehabilitation took place, this activity was secondary to the development of office, retail, hotel, recreational, and convention uses that were designed to increase the fiscal capacity of cities to compete with suburban areas.

Residential reinvestment in the downtown was often viewed as a way of rounding out the activities or taking advantage of what was viewed as a relatively small market. Rarely did the extensive attention paid to the downtown or the extensive private development in the downtown extend away from the core to traditional neighborhoods of low- and moderate-income families.

The present concern for neighborhood planning is specifically a concern for these traditional neighborhoods, and the interest focuses primarily on the needs of low- or moderate-income families. Engaging in development in these neighborhoods is not primarily aimed at improving the economic base or generating jobs or increasing commercial or industrial opportunities, but rather it is aimed at improving the living conditions and residential environment of city residents in existing housing. Since the job of economic development and development of the central business district is still an on-going task and the resources for development often come from the same rather-limited pot (Community Development Block Grants, Urban Development Action Grants, and such), cities are forced to make choices. Cities must choose between investment in the downtown, which in some cities is beginning to pay off in a reversal of blight (at least for a limited part of the core), while other cities are faced with demands for investing in nonresidential development in the core as well as the development of the neighborhood business district.[2] The choices that cities have to make about the use of the limited resources require that some priorities be set and some goals be put into perspective.

There are three essential types of goals in neighborhood planning— social development, physical development, and economic development. Each set of goals has a set of tools and associated costs and benefits. In planning at the neighborhood scale, the question: For whom?—Who enjoys the benefits? Who bears the costs of a particular policy choice?— is more sharply posed and can be more precisely answered. Some of the choices are compatible. For example, in neighborhoods it is important to achieve social development (improve confidence, employment, social efficacy, and such) as well as to achieve physical goals (stabilization and rehabilitation). However, there are some false choices as well. For example, if a city chooses to improve the life of residents in the city by developing jobs, they actually may create an opportunity for residents to gain the wherewithal to move out of the city or at least out of certain neighborhoods. On the other hand, if they choose to develop residential neighborhoods to the exclusion of economic development then they may essentially be rehabilitating in the absence of the ability of area residents to afford the housing. This physical improvement will, as in past cases, lead to new deterioration. Therefore, it becomes important for cities to rethink existing priorities; to identify where the most serious problems are; to locate the real opportunities; and to match the resources that can be brought to bear on the more serious problems and on the real opportunities. While there is not a general answer for this frequent dilemma, it is nevertheless the kind of policy choice that has to be played out in neighborhoods. It has to be considered both in the neighborhood-specific way (since neighborhoods vary) and in the resource-origin-specific way (since some funds available to local governments have limitations on how they can be spent).

Resource Allocation

General revenue sharing and Community Development Block Grants as well as other major federal initiatives (the Law Enforcement Assistance Administration and the Comprehensive Employment and Training Act) have increased substantially the amount of discretionary funds that local communities receive to deal with urban problems. In the past, cities received funds for specific categories of problems. These categorical grants were accompanied by guidelines that not only specified in which areas these funds were to be applied but specified particular program designs and tools there were to be used.

This external design of programs perverted local planning in several ways. First, the areas in which programs were located were often chosen in Washington based on criteria that often had little to do with local boundaries or social reality. Boundaries were drawn in grant applications and planning documents to meet program guidelines in a way that made the particular city appear to be more needy than some other city competing for the funds.

Second, this process of competing for funds forced cities and neighborhoods into highlighting and playing on their worst features rather than their best ones since funds were allocated based on need. Neighborhoods competed in documenting how bad things were in their city. This encouraged a so-called sandbox approach to the allocation of most funds. Citizen expectations were raised but planners became openly cynical about potential results.

Third, local communities had little to do in the way of neighborhood planning as discussed in this chapter and in other parts of the book. Planning for most cities was grantsmanship where the staff looked to Washington for ideas in good currency and simply chose to apply the new ideas according to the guidelines. The fact that the program was neither relevant nor properly tied to local sentiment could not be confronted lest the city fail to get funds from Washington.

Finally, many cities planned for local redevelopment and social services without any specific allocations of large portions of their own operating resources. This reduced the incentive to plan or design programs to deal with the problems. As a result various agencies went about doing things that were contradictory or ineffective for the larger goals espoused in planning documents.

With the advent of greater discretion for local communities, cities find themselves, of necessity, engaged in planning at a subcity level not only for which program initiatives to undertake but how to choose among them and how to design programs that meet their own contextual constraints and deal with their allocational and distributional choices. Because they are now accountable for program design and program results, the need to do real programming and planning is at the heart of the emerging interest in neighborhood planning.

Neighborhood planning creates a new management and development responsibility in local government that goes beyond the old redevelopment agency (that is, urban renewal) and beyond the custodial activities common to public works and other line departments and agencies in city hall. This resource-allocation function includes not only program design, implementation, evaluation, budgeting, and the like but also creates the need for new organizational structures (or revised ones) and new professional roles.

Population-Change Management

Neighborhoods are for the most part social units. Unlike cities that are political units or regions that are economic units, neighborhoods are defined and define themselves in ways that serve primarily social functions: networks of neighboring; areas of common social, cultural, or class background; areas of historical significance are all primarily social definitions. Efforts to intervene in neighborhoods and to assist and design programs to deal with neighborhood problems necessarily require intervening in a social context.

Any neighborhood change involving not only the number of people but the composition of the population requires some consideration and understanding of demographic dynamics. To a substantial degree, dealing with, promoting, or planning neighborhoods involves management of the population shifts that often occur as neighborhoods age and change. This issue is currently best illustrated in the present experience in neighborhood reinvestment where middle-class resettlement is concerned. The promotion of reinvestment often involves the dislocation of the existing population (usually lower-income), by higher-income households with different needs, desires, and tastes. While this area obviously has become a controversial issue not unlike so-called Negro removal of the 1960s, efforts at promoting reinvestment in urban neighborhoods necessarily require attention to the impact of various programs and development initiatives on the composition and mobility of the population.[3]

Local planners for the most part have been spared consideration of these issues. They have often planned in nonresidential areas or have been insensitive to the consequences of redevelopment on their population. Planners now find themselves grossly short of information on the detailed composition of the population, information on a neighborhood level, information on social preferences relating to development issues, and information about the housing needs of various age groups and household types. This situation is proposed to be partly rectified in the 1980 census in which the Neighborhood Statistics Program reports data for neighborhood units that are defined locally. Researchers are also looking for ways of making the Annual Housing Survey a better tool for planning.

With the emphasis on rehabilitation and reinvestment and the growing willingness on the part of non-middle-class people to move into traditionally low- and moderate-income neighborhoods and into areas of racial and ethnic mix, we now have an opportunity for the first time to promote racial and economic integration at a significant scale without the high cost and difficult siting issues common to housing efforts in the suburbs.

Achieving some integration requires that we reexamine the assumptions we made about population homogeneity and reevaluate the negative conclusions we made about the possibilities of integration based on the difficult circumstances and frequent failures of such efforts in the 1960s, when we were trying to promote integration of older city neighborhoods while opportunities for movement to the suburbs were increasing at a record pace.

Models of Citizen Participation

For most of the last two decades neighborhood organizations that participated in public policy used the advocacy (often confrontation and mass protest) approach to deal with the local political environment. These organizations were not concerned with development activity except to stop it. They were not involved in management issues. They had limited skills in some combination of management, negotiation, financing, development packaging, contracting, and so on. These organizations often grew out of particular crises and had a life that did not extend past the duration of the crisis.

Since the Nixon administration in the 1970s virtually dismantled much of the direct and indirect support for these organizations, many groups went into a metamorphosis to reemerge as organizations that were concerned fundamentally with issues of development. These were organizations that tried to fill the vacuum (with many of the same people) left by the emasculation of government antipoverty programs, model-cities programs, or organizations that emerged in other neighborhoods trying to fight off blight and reassert neighborhood control over their destiny.

The Carter administration's urban policy called for a partnership between the public sector and the private and volunteer sector (which includes neighborhood organizations). Even though the programs that are designed to implement this policy were stillborn in Congress, evidence of partnerships abound.[4] While some local governments have resisted formal recognition of and alliance with some organizations, other local governments have used these organizations as agents for local government to provide management, development, and counseling services to neighborhoods.

As a presidential candidate, Ronald Reagan embraced the rhetoric of neighborhood action and control, but his administration has dismantled some of the more promising neighborhood initiatives of the Carter administration—notably the Neighborhood Self-Help Development Program. Chapter 12 articulates a thoughtful conservative posture toward neighborhood policy, yet the administration, which is philosophically in tune with the author's analysis, has failed to act on it in ways that would be constructive for the future of residential communities.

Enough partnerships have emerged to suggest that we give some serious consideration for models of volunteer and government partnership and organizational structure that can play an even more significant role in neighborhood development. One model that bears significant attention is the Office of Neighborhood Associations (ONA) in Portland.[5] ONA serves as an umbrella group for neighborhood organizations in the city to make direct imput and to receive direct feedback from the development of city policy for all Portland neighborhoods. The Office of Neighborhood Associations, as a formal part of city government, has a right of access to information and other privileges accorded to a public agency. This right assures that the partnership is not sporadic and that volunteer interests have adequate resources to plan and organize long-term efforts.

It is important to know, however, that even though citizen involvement can be positive and is a precondition to effective neighborhood planning, all citizen involvement is not constructive, citizen groups can be exclusive, parochial, obstructionist, racist, and negative in other ways that have to be managed by local government if equitable change and development is to occur.[6] Part of the citizen-involvement aspect of neighborhood planning will have to include particular attention to ensuring that neighborhood organizations are representative, that all neighborhoods have some form of organization, and that citizen organizations just as public agencies must act within the law and within the public interest.[7]

Regulatory Policy

Many of the factors that play a role in the success of neighborhood planning are matters of regulatory concern. In the future development of neighborhood planning, orchestration of the regulatory functions of municipal government will become increasingly important. During an era of shrinking public budgets, cities are learning rapidly that they must turn more to nonservice strategies for addressing local needs. The regulatory levers that need to be integrated into the processes of neighborhood planning include code enforcement, insurance and mortgage disclosure, architectural standards, real-estate taxes, building inspection, rent control, siting of public and social-service facilities, and zoning. These regulatory policies all are concerned with which actors can participate, what incentives or sanctions exist, how much it costs, and so forth. Efforts to improve neighborhoods can be affected substantially by how well cities handle their regulatory functions. What we have learned from studies in a number of cities is that a combination of inertia, misguided or contradictory reforms, and concessions to intermediaries and special interest groups have combined to prevent many regulatory activities from being helpful and supportive of neighborhood development. Code enforcement, for example, when handled like a meat ax can serve to drive out marginal home owners or discourage small investors. Rent control if not sensitively administered, can lead to declining maintenance of rental property. Taxes that reflect gross inequities can lead to cynicism, disinvestment, and abandonment. Therefore it becomes necessary to develop a regulatory strategy that is flexible on certain regulations. Rehabilitation standards might be flexible to reflect neighborhood standards rather than the highest engineering standards, for example. The city or the state might provide incentives for private self-help and provide strong sanctions against uncooperative and recalcitrant owners and investors.[8]

When regulation is carried out using these goals it becomes a way for cities to help neighborhoods improve themselves in ways that are meaningful and relatively inexpensive. Using regulatory tools in conjunction with the allocation of certain resources (for rehabilitation, for example), can be much more effective than the simple allocations of larger amounts of money.

Public/Private Interface

Because of the difficult situation in which many cities found themselves in recent years, cities have often been very generous with their incentives to private developers who are willing to reinvest in the city. Many cities (sometimes with the help of state governments) have developed generous incentives involving taxes, discount financing, development rights, service improvements, land writedowns, and other mechanisms to reduce the amount of risk involved in investing in the city or assuring higher profit.

The recent experience in urban reinvestment suggests that the risks, while still significant, are not evenly high across the city. In some sections of the city investing is relatively risk-free; in other parts of the city the risk is still substantial. Neighborhood planning, indeed all city planning, should now feel obligated to look more carefully at how best to target incentives so that unreasonable incentives (often out of resources that could be more wisely spent elsewhere) are not given to investors who continue to say the risks are substantial when in fact they are not.

Excessive incentives represent a misallocation of resources and poor regulation. They encourage overdevelopment and mismanagement on the part of private investors. They lower the respect (or raise the level of cynicism) citizens have for their government when they see developers making large profits partly at their expense while investors and residents in more distressed areas are told that there are no resources.

What cities will have to do is to look at their different neighborhoods, economic markets, commercial and other districts and make an assessment about where each of them stands relative to opportunities and risks for private investment. Making such a determination would not only be a substantial public service to the private sector, but it would give the city stronger grounds for making allocations for managing regulation and it would generate a more cost-beneficial local-development policy. It would likewise serve to even out what is often an imbalance between attention and resources given to central business and economic development on one hand and neighborhood development on the other.

The Emergence of Innovation

This chapter would be theoretical were it not for the substantial number of innovations that have been tried in numerous cities around the country along the lines suggested in the elements above. It is much too early to evaluate how successful these initiatives will be. No city has yet to develop the comprehensive approach suggested here, but many cities have made innovations that deserve watching and that at least offer the support that there is a field of neighborhood planning emerging. Just a few of the initiatives are outlined here:

1. Several cities have developed policy-planning and development agencies usually in the office of the mayor, to manage the neighborhood and development policies of the city along the lines suggested here. These offices are often called something like the Office of Program Planning, the Department of Housing and Community Development, the Office of Program Development, and so on. Baltimore has gone a step forward by combining all of the relevant agencies—both the new agencies associated with community development and the old-line agencies associated with city and neighborhood services—into a single super agency with a commissioner who has substantial control over housing, economic (except industrial and harbor development), and community-development issues in the city.

2. Several cities are now coming to view the substantial responsibility they have for what happens to the composition of a population in neighborhoods in which they are actors. This has particularly emerged in the context of reinvestment displacement. Cities like Seattle, St. Louis, and San Francisco have developed formal inquiries into the impact of development policy on population composition. Boston has surveyed its neighborhood residents on a wide range of development issues and San Francisco has required that major projects submit an impact statement that outlines the impact of the proposed development on the neighborhood's social and physical development.

3. Several cities are using community-development agencies as contractors for the delivery of public services. Baltimore uses community agencies to provide counseling for a range of development programs. We have previously discussed Portland's Office of Neighborhood Associations; and Detroit allows neighborhood organizations to apply for funds to do extra neighborhood services that are defined as priorities by the neighborhoods themselves.

4. Several cities have or are proposing to use their bonding authority to raise capital to provide mortgages for housing rehabilitation. The cities propose mainly to serve either as direct lenders or as secondary lenders to provide capital when it is scarce or very expensive or to target it to particular groups or areas. This gives them some leverage with local lending institutions as well as guarantees that there is adequate capital to meet the needs generated by the improved confidence residents have in their neighborhoods. Examples in this regard are primarily Baltimore and Chicago. Other cities are currently considering such programs.

Limitations of Neighborhood Planning

Despite an emerging interest in neighborhood planning and a growing acceptance of social planning, there are some limitations that we have to recognize. The first is that neighborhoods are very different from each other. They have very different meanings and boundaries within cities as well as among different cities. This fact makes it very difficult to categorize neighborhoods or generalize about strategies and approaches appropriate to deal with neighborhood problems.

The second limitation is that neighborhoods are in fact social units. The functional transaction is the rental agreement or home purchase, which is based on some consumer values interpreted differently by different consumers in the metropolitan area. Neighborhood status and values are a function of the attitudes of consumers about the given area and their differential willingness to stay, leave, or move in. The physical condition of the housing is less important than we have assumed.[9] Our traditional tools for planning are framed to relate to economic markets or to institutions' behavior. Yet what chapter 6 clearly illustrates is that the effectiveness of neighborhood policy is a function in large part of how the policy relates to long-term residents, newcomers, and others. Furthermore, whether private reinvestment occurs is not a function of impersonal market phenomena but the psychology of specified actors.

A third limitation is that while citizens are somewhat hopeful about their neighborhoods, there is nevertheless a strong cynicism about cities in general and specifically about city governments and private institutions. This cynicism may limit (or at least make more difficult) efforts to mobilize the citizens and may prevent the cooperative efforts so essential to the success of neighborhood planning. The facts suggest that neighborhood planning may be as much confidence-building as institution-building.[10]

Finally, in virtually all cities there are political, ideological, racial, and class meanings attached to neighborhoods that have both negative and positive aspects. On the positive aspects these meanings provide an organizing focus that planners might use and that helps define needs and set boundaries. On the other hand, these meanings may make it difficult to plan for neighborhoods where parochial interests are so strong and where efforts at exclusion or competition prevent the effective mobilization of interests, economies-of-scale, or cooperation among neighborhoods. It also becomes difficult to identify a public interest for the city when in fact there are as many public interests as there are interests. In addition some organized publics are not organized neighborhoods but rather organized interest groups that have no spatial analogue (that is, the elderly, large families, and such).

We are also aware that there are a number of neighborhoods (including many low-income and minority areas) where the level of cohesion is so low and transience and pathology so great that neighborhoods are not presently able to play a functional role to protect or advance their interests. In such places working with the neighborhood is difficult and the tendency to work with intermediaries, to plan *for* them, or to focus only on social services is very strong. Given this situation, neighborhood planners will have a tendency to segregate the city into groups of neighborhoods that on the one hand have some self-determination because they can enter into partnerships for neighborhood development and a group of neighborhoods on the other hand that get planned for with the limited and disjointed tools presently established.[11]

Conclusion

It is risky to try to identify the central elements of any emerging body of knowledge or practice. However, the rise of neighborhood consciousness and the changing contextual features of urban development suggest that we are going to have to deal with neighborhoods as a fundamental organizing entity for a long time. There are resources to be allocated; there are compositional issues in the population to be understood; there are regulatory actions that have to be taken; and there is a private market that has to be influenced. All of these combine to assure us that neighborhood planning will be around for a while.

What we have done in this chapter is try to outline what we feel are some of the major elements and issues that will need to be dealt with in the future. This is only a beginning, however. Further research is needed to provide better documentation for what we know about these elements both from past experience as well as from our present experience. We also need better data gathered that deal with the concerns that exist at the neighborhood level. For a long time we have only dealt with cities or regions—or we have dealt with substantive problems and not with the places in which these problems are profoundly felt and in which the agony of the problems are worked out by residents. Neighborhood planning offers us a chance to do better.

Notes

1. See Phillip L. Clay, *Neighborhood Renewal: Middleclass Resettlement and Incumbent Upgrading in American Neighborhoods* (Lexington, Mass.: D.C. Heath and Co., Lexington Books, 1979), pp. 11–56.

2. See Gerald Manners, "The Office in the Metropolis: An Opportunity for Shaping Metropolitan America." Massachusetts Institute of Technology-Harvard University Joint Center for Urban Studies, 1974.

3. See National Urban Coalition, *Displacement in City Neighborhoods in Transition* (Washington: National Urban Coalition, 1978). Also see Dennis Gale, "Dislocation of Residents," *Journal of Housing* 77 (June 1978):232–235.

4. See Roger Albrandt and Paul Brophy, *Neighborhood Revitalization: Theory and Practice* (Lexington, Mass.: D.C. Heath and Co., Lexington Books, 1975). Also Rachel G. Bratt; Janet M. Byrd; and Robert M. Hollister, "The Private Sector and Neighborhood Preservation," Neighborhood Policy Research, January 1983.

5. Other cities that have granted significant planning authority to neighborhood districts include Denver, San Antonio, and Honolulu.

6. There are numerous cases of neighborhood groups (often the ones organized by new or middle-class residents) who oppose subsidized housing, the siting of social-services facilities, and the provision of facilities or services that might serve low-income families. They may also engage in activities that foster affirmative discrimination (that is, private

circulation of house lists, demand for expensive and restrictive building regulations, and such).

7. Leaders of minority groups often oppose neighborhood policy because they feel it is directed toward protecting or advancing the interests of white ethnic groups over those of black. Others view attention to neighborhoods as a way of avoiding dealing with the serious needs of families. They also charge that to the extent not every neighborhood is helped, neighborhood policy helps some groups to the exclusion of others.

8. See Clay, ch. 7.

9. Clay, ch. 3.

10. See Rolf Goetze, *Building Neighborhood Confidence: A Humanistic Strategy for Urban Housing* (Cambridge, Mass.: Ballinger, 1976).

11. For a discussion of the triage approach see chapter 10 of this book by Conrad Weiler.

Index

About the Contributors

Geno Baroni was formerly Assistant Secretary for Neighborhoods, Voluntary Organizations, and Consumer Protection at the U.S. Department of Housing and Urban Development. He was director or urban affairs at the Catholic Archdiocese of the District of Columbia. A leading figure in the neighborhood movement, Father Baroni formed and directed the National Center for Urban Ethnic Affairs in Washington.

Rachel G. Bratt teaches housing and community-development courses in the Department of Urban and Environmental Policy at Tufts University, where she is an assistant professor. She currently is doing research on housing issues and on public-private partnerships in neighborhood development.

Kent W. Colton was staff director of the President's Commission on Housing and has taught at the Massachusetts Institute of Technology and Brigham Young University. He is currently with the Mortgage Corporation in Washington.

Dennis E. Gale is associate professor at The George Washington University in Washington, where he teaches planning. He has conducted extensive research on housing and the gentrification of neighborhoods in Washington.

Rolf Goetze was formerly director of Housing Rehabilitation Programs for the City of Boston; he is now a consultant in housing and urban development. He is the author of *Building Neighborhood Confidence* and *Understanding Neighborhood Change*.

Robert B. Hawkins, Jr., is president of the Sequoia Institute and chairman of the National Advisory Commission on Intergovernmental Relations.

Albert Hunter is professor of sociology at Northwestern University, where he is also affiliated with the Center for Urban Affairs. Professor Hunter is the author of numerous articles and books on urban sociology.

Robert Kolodny is president of Urban Strategies, Inc., in New York City. He formerly taught in the Department of Urban Planning at Columbia University as associate professor.

Neil S. Mayer is senior research associate at the Urban Institute in Washington. His research on voluntary organizations has appeared in numerous journals and books.

Dowell Myers is assistant professor of urban planning at the University of Texas at Austin. He has conducted research for the Department of Housing and Urban Development on demographic aspects of housing.

Timothy Pattison is assistant director of the Neighborhood and Economic Development Agency of the City of Boston, where he is responsible for research and policy development.

Conrad Weiler is currently head of the Political Science Department of Temple University. He has conducted extensive research on displacement and has been active in the National Association of Neighborhoods as well as serving as president of the Queen's Village Neighborhood Association in Philadelphia.

About the Editors

Phillip L. Clay is associate professor of Urban Studies and Planning at the Massachusetts Institute of Technology (MIT) and assistant director of the MIT-Harvard Joint Center for Urban Studies. He is author of *Neighborhood Renewal*.

Robert M. Hollister is associate professor and chairman of Urban and Environmental Policy at Tufts University. He is also executive director of the Boston Neighborhood Network.

DATE DUE

JUL 1 0 1990			